TALKING THE WALK

MARILYN CASSELMAN

TALKING
THE
WALK

THE
GRASSROOTS LANGUAGE
OF
FEMINISM

FREEBORN PUBLISHING

NEW YORK   MONTREAL

Published by Freeborn Publishing
P.O. Box 20195, New York, NY 10014
www.freebornpublishing.com

Cover design and photographs by E. Freeborn

First Printing 2008

Library of Congress Cataloguing-in-Publication Data
Casselman, Marilyn.
Talking the walk: the grassroots language of feminism / Marilyn Casselman.

Includes index.

ISBN 978-0-6151-9409-7
1. Feminism – United States, Canada.   2. Feminism – Canada, United States.
3. Language and culture.   4. Knowledge – Feminist.   5. Feminine
Principle.   6. Women – Social conditions.   7. Patriarchy.   8. Wisdom –
Women's.   9. Story – Women's. 10. Narrative – Women's

Title

To the memory of my mother, Marion Grace.

And to April, Briana and Hannah,
my daughter and grandchildren.

Preface

I have written this book for mainstream women: the many who wonder about feminism but are not sure if they want to know. These are the women who I believe have missed an important component of what should be part of our general education; therefore, part of our common knowledge and cultural narrative. My motive is a feminist one: to describe where we stand in the structural scheme of patriarchal power; how to develop your position in it; why you should think and speak for yourself; and how to do just that. I approach the subject as it is meant to be used in day-to-day living, at the grassroots level.

The material is basic and concentrates on the themes of patriarchal power, standpoint feminism and the story of our lives. It is historical only in terms of intellectual and anecdotal needs and does not encompass the particularities of race, class and gender group identities. That would not be a book, but an encyclopedia.

Although this is a personal work, written in my own voice and from my own point-of-view, I am happy to say that I have found major meanings in our literature and culture. It has taken shape through a lifetime of reading, media, listening, conversation and the observation of female-male thinking, behavior, and experience, including of course, my own.

Though not an academic nor scholarly book, it is indebted, as all women are, to works of feminist scholarship. It does not claim validity through dependence on evidence, statistics or theory, but on insight and the external sensitivity to the reality of living on this planet female. Its contents fit my own sense of how to use this knowledge, which I have acquired throughout my life. It is not a "critical" work based on the work of others, history or linguistics (although refers to these from time to time). It is not a research study, nor does it emanate from women's studies or feminist theory.

Finally, the work does not pretend to serve the womanly role of being all things to all people. The experience of a lifelong feminist has its own nature. It does not mutate because of backlash politics; does not weaken by marginalization or group pressure; does not become confused because of sociological, psychological, historical, anthropological, political or theoretical feminist arguments. It remains as it is – amplified, nuanced and colored by insight and new rationale and tempered by the passage of time. But it is fundamental at the core. Feminism is an essential sense of my being.

The debts I owe in the evolution of this project begin with the feminists of my generation, those who preceded us and those who have followed in our footsteps; and to every other soul, who by whatever method and in whatever context has challenged my mind, emotions and ability to outgrow the "toy-box history" of women's consciousness, as George Elliot puts it in *Middlemarch*. So to all Amazons, artists, narrators and provocateurs, thank you.

I am grateful for the generosity and confidence of family and friends during this long process: Judith Casselman, Dr. Alice M.E. Cheatley, C.M., Aline Bourdages Dresdner and GailGreenhalgh; Beth Adler, Barbara Pfeffer Billauer, Elisabeth Coleman, Haidee Granger, David Haber, Linda and Ted Hart, Gerry and Judy Hill, Hannah Horovitz, Eva and Walter Iooss and family, Morna Murphy Martell, Samia Moosa, Monika Moritz-Akin, Ann Mulhall and Lawrence Austin, Jane Needles and Ted Bradley, Frederick Noonan, Lois Noonan, Carol Ann Ross and Chrisjean Whitten Tiberti – all of whom helped me, in one way or another, to hang in there.

Thanks for feedback along the way to Gail Bruce, Eunice DeGruechy, Anna Fahr, Renée Gregorio and John Brandi, Arpi Hamalian, Jeff Haughton, John Harrop, Maya Islas, Jerome Kuehl, Sophie Mardirossian, Camille Perrottet and Sara Stuart. Thanks to Victoria Clark, Terry Lawler, Sheila Mohammed, Shree Mulay, Eugene Price and Cy-Thea Sand for help organizing the original seminars and to all who have participated. And for their generous assessments and comments on the manuscript, to Dale Rhonda Burg, Linda Roberts and Tess Fragoulis, my gratitude.

CONTENTS

INTRODUCTION

The struggle for women's rights was one of the defining events of the twentieth century and feminism was the intellectual engine that powered it. Yet millions of women today have no idea what any of this means or why these battles were fought in the first place. And feminism? Most are even averse to hearing the word.

Feminism is women's knowledge, so the vital question is this. Why do we deny ourselves the opportunity of expanding our minds with information that is critical to our own survival and well-being? This book is meant to help answer that question.

The suppression of women's knowledge has been going on throughout recorded history. It is not surprising, therefore, that the recent narrative of women's experience, talents, values and wisdom is not reflected in today's culture, just as it has not been in the past. What counts in life is interpreted by the male voice according to male values. The truth of women's reality is not reflected back to us because it is not there to begin with. It is not regarded as important enough to be part of the foundation of our own cultural and political reality. If it was, fear of feminism would not exist. If it was, the average women would know something about it.

We live in troubled times. Issues critical to women's lives exist on many planes. High level, big-ticket "I can't do anything about it" problems stalk us every day. War, the weaponization of the planet and the threat of nuclear jihad; terrorism and obscurantism; famine and starvation; ecological disasters and the unfettered mindlessness of globalization. Each of these affects women in a particularly disproportional way.

Then there is the laundry list—issues closer to community, home and to the bone. Issues at the personal, local and national level that meet us coming and going every day, whether we acknowledge them or not. These are just a few:

•The demographic crisis in Western democracies and places like Russia and Japan causing pressure on women to have more babies. And if we don't? Read *The Handmaid's Tale* by Margaret Atwood published in 1985 (still one of the Most Banned Books in America) to get a glimpse of the alternative.

•Stem cell research. From whose tissue and DNA, did you say? How do they get this "raw material" and from *whose* bodies?

•Image and the pressure to remain thin. Starving, binging, puking, compulsive exercising, the addiction to plastic surgery. The obsession with appearance and youth.

•The disappearing divide between church and state. All religions are prejudiced against women as basic doctrine.

•Aberrant, self-debasing sexuality practiced by young women and girls—as though their reputation won't follow them. To say nothing of the related psychological and physical health problems.

•Affirmative action. States are pre-empting federal anti-discrimination laws. This affects women of every race and class.

•Computing, social networks, digital imaging, online media. There are major privacy issues at play here. Think twice about what you put out there. This fun system has its own vicious karma. And whatever goes in, stays in: forever.

•Repressive economic conditions, called "the gap between rich and poor," as though it was the result of some natural erosion. The feminization of poverty is real and single mothers are at the bottom of the income scale. In the workforce, women in the U.S. average 80 cents of every dollar earned by male counterparts (U.S. Government Accountability Office, *GAO Report 2006*) ; figures in Canada are 71 percent and lower, depending on education level.

•Bias against women in science, engineering, mathematics. The "innate differences between sexes in aptitude for science and mathematics" canard—a hot media topic today—can be traced back to Pythagoras (c.572–497 B.C.). "There is a good principle which created order, light, and man, and an evil principle which created chaos, darkness, and woman." (*Source: Columbia World of Quotations*)

•Unfairness at work. The limits to women's higher advancement and the common perception that men are more capable managers than women, which is untrue.

•The distribution of labor in the family and home.

•Work-life Balance. This relates to women who have careers and families and whether or not they should work themselves to death. And for what, exactly?

•The legal right to an abortion is one of the most important aspects of women's liberty. Either other people and the state control what's happening in your body, or you do. Morality is not the issue; politics is. If emotional problems interfere with seeing this subject clearly, chill out and use your imagination. Circle back up to the first item on this list, the demographic crisis. Anyone who wants to be that breeder should go right ahead. But make it your own personal burden. Don't presume that anyone else should carry it for you.

•The pandemic violence against women doesn't just mean "over there." Raise your hair on end by reading *The UN Report on Violence Against Women,* October 2006, which documents the horrendous brutality and sadism that men afflict on women around the world. The statistics for the U.S. and Canada are no better than those in underdeveloped countries; they're just different. And the costs of violence against women? In Canada, a 1995 study estimated the total was over a billion a year; and the 2003 report by the Centers for Disease Control and Prevention estimated that the costs of intimate partner violence in the U.S. alone exceed $5.8 billion per year. So women not only suffer the blows, but pay for them, as well.

And think of this. There are actually "trends" in violence against women. Mass rape as a strategy and weapon of war in the former Yugoslavia, Sudan, Darfur, Congo is an example. Female abduction, slavery and trafficking as a result of globalization and internet technology is another. Some three to four hundred women have been raped, mutilated and murdered in and around Ciudad

Juárez near the Texas Mexico border in the past few years, and this is yet another.

Feminism is core knowledge. It relates to almost all subjects and connects with almost everything else. It is flexible, powerful and dynamic: and that is why it changed our world to the degree that we all recognize it. And it is this knowledge that must be brought to bear on all of the items in the laundry list above and the myriad issues, large, small, complex and unfathomable that we individually and collectively face every day. Or we may not face them. That doesn't mean they aren't there.

The Need for Women's Language

Culture is the mirror in which we construct and reveal ourselves. Because there is a void where our history is supposed to be, our culture is a projection of women's insignificance and subordination. In virtually every personal, social and political encounter, women's physical and cognitive image is impersonated in a powerful lens ground by the male culture. In this light, we are abbreviated entities, making innumerable small contributions in the exaggerated objectives of our own society. From this point-of-view, women's narrative is that of cultural irrelevance. Five thousand years of collective wisdom and creativity is buried in the paradox of our cultural insignificance contrasted with the truth of our irreplaceable roles in all aspects of human affairs throughout time. The story of our presence in this grand scenario is a void; a lacuna.

We can stay in this hole or get up and out of it and onto the path. The path, in this case, is knowing the story of feminism. Even though the word has been integrated into the Western vocabulary, its concepts, values and implications are consistently trashed, scapegoated and vilified in the cultural narrative. This is our intellectual legacy and actual experience and history being suppressed; and it means that we do not have access to understanding our own oppression, nor the reasons for our advancement. So do we just let this go? Blow it off? Can we bear to lose our heritage again—as we have consistently done in the past?

Many women believe they're equal and that is a very good thing. It would be a mistake, however, to think we've got it made. Equality is not a default position. In fact, there is a continuing crisis in the equation. As you read this, someone, somewhere, is undermining, curtailing or reversing the rights of women. Equality is an ongoing project, which right now, is stuck in a rut somewhere between revolution and evolution.

I believe that the phenomenal gains of the twentieth century could easily slip away if we are not vigilant about protecting them. Our higher consciousness and position in life are still being thwarted by the historical nature of sexism. The end result? Loss of potential. Untapped power. Denial of our full humanity. And inherent in this situation is the loss of vision that gave rise to the women's movement in the first place.

Women's identity should be a groundbreaking force that is reflected to our own advantage. We are not men. We must SPEAK in our own language—the authentic language of what it means to be a woman living in this society.

The story of higher female consciousness is the unspoken narrative of our culture. I have found that mainstream women do want to be able to think and talk these things through; to talk about the issues of femaleness and her own role in the world. And by mainstream, I mean grown-up, adult women of any age—the female panorama of normal people. I believe women want to be taken seriously and that they are interested in the imperatives of women's standing in both the personal and public domain.

Women are the recognizers of others, the makers of community and the seekers and speakers of humane language. It is this language that we do not hear spoken back to us; that does not resonate in the cultural dialogue. As long as men maintain their domination and broadcast their tyrannical babel, this negation will persist. I do not believe men's tools and abstractions fail because of inherent weakness, but because women's expression neither informs their intelligence nor counsels their tangents. They are deprived of the language of women's great aptitude in the living of lives. When the complexities of politics and power are leavened by both the obvious and extenuating language of women's reality, only then will we have a culture that transmits knowledge worthy of calling ourselves free. Or equal. In this case, it is one thing.

"What Is *TALKING THE WALK*? What Does It Mean?"

TALKING THE WALK ("TTW") is the reverse of the old saw, to "walk the talk," which means what you do, corresponds with what comes out of your mouth. Here "the walk" relates to the fact that all women in this country take advantage of the opportunities and benefits which have resulted from women's rights activism. We live in our new social, economic and political reality because activists created this possibility. So if it's good enough to walk it, it's also good enough to back it up with the talk.

TTW means being aware of the concepts and facts that underpin women's self-direction—and voicing this consciousness. If we are to retain our gains and change the nature of our culture and politics to reflect the fact that women are controlling their part, we're going to have to SPEAK. The subtitle, *"The Grassroots Language of Feminism,"* refers to establishing the language of feminism as accessible, acceptable and usable in the daily circumstances; in other words, giving feminism a more popular face.

"Why Do I Need This Book?"

TALKING THE WALK is a confidence building and language development project (book and related seminars) that reflects and serves the needs and interests of women in general. It is a framework of essential concepts designed to break the grip of male dominance on the mind. These ideas result in the expansion of language and increased self-assurance.

It is aimed at the intellect and the gut, not the emotions. It is a vehicle to expand intelligence, not reduce or petrify it. It brings into play the gears of critical thinking, to help shape one's particular point-of-view.

It is written to transcend the negative images of feminism and restate its meanings and motives in language that is accessible to all people. My goal is to unify women's attitudes about our commonalities and inherent power to change the reality around us for the better.

TTW is a book for practical use and not a sociological model. It is intended as an aid to develop thinking and language which speaks for women's world from our own point-of-view, while freeing ourselves of the subjective subordinate case (I come after you). With the truth of our own language, we carry the story of women's incomparability and accomplishments with us always, to be passed on to the living and to be left with them for the future.

The Framework

The organization of the material in TTW is meant to change readers' ideas about how we think of ourselves personally and as women in the world. It provides for reconfiguring and clarifying things we already know, but have not had the liberty, or motivation, to contemplate. It is meant to set new sign posts and paths for thoughts and feelings we didn't know we had, until the possibility presented itself to make these things known.

It is also meant to generate an appreciation for intellectual conflict. Conflict is advocated as a muscle we use for healthy disagreement and debate and which allows us to recover our linguistic endowment. In the past this has been denied as a result of our subordination.

The Framework Effect

When we imagine a mental construct that liberates us from the imposition of others' concepts and values, life opens up the horizons of personal expression. Retooling our general identity as women, in terms of a set of practical ideas, contributes to the reinvention of meaning. It sets up a mental gallery we can use to dispatch negative interpretations and rethink our experience according to what is important to us—not to men. Politically, it identifies us as women first, putting our existential issues into perspective in intellectual and social terms.

Overall, the framework is structured to aid in the manifestation of our own wisdom and innate knowledge—and keep it at our core—despite the permanent siege on our identity and harmony. Grounded in the feminist standpoint, we can embrace the kaleidoscopic possibilities in life while maintaining our own convictions and values. By committing to its principles, we are in a better position to absorb the information around us and turn it into knowledge which will serve us, not subjugate us.

The Process

TTW is designed to develop this knowledge; this language. The objective is to recover our buried legacy and create an interest and identity which enables women to speak what they truly mean. Thinking through the text provides the initial experience and skills to build a personal language that connects the inner and outer worlds and strengthens confidence to influence the forces that affect our daily lives. It is a method for internalizing this knowledge: absorb it, retain it. And to advance it: use it. The nuts and bolts of feminism: principles, concepts, facts, truths.

Part I, "Speaking of the Theme," introduces the topic of feminism in terms of what is fundamental knowledge from my point-of-view.

Part II, "The Big Picture," addresses the fact that we live in a patriarchy. The content is framed to clarify, in simple terms, patriarchal operations and intentions; and open up paths of critical and responsive reaction.

Part III, "The Better Idea," proposes the challenge of feminism and the feminine principle as trustworthy concepts to ground us as individuals and women of the world; and to use this standpoint from which to speak truthfully about our lives and the people and reality around us.

Part IV, "The World According to You," is a set of practical exercises in revising the common narrative to correct the historical misrepresentations about living female. It starts with an appraisal of the construction of values. Then, through the use of story and samples of literature, we examine women portrayed as irrelevant, dirty, illiterate, unprincipled, incompetent and sluttish. The reader then employs a technique to create the language of her own values and experience, in opposition to the biased and prejudicial aspects of the text in use. This is the start-up phase of creating women's original cultural narrative with the TTW method and emphasizes the need to reinforce the feminist standpoint operation in real life—with men. Here the point (standpoint) is to speak about what we have learned about what we (more than likely) already knew, but about which we have been heretofore silent.

"What Can TTW Do for Me?"

Feminism and language are both dynamic forces. Together they build confidence and knowledge that will benefit you personally, professionally and in your daily dealings with the outside world.

Personally, this book will help you get centered and realize that your core power lies in the innate strength of being a woman. It will help you clarify your intellectual framework to understand the circumstances limiting your experience and ways to overcome them. It will help you build your own true voice, and develop the language of common sense about your individual significance and status so that others can understand it. With higher conversation skills, end a lifetime of deference to men.

On the job, at work and in your career development, with feminist knowledge your ambivalence about your position will disappear. You will be better able to assess any situation; from a stable standpoint, create a positive environment for yourself and others. It will enable you to hold your ground in negotiations and in the resolution of issues. When you maintain your position of internal power, sexual harassment and sexism immediately become a no-win strategy. And relieved of the internal pressures of male dominance, you will be better motivated to pursue opportunities in the world.

In the outside world you will be prepared to deal with the social, political and cultural realities of gender prejudice and misogyny. Equipped with language, you will be able to express what it means to be a woman—by defining your sovereignty, practicing advanced citizenship, and defining this society. In this daily affair with the world, you will be affirming your female legacy—passing on your knowledge at the grassroots level to our daughters and sons, to upcoming generations and to the future.

We have a whole new human archive to create and an entire culture to shape up and cure of the delusion of male superiority. So let's get on with it. Let all of us utter the unutterable and end our collective bondage in speechlessness.

> ... the welfare of society is not built on extraordinary exertions; and were it more reasonably organized, there would be still less need of great abilities, or heroic virtues.
>
> Mary Wollstonecraft,
> *A Vindication of the Rights of Women*

PART ONE

★

SPEAKING OF THE THEME

CHAPTER 1

FEMINIST KNOWLEDGE

F eminism is a category of knowledge. It is essential, stands alone, and is constituted in the underlying principles and causes of the female reality. Women's inequality is understood around the world because of the dynamic thought emanating from the concepts of feminism.

Feminist knowledge is the history of our past, of working our way out of our own underdevelopment and of developing enlightened thought about our conditions and possibilities. It is the history of the development of this knowledge and the knowledge itself—statements and facts about things we need to know in the common experience of living on this planet female.

The thrust of this knowledge was powered by the liberation of women's consciousness from the ideology of male superiority. The second wave feminist movement (1960s and 1970s) forced new forms of consciousness which caused us to advance our thinking and develop a vast amount of knowledge about ourselves and our relationship with the world. With liberation came the emotional and intellectual development necessary to determine our own values and create a vision of what our lives were supposed to be. Feminism is a set of values, therefore. As such, and in the face of entrenched resistance to women's freedom, it is also a moral imperative based on reason.

Many basic understandings developed in the women's movement are yet to be recognized. Generally, mainstream women claim to know very little about feminism or they know all the wrong things. (See Chapter 4.) In the mind of many, feminism has taken on the character of Villain. So first I'll state what feminism is not. It is not rape, abortion, pornography, lesbianism, yelling, hairy armpits or so-called "man bashing." Feminism is not a problem. These are intentional distortions by anti-woman forces to create fear and *that* is a problem. Fear of feminism—turning it into an element against ourselves—is really fear of acknowledging the motivations, harms and inequities of male power and domination in its myriad forms. Acknowledging this fear is part of feminist knowledge.

The core of feminist knowledge is understanding sexism and the patriarchy and how they operate socially and personally. But sexism is just a word and needs to be understood at *its* core. This is not just about "rights." One must get the gist of sexual politics and the related questions of power, ideology and culture.

Today, feminist knowledge—the sum of everything we've learned, combined with our history—is information we all need to acknowledge so that we do not keep slipping backwards. Understanding the many places that feminist knowledge affects our individuality, our lives and the world—and the transmission of that knowledge—are the keys to combating the forces of regression that have been with us throughout recorded memory.

Feminism, Actually

Feminism is what, again? **Feminism** is a mental environment. It is also the policy, practice or advocacy of political, economic and social equality for women.

A **feminist** is any person who advocates women's rights, meaning that her beliefs, actions, political position and critical perspective cohere with the definition of feminism to some degree. This group includes old, middle-aged and young women; girls, boys and men.

The **subject** of feminism is women and the **substance** of feminism is the political, psychological, spiritual and experiential expression of women. It is about women, for women and speaks on behalf of women, even those who oppose it. Where there is feminism, by definition it is working in opposition to patriarchal domination and seeks to secure women's liberation from the dominance—deliberate or unwitting—of men. Such is the **purpose** of feminism.

Feminism is the **controlling idea** in women's advancement. By avoiding this indisputably solid concept, one is implicitly—and almost as often, explicitly—disowning her interest in her own political rights and intellectual power.

Philosophically, practically and morally, feminism is not a problem. It is a solution. The **theoretical framework** has been constructed and the principals of feminism have been established. Feminism is an ethical doctrine and in theory pertains to all women, the way the "female gender" as a patriarchal structural division pertains to all women. The intellectual, emotional and creative superstructure for feminist ideals is here to stay and it will be maintained and furthered by art, literature and scholarly pursuits. In these times of backlash and rising fundamentalism, we are fortunate that responsible people have created archives and repositories for what most women have already ignored or denied. Many of these are in women's studies departments, but we do not go to academia to learn how to live. We have to do that ourselves.

Feminism is concerned with the radial restructuring of society—to end, once and for all, the political and cultural impotence of women. The **goal of feminism**, therefore, is that women understand their position, develop their knowledge and power and bring to bear their unique influence to create a culture of positive social and human evolution. Changing power relations will cause human society itself to develop into something yet to be defined.

Feminism is a **matrix**. It exists to help you manage yourself internally and make informed decisions about your life and the lives of those around you.

Feminist knowledge is an **angle**. It opens up a whole new world of thought, observation and imagining, which is of great interest and complexity. It shapes the life of the mind and underpins your personal identity. It causes you to use your brain in a different way. It allows one to discover that there are alternatives to every disappointment, disillusionment, bafflement, fear and weakness and then some. And to discover creativity and insights never before considered. Personally, I can't imagine not being a feminist. For me, it would be like staring into the void.

Feminist knowledge is a **source of power and strength** as a basis for conducting your affairs in the outside world with stability and control—and interpreting the human experience. It improves your ability to realize important information about your environment that would otherwise not be apparent. It helps us recover lost knowledge about our internal life and return that knowledge to the world—and to the general information of the culture.

Feminist knowledge is a **tool**. It is flexible, portable, powerful and self-sharpening—and it already exists. A young physician, with whom I am acquainted, goes to Africa every year to work with a volunteer medical project. She told me that she explained feminism to a group of village women. The villagers were delighted to learn this, and said it gave them a way to think about their problems. They got it instantly—an indication of all that was lurking in their minds and waiting for a way to be realized.

> With feminist knowledge comes the realization that we can look
> at the world from a subordinated point-of-view or from the
> position of understanding the arrangement of that subordination
> and its implications and deciding how you want to live your life
> in light of that knowledge.
>
> Vivian Gornick

Feminist knowledge pertains to all races, ethnic origins, classes. Rather than being exclusionary and obfuscating, feminist knowledge is an indispensable tool for every woman to wield in this complex world. It has been discovered and conveyed within and by different groups in different systems. This was manifested in the second wave when the intertwining diversity of women of all races and socioeconomic identities created movements in their own independent and collective fields.

The change in this society as a result of the women's movement in the 1960s and 70s shows the great transformative power of feminism. Lifestyle feminism; theoretical, cultural, radical feminism; anarcha-, cyborg, eco-, existential, individualist, liberal, Marxist, postmodern, psychoanalytic, religious, separatist, socialist, transnational feminism. And, as it has not made it into the lexicon, add **grassroots feminism**, which is the conception of this book. All have a different focus, each draws on distinct resources, all have core feminist principles in common. All these interpretations are related and have served to bring new ideas into the blend of human knowledge. As a result of their enormous brilliance and energy, feminists can claim great legal and social victories. But have no delusions about economic, social and cultural parity. It doesn't exist.

This identity, "women," has grown into massive strength. This is true of our personal, racial and cultural identity and collectively in the women's rights missions here and abroad. All have brought forth feminist knowledge and feminist consciousness. As fundamentalism marches onward, and we keep slipping backward, where do we see that leaving women? Understanding the many places that feminist knowledge affects our individuality and our lives—and the transmission of that knowledge—is the only way we can combat the forces of regression.

Increasingly, the intellectual and political development of women has resulted in a different meaning of power and a different relationship to power and this has enhanced the understanding and implications of the "we" of feminism. And creatively, women from every corner of the nation have generated a mind-boggling collection of literature, art and creative works which resonate the feminist identity and experience. We can either use this extraordinary archive to root the principles of women's justice and humanity in the land—or we can just let it blow off into the wind.

Issues Inside Feminism

Feminism has its share of problems—in addition to its characteristic defect of tanking every time it gets a head start. There has been plenty said about this, so I'll mention just a few points in order to provoke some thought and even better, self-criticism.

•There is the problem idea of "feminist purity," the search for theoretical consistency which would make it beyond expansion, growth, improvement, transformation and better ideas, also making it immune to criticism from within.

•There are the unsustainable notions of radical feminism that propose the rejection of existing society (where do we take this?) and which challenge men to transform themselves at the most fundamental levels of their identity (indicating a total naivete about the nature of men and male power).

•There are confrontations between hard core and soft core feminists, important in the third wave or "next generation." (Think pop icon Kate Bush vs. post-punk, goth rocker Siouxsie Sioux; or alternative Tori Amos vs. grungie Courtney Love).

•And there have been flip flops in the movement like swapping outer activism for "inner change" (for instance, Gloria Steinem's *Revolution from Within*).

•And most consequential and disturbing is the pervasive passivity of the feminist voice.

Feminism has paid off big time in terms of economics and power. In terms of work, most middle and upper class women see little standing in the way of their careers, and many face no more barriers than men in business opportunities. But no one mentions feminism—only that women are serious players in "some sort of correlation to feminism but in a superior way." In fact, it is in the zone of feminism that all work and career-related struggles of the past have achieved stabilization. This has occurred within the mechanics of the law which have furthered women's possibilities in the all-important livelihood department. It is because feminists routed "feminine" ideals that the workplace and institutions can no longer function in their usual, male supremacist ways. And it is an ongoing struggle. There are class action suits for sex discrimination against Boeing, Smith Barney, Wal-Mart, Costco Wholesale (filed January 2007) and others representing hundreds and thousands of women. (Morgan Stanley was settled in 2007.)

Is this shunning a female strategy? Does denying the relevance of feminism indicate the fear of having to acknowledge a debt? Is the pay off from a very specific campaign and efforts of very specific women now being treated as an entitlement by those who have come after? All women should get what we deserve, having been deprived by the historical burden of unfair and cruel gender fraud. But we should also be able to speak coherently of the conditions that existed just awhile ago (think of trying a job class action in the 50s), exist now and will continue to exist until our culture echoes back what is being presented in this book.

•The last thing on the short list of issues inside feminism is forgetting, a primary mode of problem-solving. In the 1970s, the ease of women's acceptance in man's world DID NOT EXIST. Forgetting this fact, and forgetting to be curious about the background of one's own present, is full partner with the weakness of the feminist voice. Willful mindlessness still reigns as a primary mode of problem solving.

The Language of Feminism

Feminist knowledge exists because of the development of language which has progressed along with activism. Assuming the responsibility of self-determination, full humanity and obtaining our rights, meant that feminists had to figure out what they really believed and how to say it. This development began in the U.S. in 1848 at Seneca Falls, New York. Involved in the movement for the abolition of slavery, Elizabeth Cady Stanton, Susan B. Anthony, and others, were able to recognize the injustice in their own lives. Just as slaves were the property of landowners, they were able to recognize that they themselves and their daughters were chattels of their husbands and fathers. Thus, the struggle for women's suffrage was born (the first wave) and out of this movement, women's language developed organically.[1]

---

[1] The word itself, from the French, "feminisme," was introduced in the in the early 1900s and came into popular usage in the 1960s and 1970s. *Source: Ask Amy, feminist.com*

The second wave articulation of feminist ideas and activism began with women challenging men in the civil rights, antiwar and social change movements in the 1960s and simultaneously, by educated, middle-class women such as Gloria Steinem and the late Betty Friedan and their many cohorts. Thousands of women of all races and classes have contributed to the language of feminism in the past four plus decades.

Feminist language was invented and constructed to describe women living in the reality of patriarchal domination. Feminist language states, explicitly and implicitly, each individual's right to liberate her mind and herself from the tethers of past and present male oppression. It implies responsibility and the assumption of equal power with men to regulate and control society. It is about describing a new way of living as a woman and should be an intellectual and emotional influence on how we witness the world: how we know it and how it knows us.

Feminism is the mind in action. The feminist objective is to forward the meaning of women's experience in the context of the larger world; to establish ideas and demonstrate credibility. The point is to develop and modify the picture of reality from our own female perceptions. It is not the domain of male-identified authorization, but is opposed to it.

The challenge that the modern feminist dialogue posed to the culture was met. However, the challenges of the interrelationships of power between groups and between women and men are more complex; that is to say, how we personally relate to this power and how we practice it. Although feminism is a reality, it is not an established one in the larger sense of the cultural narrative—and this is the issue that motivated this book.

Women's unwillingness to articulate their position in their own favor indicates the perniciousness of self-prejudice, as well as the absence of understanding the major influence on women's lives in our time. This is unacceptable on any rational terms. To alter this, we have to learn how to SPEAK as our own advocates.

Language is dynamic. It builds confidence which brings new knowledge that in turn, automatically changes the way we speak. We use language to leverage ideas in our own interests. In turn, it brings greater clarity and creativity to the narrative of our own lives.

•

The following is taken from a statement issued by 60 Million Girls, a foundation launched in the fall of 2006 to empower women and girls in underdeveloped counties.

> Education of women is the key to economic productivity and political stability. . . . Women comprise half of the world. We can no longer do without their intelligence, their imagination and their talents.

Will they inform these students that girls around the world have been kept ignorant by male design and malice? About the millennia of male oppression and the exploitation of women's labor? That political stability does not bring the end of women's oppression nor bring them justice? No. And seeing "they" won't, who will? And who will teach this to our own girls in North America?

CHAPTER 2

WHO IS THIS "WE?"

Hey! "Just who are you talking about when you say, we?!!" We're all we. I'm we. Mature, middle class, Anglo Saxon female, whose ancestors arrived from Europe and the British Isles as early as the mid-1600s. German colonials in what became America; immigrants from the British Isles who became Canadians. As to the traces of Indian blood running in my veins, it rose up from the land where the Cree people live and in my case, probably Quebec. If I did not have my "informed urban" perspective on the topic of this "we" identity, then it would be that of a me who stood somewhere else. This is because I am accountable to myself as a woman and to other human beings on the level of my own competencies. I have a free will and use it to suit my mind, personality and the environment around me. This book is the story of that me, who is also "we."

•

When I was a child living in a remote town in Canada, Einstein had landed in the United States and my mother, aunts and their friends used to talk about him, "the most intelligent man in the world." I was highly impressed by all this and formulated this thought: if Einstein is so brilliant, he won't think he's better than I am. I was six or seven at the time and this was my first hunch about equity and natural law. Then, growing up female, I matured into a society that belittled, suppressed, devalued—and cheated—women; and the philosophical forecasts implanted in my childish Einstein flash fueled a near total rejection of "what was expected" of me. After my insurrection, I marked time, inventing my own survival kit of savvy and surly, living on the precipice of getting sucked in, again, to what I had already escaped.

I could scarcely believe my lot when the women's movement rolled around, giving voice to what I was trying to think. Hundreds, then thousands, created the news of women's lives and told us about our losses and our cause. Participants and observers both, we were part of the flowering of women's vision and the development of character and personality. We said, "I'm not going to live like this any more and must stop." And so we did. That "we."

Now, after decades, and living the legacy of that great social movement, I've learned to accept my autonomy for what it's worth and live with gender indignation as just another part a life. Nothing's perfect. What I do not accept is a society devoid of women's self-controlled narrative and the speechlessness of women themselves. Nor do I accept the appalling idea that this contemporary women's knowledge should have to be invented all over again at sometime in the future because of fear, neglect and muteness. That we.

On Whose Authority?

Many claim the right to determine what women say in this world. This inevitably gives rise to the question, "Who do you represent and by what authority do you speak?" This presumes a hierarchical system in which I occupy an assigned rank and position.

In the sixties and seventies when my generation was blazing the feminist trails, we made everything up as we went along. There was no other choice. Except for a few texts and rampant rhetorical and political aspirations, it was the only way to escape the prejudices and obliviousness that decided the course of our lives. During those years, I constructed a worldview of problems as solvable, dreams realizable and possibilities available—as did thousands of others, for whom I do not speak. The movement captured the entire nation's political consciousness. That was then.

It didn't take long for the ideas to be first, reversed and worse, denied. The backlash to women's power was swift and virulent. Feminists were vilified, concepts trashed. Feminism itself is now a theater of contention. Generations argue about "waves." Factions argue about ideology—rejecting society, integration in the system, social reform, inner change or outer activism, and feminist purity (that from the feminist police), among many other things. One item I read even suggested that women "should moderate these days," because not just feminists are listening! As if any feminist movement ever arose for any other audience but everyone in the first place. Then there is the "feminism is dead" cabal. These sorry funeralists confuse the waning of the movement with the ideas of feminism. Contrary to their dismal hopes, the latter are indestructible.

Feminists speak on their own authority. Feminism developed out of individual initiation, subjective experience and self-development. Feminists came up from across the spectrum of poverty, working-class environments, the middle-class and privileged circumstances. Regardless of their origins, they all bore the legacy of women's historical underdevelopment—just like everyone else does. That we.

Feminists made it their business to discover the links between their personal lives and the oppression of women. As they did so, they grew stronger, personally and politically, in the environment and synergy of the women's movement. They developed a particular way of seeing and assumed the responsibility of negotiating the myriad connections, juxtapositions and dynamics that turn on the pivot of sexism and the male agenda.

Feminists found they had a secret power. It was the individual and collective will to act and the willingness to take a stand and to speak about patriarchal power, subordination and misogyny; and to combat fear and opposition to the power of feminism to change minds.

This resulted in the construction of knowledge which is the result of the experience of being feminists and of living with that reality. The authority lies in this knowledge, this living reference. And with it comes the responsibility to provide the answers which have concluded in the enhancement of our lives and changes in society, to those who do not know what these answers are.

Feminists do not acquiesce to patriarchal policies that include the subjugation of women regardless of race, religion, group or community. If one's views on gender are complicated by these, tough. Deal with it. And if this creates antagonism among groups of women, then solutions to the problem will lie in women's development—not by attacking those who have broken the ground and cleared the path for advancement.

Feminism is not the domain of any male-identified authorization nor is it granted by anyone who imagines that they are in charge. There is only one authority and that is inside the head of the woman who puts herself on the line. Who walks the talk and talks the walk. The basis of its validity lies in the belief in individual liberty and participatory power in a free society. Informed, individual views in a free society are valid precisely because they come from within and not because they hold a preconceived or preconditioned authorization. We do not ask permission. Just as there is no "authority" appointed as the sole guarantor of women's interests, nor is the right to speak on behalf of women's interests bestowed or "granted" by some imaginary agency.

Authority lies in the experience of being a feminist and the knowledge that feminist thought broke the codes of patriarchal ideology and power. This self-sufficient, problem-solving genius, however, lay in human creativity whose most profound insight is that we all must straddle the road to wisdom and the path that takes us back to fairyland. That "we."

Many People, Many Paths

The leadership of the second wave grew out of necessity and where it was needed. Much of the leadership came from the grassroots. The movement was the mainstream; it didn't matter where you came from. People inspired others with ideas. Others volunteered where they were needed. There was no model for it. It was organic.

Thousands of projects were launched. Women established coalitions, collectives, safe houses and women's centers; published books, newspapers, magazines; organized conferences, campaigns, demonstrations; fought for reproductive rights, against poverty. ". . . Set up battered women's shelters, rape crisis centers, programs for women with substance abuse problems, tenants' unions, neighborhood groups, day care and medical programs, afterschool programs and welfare rights groups."

Over the years there is not one sector, field, issue, cause, need that has not been addressed by women. Their investment in time, money and creativity ranges from the basic—such as providing suitable clothing for underprivileged women entering the job market; to the spectacular—like readings of Eve Ensler's *The Vagina Monologues* in hundreds of venues around the globe every year; to philanthropic—like the Liz Claiborne Foundation to help young girls maintain their focus while coping with destructive social pressure from interacting with boys; to the bold and volatile—like the group of Vancouverites struggling to establish a public memorial to the 14 women killed at l'Ecole Polytechnique in Montreal in 1989. (The project itself has brought death threats to the organizers.) There's Emily's List, a group which funds women's political campaigns; and an organization in my neighborhood which lobbies city hall for women's interests in housing planning. And the list goes on. This activism, which is occurring every day all around the country, is evidence of the success of feminist ideas and practice which drove the movement for women's rights.

Feminism is always happening, somewhere. Whatever the form, its structure arises out of serving particular needs from a particular point-of-view. Every variety of women's activism that has happened in the past is happening today on some level or another. Then there is the range of new activism that young women are making happen—activist training, boycotts, canvassing, media collectives, hip hop bands, performance groups, petitions, pregnancy prevention, protests, rock bands, sit-ins, speak-outs, street theater, teach-ins and many, many more. There are always people interpreting their version of women's equality and rights to others.

Whatever the group—in a free society, that is—they are going to organize around their own issues to redress wrongs and gain position. The reasons and solutions derive from being involved. In the process, we educate ourselves and raise our own consciousness and those of others: human development. Feminist knowledge is a classic example of such a process. Feminism was and is a grassroots movement. In and of itself, it provides the motivation, the impetus and the synergy.

Not Us!

And then there are those who object to the word "women" used in the collective sense, period; as though women haven't identified with one another since time immemorial. We: the common hurdles. The essential biology. The core values that make us happy. The stakes and risks that we own and bear. That we.

We all live in the same power arrangement and each of our positions has the same patriarchal backdrop regardless of race, color, class, creed. Herein lie the dominant-subordinate political and inter-relational roots of every woman's problems. This truth does not disappear just because one takes umbrage at the use of the word "we" in describing the female reality.

The reluctance to accept that a woman has the authority to talk about women is a reflection of the grip that the patriarchy has on our mental territory, i.e., them controlling us. All religious dogma, all literature and the entire cultural narrative define women in patriarchal terms (with the exception of recent writings and creations by the unconstrained). So attached are we to our subordinators that we believe we lack the authority to describe our situation with comparative pronouns.

Nowhere is this umbrage more obvious than in the minds of conservative women; the ones who want to turn back the clock. These women identify with the men whose inflated egos felt the blow that second wave feminists delivered to the social and political status quo. Their men were unable to protect them from that reality and the whole lot has never been able to recover.

Conservative philosophy means the maintenance of patriarchal principles and practices. Instead of developing their intellectual independence and investigating their unexplored and unarticulated thoughts, these women carry the lead for their ignorant and canting male superiors. Instead of participating in the dynamic conditions necessary for human beings and society to evolve, they spend their lives trying to nail back down the fragments of patriarchal ideology. Unable to transcend their own backwardness, they wallow in a mire of confusion and deceit which is amplified by humiliations like the declaration of the Southern Baptists (America's largest Protestant denomination) in 2003, that the subordination of women to men is an essential Christian belief (presumably conferred by divine ordinance). This running-scared edict was a response to feminism.

The progressive feminist agenda provided all women access to power and decision-making authority. Many in this group have taken advantage of it—in a subordinate mind state. Afraid of what would happen to their "value" if they caused trouble or rocked the male equilibrium, they chose to use their power against . . . other women!

This is a horde of hypocrites. These people talk the submissive rap, but have little faith in the patterns and prospects of pre-liberation. They're not going back there. That's for other suckers—not them. While they work the front lines of repression for men who like their women submissive, they live secretly progressive personal lives. They control their own lives, work, get rich, travel and do all that free women expect to do, while promoting an agenda which solidifies male power. They obviously want the things normal women want—freedom and independence—but believe it's reserved especially for them. Privilege, position and ideological corruption cause them to forget our common interests and to use them as a division in service of the powers which they, themselves, ultimately serve.

The visible and vocal wing of traditional conservatism is led by movers and shakers like Phyllis Schlafly, founder of the Eagle Forum, Beverly LaHaye, founder of Concerned Women of America; and operate out of organizations such as the Clare Boothe Luce Policy Institute and Heritage Foundation. Even more visible are the new female pawns promoted by right wing media groups and schools of false arguments—the ones they trot out onto the podium or in front of talk show cameras, to offer the opposing view to women's rights, of all things.

So bewildered are they by the "we" of it, some of these women claim they are feminists! They have to identify with the feminist concept to have any credence at all outside the anti-woman orientation of their own lot.

An example of how unhinged this gets, can be found in Feminists for Life, a national anti-abortion organization. This outfit, whose slogan is "refuse to choose," claims it does not want to criminalize all abortions, it just supports "legal protection for women and children"—from abortion! This double talk is language divorced from meaning altogether and is generic to this group's identity problems. Instead of expanding their sense of the world, they have lost any semblance of rationality. In another tawdry contrivance, the founder of one of their chapters purchased the birthplace home of Susan B. Anthony in Adams, Massachusetts. The organizers argue that "Susan B. Anthony . . .would feel comfortable with the positions of Feminists for Life of New York." (Stacy Schiff, "Desperately Seeking Susan," *New York Times,* 13 October 2006.) The entire concept of this organization is as ludicrous as inventing "feelings" for a dead suffragette.

There is no such thing as a conservative feminist. Anyone who promotes the patriarchal agenda at the expense of women's autonomy—who imposes her will upon another woman to make her a breeder, for instance—is not a feminist. In this culture, conservative-speak is still considered to be the authoritative take on women's reality: their views are assumed to be the norm. This twaddle must be denormalized— and it can't happen too soon.

> The vision of all this . . . seemed to Dorothea like a sudden letting in of daylight, waking her from her previous stupidity and incurious self-absorbed ignorance about her husband's relation to others.
>
> George Eliot, *Middlemarch*

CHAPTER 3

THE FEEDBACK LOOP

In 2006 I held seminars, based on this book, with two very different groups. One was in a women's studies center at a Montreal university; the other at a professional organization in New York. The participants were a multi-racial combination of academics, students and business women. In presenting this material, two trains of thought about "we" emerged: the academic agenda and the race-class dialogue.

The Academic Agenda

At the university, two striking statements were made. One was the argument that there should be a unified theory of feminism, race and class,[2] the other was that the goal of feminism is the destruction of the patriarchy. Both of these have their roots in Marxist doctrine.

The attempt to define feminism from a socialist perspective is nothing new. It began at the beginning of the second wave movement with the relationship of the nascent women's movement and the male-dominated left in the civil rights and anti-war movements. The idea was to combine the ideology of women's rights with that of all oppressed races and classes who were on the rise. However, it didn't work then and it won't work now. The idea that one must conflate feminism, race and class—three aspects of oppression—is a leftist and leftover contrivance. Social change does not mean social -ist. Feminism developed itself out of intuition and qualitative

---

[2]To reduce women's individuality into an all-or-nothing theory should fail by definition. Reductionist models of women's reality have already worked to our timeless and universal disadvantage. Must we have another one?

experience, not Marxist ideology. Whatever threads of socialist ideology have been woven into feminist ideas were appropriated by feminists, not imposed on feminists.

The alleged "unified theory" should arrive at an overall socialist perspective from the point-of-view of whom, exactly? And seeks to find solutions to what, specifically? Why and how would I relate to such a theory? In other words, what has the supposedly superior knowledge of Marxism got to do with feminism? "Workers unite!" did not demand equality for women. Marx's concept of labor did not include homemaking and raising children or the need to balance those with an independent quality of life. If the investigation of a unified theory of feminism, race and class is irresistible, one should do it in the department of failed ideology—flogging the dead horse of Marx and post-Marxism ad nauseam—and prove the negative. Perhaps they'd discover that feminism is a life raft that will deliver this corpse of male delusion and give it a proper burial.

The superimposition of race and class theory, or a fusion of these with feminism to meet the demands of a "unified theory," imposes censorial conditions on feminist knowledge, instead of contributing to the expansion of human understanding about how our collective identities develop organically side by side. To suggest that I, as a white American feminist, should separate from my race, my history, my culture, my path, my standpoint, because of a dogmatic demand fostered by the pandering forces of political correctness to fuse all races and classes with my own experience is not only intolerable, it's out of the question. Throwing up accusations of slavery, privilege and colonialism in the belief that I will change my identity, or fuse it with someone else's and deny my life experience, is equally silly. I will happily continue to be what I am and write and talk about the things I chose. Feminism by definition is the expression and experience of one sex. The class and race of feminists add to that body of knowledge, each from their own particular angle.

Destruction of the patriarchy? This notion comes up outside of academia, as well as within. When it does, one is lead to ask, "to be replaced by what? Utopia?" "A matriarchy!" is the standard reply. "There have been matriarchies in the past!" That they did not survive is pertinent. Why, after 5,000 years of patriarchal dominance, would that be viable now?

The patriarchal destruction, slash, matriarchal replacement concept is a knee-jerk discussion and polar opposite. In the supposed new-age matriarchy, women's entire work would be beating back men who were trying to reestablish the patriarchy. I do not believe in the -archy by anybody. Enlightened humans understand that authority to govern social and political affairs is a shared responsibility and not something that either sex has the right or responsibility to dump on, or wrest from, the other. Life is relational. We have to learn to live with each another as mature beings.

In academia, the destruction of the patriarchy notion is an outcome of the Marxist mentality. Marxist-Communism was a revolutionary movement whose intent was that the people overthrow the state machinery and seize power. The idea that our goal should be to destroy the patriarchy is an extension of this ideology. So far, I've seen no developments to that end on the North American women's front. In the winter of 2008, we have ninety women in the United States Congress. That's the way it works here. It's called change.

Higher learning institutions are patriarchal and the minds that are developed there are shaped in accordance with male codes of epistemology and within the strictures of that control. Men's values dominate the entire structure and content of learning. Whether female academics like it or not—and fight it or not—males force questions down their throats and answers out of their mouths. So most women are left with their inner thoughts never spoken to another person—at least not in terms of our higher education.

The creeping hand of male control operates in the intellectual structure of young women's minds which are developed in an environment of hegemonic masculine ideology. This co-option causes them to support any number of bad ideas. Replacing the word women with "gender and sexuality" studies, for instance, is one. This tactic deletes, marginalizes and decimates feminist knowledge. Abandoning the concept of women's rights for "human rights" and promoting the panaceaic "we are all one" of humanism are others. It was even suggested to me in a seminar that feminism as a concept should be eliminated altogether. "Would not ecological subjectivity bypass gender differences?" she said. Ecological subjectivity? If you want to go on that trip, don't forget your compass.

This society should be smart enough by now to understand that the human rights and freedom puzzle merely buries women's interests. It does not address nor fight for them. Human rights are male rights and the concept is a smokescreen for the inequities women suffer at the hands of man all around the world. Only knowledge and acceptance of women's fundamental sovereignty and equity—and of male oppression and subordination—begin to give even a glimpse of what is required for justice and equality for women.

•

The supposed privilege of academia to control knowledge gives rise to another misguided mind set. That is the one which claims the right to determine what feminists say. An example of this authoritarianism arises in a paper by R. Bahramitash, "The War on Terror, Feminist Orientalism and Orientalist Feminism" (9/5/2005) in which she chastises both Geraldine Brooks for her book, *Nine Parts of Desire* and Azar Nafisi for her *Reading Lolita in Tehran*, as ". . . 'independent' [her quotes], self-proclaimed feminists" and propagandists for the "colonial strategy of focusing on the Muslim world's treatment of women."

Feminist knowledge is used as the scapegoat in the dogmatic arguments going on about individuality, democracy, multiculturalism and cultural relativism. Colonialism, liberalism and their neo-prefixed versions are big buzzwords on campus these days and female scholars are attracted to these phenomena to use as scourges against Western feminists.

One of their pet peeves is Western women's organizational and financial support for Afghan women, which the neo-theorists claim is part of a new liberal colonization effort, aimed at developing countries. I've heard this in seminars and assemblies; on television and radio news and news magazines in Canada and the United States. By way of theoretical contrivances, the detractors fuse women's activism with the neo-conservative and opportunistic foreign policy propaganda regarding women's issues which emanates out of the Bush White House.

I am not impressed with the scholarship of white, foreign-born or "nonwhite" academics who construct bogus arguments on the backs of American feminists. Nor am I moved by accusations of white privilege which imply that all the sins of colonialists fall on the daughters. Diversity of thought is one thing. Ill-conceived notions are another. If these academics think that Western women going abroad (or helping others here at home) is nothing but a neo-colonial smokescreen for dastardly and hidden motives, then they've missed a whole level of education they should catch up on. The topic of this pursuit could be called "the consequences of civilization brought about by colonialism; and the more recent phenomenon of women's advancement in the very societies of which these academics are now a part." Within this discipline, in the barbarism section, they could reflect upon their own motives for using colonialism as a bludgeon against contemporary Western feminists. As part of the project, documenting the experience of the alleged "colonized" of Afghanistan, would be required to learn what Afghan women themselves bring to the arrangement, such as their own hopes, determination and efforts to improve their lives.

The constraints that engender women's knowledge in a vacuum and prevent academic women from actually manifesting their learning in the society, culture and community is a problem they'll have to work their way out of. And as for the academic disdain shown toward the "independent feminist," which would pertain to me, let me put it this way. When I'm talking to someone who knows little or nothing about this subject and they understand me—that's peer review. Academic approval not necessary.

·

Another part of the problem nestled in academia, is that the language usually used to describe the concepts which underpin the advancement of women's rights is theoretical rhetoric. Unless feminism is being bashed in street or media slang, it is described in tedious, impenetrable jargon. Both turn people off and scare them.

The feminism of what is, when you live it, is knowledge. What isn't knowing it by living it, is academic theory. It comes after the fact. Once you get into the theory of what feminism isn't (academia), you start inventing dogma about what it should be and depend on patriarchal constructs to come up with your thesis. Thus you rationalize things along the lines of stale male meaning, instead of thinking them out for yourself. You do this instead of discussing your commitment to acknowledging who you are as a woman, how you relate to your position in the patriarchal hegemonic system which higher education is, and what you're going to do about it. Doing this would mean discussing your experience and relationship to the subject; not theory, but something you are actually learning how to know. As for the students in this ironical situation, they would be better off turning their women's studies into a lab—a living lab. Feminist knowledge is rooted in experience; in where you stand. In risk. Within the process you awaken yourself to powers and initiatives you didn't know you had. You learn that the essence of feminism is a set of universals; that women's condition encompasses all race, class and sexuality issues and that we all live out our own lives in our own skin. That the "other," which theorists are so fond of referring to—as though it were an objective correlative for people—means those who live it out with us. It has to be close to the bone. Otherwise, it's just hot air.

The Race-class Dialogue

One of the other defining events of the twentieth century was the Black civil rights movement which dismantled the Jim Crow[3] system of racism in a few short decades. Considering the impact of that and the feminist movement combined—"permanent transformation of the social fabric of this country and countries around the world"—it is hardly surprising that black and white women have an ongoing debate about feminism.

Basically, the argument goes like this. You, white woman, must include everything important to women-of-color (black, actually; other races and ethnic groups go virtually unmentioned in this conversation) in your thinking and dialogue. This position has its origins in the question of why women's liberation in the United States was not a racially integrated movement. In her book, *The Trouble Between Us*, Winifred Breines discusses the topic at length. And no, by the way. I don't have to.

What didn't happen—an integrated feminist movement—is what isn't. Trying to establish a cultural analysis of the thing desired but which did not manifest—in this case, a fusion of the values and identity of women with every class, race, sexuality, religion, nationality, disability—is attempting to assemble the pieces of a puzzle that does not mesh with reality.

No feminist I know is blinkered about the aberrations of slavery and native genocide. Nor are they immune to the fact that the different races with whom we live, have had to concern themselves with life and death issues that have made loyalty to their race or tribe overshadow the gender problems that affect all of us. However, I do not stand at the intersection of my gender and everyone else's ethnicity, culture, socioeconomic status, sexual orientation and the myriad other qualifiers that mark us as individuals and groups in the many dimensions we inhabit. We each occupy a particular territory and that is where our stakes are. We cannot, and do not, internalize or conceptualize everyone's struggles and rush out to fight their battles. Instead, we all do our part to emerge free from our own underdevelopment and that inevitably includes working with and helping others to the extent that we are able, within the context of our own individuality. But it's not a package deal. One cannot superimpose their identity on others because of their own theoretical or political imperatives. Human progress is an unfolding. It's a messy thing and has its own nature. It's un-theory.

---

[3]Jim Crow laws were state and local laws enacted in the Southern and border states of the United States and in force between 1876 and 1967 that required racial segregation, especially of blacks, in all public facilities. It also affected Asians and many other races. "Jim Crow period" or the "Jim Crow era" refers to the time during which this practice occurred. The most important laws required that public schools and most public places (including trains and buses) have separate facilities for whites and blacks. *Wikipedia*

> I can't talk about what it's like to live in a white person's skin.
> I only know what it's like to live in my own skin.
>   Participant, *TALKING THE WALK* Seminar

What did happen is a more plausible way to frame the discussion. The feminist movement defined itself by proving itself to be what it is. Different groups on different paths and parallel tracks, interrelated and often intertwined on many common terms, conditions and contexts. We were all in the zone: getting out of ourselves and moving ahead because of the dynamic conditions we were all creating as a result of our mutual needs and demands and our ability to influence one another. It is self-evident that each of us came with an identity that could and did inform each other—the way Winona LaDuke, or bell hooks, or Homa Arjomand, or young women, or the participants in my seminars, inform me today.

The women's movement was an and-and situation, and it still is. The complexities of individual priorities and human relations and motivations of groups and races are not the problem here. The struggle was and still is against the male agenda dominating women. Understanding this, while engaged in the struggle, one must also continually adjust the elements of her own stability. This precludes a utopian "togetherness" and certainly precludes a "unified theory" of what it means to be a political woman. And none of this alters the fact that all women live under varying degrees of patriarchal control and pressure. What kind, or to what degree, doesn't matter. What does matter is that we acknowledge it.

Sexism, which feminism deals with, is inevitably intertwined with race and class. bell hooks argues that "race and class oppression are feminist issues in that they all depend on domination and one form of domination cannot be eliminated while the others remain. Sexism can be considered the primary oppression because it is the most widely felt both by the exploiter and by the exploited." Audre Lorde (1934-92) argued that it is "crucial not only to acknowledge difference between women but to see it as a basis for women's empowerment. Women's interdependence can generate creative power that will lead to freedom and a new way of being women." Amen to both, and to the old adage that Rome wasn't built in a day.

Social integration does not mean a homogeneous society but all of us coexisting together in living color—each in our individual and collective way. This vision is a true broadening of what it means to be a woman living in a democracy in the 21st century. We are all living what we are and with the capability of what we can be, adding our own dimension to the historical trajectory of free women. We have broken the essential barriers. We are growing up and getting older and smarter; and transcending the history of our own subservience.

In the end, we are all people living in this country who must make sense of gender prejudice. Every group has the task of articulating and protesting the specificities of women's struggles across their own culture and over time and developing their own potential within that context. As this happens—which it has done and continues to do—we all gain an understanding of our lived similarities, differences and connections. Nonetheless, we continue to focus and apply our energy in areas connected with our own lives. Were this not the case, women's development would not be a global topic.

The Mural

A portrait of the reality of American women's collectivism can be seen in the 45' x 75' mural covering the high side of a building at Greene Avenue & Norstrand in Bedford Stuyvesant, Brooklyn, New York. Titled *When Woman Pursue Justice* © 2005 Artmakers, Inc., this women artists activist project, spearheaded by Janet Braun-Reinitz and Jane Weissman, was created by women artists, volunteer painters and high school interns from the area.

This entire project is a study in form. The painting presents the faces of eighty-nine of America's finest, who personify a chain of activism for women's suffrage and autonomy over two centuries. We see Elizabeth Cady Stanton, leader of the nineteenth century women's rights movement; Charlayne Hunter-Gault, who risked her life to desegregate the University of Georgia in 1961; Wilma Mankiller, first woman to lead the Cherokee Nation; Yuri Kochiyama, grassroots civil rights leader for political prisoners and Japanese reparations; labor leader and organizer Dolores Huerta, cofounder of the United Farm Workers; Eleanor Holmes Norton, lawyer, educator, politician and who, as an ACLU attorney, won promotions for 60 female *Newsweek* employees, who accused the liberal magazine of discrimination against women; Betty Friedan and Gloria Steinem, pivotal leaders of the contemporary movement; and eighty-one others.

This mural conveys the truth of individual women's contributions to the history and evolution of this country. They are brought together here to reveal the shared purpose of women's struggle which was to create change through their own pioneering activism. It provides an immediate grasp of what feminist collaboration is: not one issue, not one cause, not exclusionary, not elite. The message is that each woman worked in opposition to a particular aspect of the patriarchal power structure (and many went to prison as a result). Each action, which nobody forced her to take, shaped her own destiny and the world of those around her.

This art project, as well as its content, is a portrait of women's activism, cooperation and solidarity. It is a glimpse into the world of politics and an example of how knowledge about our circumstances can be conveyed in order to help us round out our sense of ourselves. Knowing that creative projects like this exist, and the things themselves, makes it easier for us to maintain our position.

•

Along the lines of the race-class dialogue, it was suggested that I was responsible for enjoining the issues of women in emerging countries. There is a big difference between solidarity and activism. The latter, activism, I concentrate where I choose. Around me every day is evidence of women suffering because of the stupidity and neglect of my own society, which will take generations to alleviate. While I find the struggles of women in other nations compelling—and as often appalling, horrifying and mind-boggling—I choose to focus on issues that face us at home and particularly on that of feminist consciousness.

An editorial in the *New York Times*, 21 July 2006 (excerpted from a series in the Spanish-language newspaper *El Diario/La Prensa*), described the dire straits of young Latina women in New York and in every region in the country. These girls and women suffer from every kind of deprivation, manipulation and self-destruction: suicide, drug use, teenage motherhood, school dropouts, family violence, social alienation. "Solving these problems will require more than research," said the editorial. "What is needed is a larger effort that includes educators, policymakers, families and communities. Here's one more statistic: one in four women in the United States will be Hispanic by the middle of the century. The time to help is now." The editorial is describing a national crisis. So who's stepping up to the plate? Who's leading? Who's supporting? Who is helping them find the answers?

Activism in other nations is what those who live there do. According to *Women's Studies Quarterly*, "Much of the current creative energy in feminist activism comes from outside of Western Europe and North America, in the vibrant networks of women's groups, gender institutes, politico-cultural performances, and the feminist coalitions in Africa, Asia and South

America." And there are many, many women from democratic countries working on these causes all around the world.

Getting involved in other women's cultures and expecting to break the ideological, psychological, tribal and social codes which define their plight is not something I choose to do. Living in the misogynistic, Judeo-Christian, white male power dominated, pseudo-democratic conditions that I do—with fundamentalism rising and the position of the U.S. in the world weakening—is quite enough for me.

Miriam Helie-Lucas, an Algerian sociologist and anthropologist and activist with Women Living Under Muslim Law, seems to agree. During her appearance at McGill University in 2005, I asked her what she thought of a certain group of American women who were promoting the idea that the Bush White House should make the liberation of women in Islamic countries part of our foreign policy. "No thanks," she said. "We need your support. Not your interference." Amen to that, too.

Political Correctness: The Bane of It

Political correctness (PC), an aspect of the political and cultural feedback loop, is self-abnegating and hypocritical behavior. Reverence toward the PC position means you bend to the beliefs of others at the expense of your own—and that's why such rhetoric always sounds so phony. PC is caving into group pressure to conform to their point-of-view. This is not dialogue. In a dialogue, thoughts arise according to one's own principles, experience, sensibilities and point-of-view in relation to the other. PC is the legacy of decades of equality rhetoric. PC responses happen when our own ideas get mixed up with preordained social values and the speech patterns of the going political fashion. In such a case, we prioritize the going dogma over our need to contemplate, criticize and debate. It's the worst thing that could happen for the cultural advancement of feminist knowledge. In PC world, even the quaintly named "masculinism" gets reverence.

PC is not as "nice" as those who practice it may think. It stifles dialogue and debate, makes people resistant to struggle, protects ignorance by denying that there are real differences between people, many of them dangerous and irreconcilable. The virtue of all-inclusiveness spares us from making tough judgments about what is right and wrong about the way people have organized their own development. Women should be particularly conscious about this, considering our history of muzzling and strait jacketing ourselves. PC is an extension of feminine naivete which relies on an exaggerated agreeableness quotient, combined with an underestimation of the value of doubt.

Justice and fairness do not arise out of blind equanimity, but out of people taking a stand against opposing forces. It requires looking into things. It is not brought about by blanket empathy or self-loathing about privilege or by kowtowing to another's cultural beliefs and practices.

PC sentiments are there to be taken advantage of; and they are. Each group has a cultural strategy whose mission is to further its agenda. The more self-righteous and the greater the willingness to oppose—the greater the power to persuade. And, of course, this is met with a corresponding willingness to be persuaded. Furthering one's agenda requires coercion and in a democracy, political correctness is its tool. The politically correct response is acquiescing to this power.

Today, attacking liberal individuality and Western values is the most popular line of attack and it is quite successful. People are proving their eagerness to react against themselves. The self-flagellation after 9/11 is an example of this. Many here in the U.S. blamed Americans because radical Muslims destroyed the World Trade Center and killed thousands of people. Americans blamed themselves because another power is working to destroy us. How crazy is that? How crazy is the self-suppression inherent in political correctness?

When we act with political correctness, we discount the pathologies bred in other groups and nations and integrate them into our society. We thereby deny the underlying strategy in all countries to oppress women.

It is with impaired judgment that after 150 years of struggle, we welcome groups that believe in the subordination and oppression of women into our society. Like trained seals, we buy into the dogma of moral and cultural relativism, embracing cultures whose males oppress and subordinate women as a matter of course, culture and ideology. The fear of being accused of racism plays a part in this—as do the accusations of fear itself. In PC lingo, you don't dislike or rationally oppose another's values, behavior and positions; you "fear" them. In fact, what PC person fears is social disapproval. Those who fear the group itself, cower in some other mode.

Backward attitudes and practices relative to women are not acceptable in this country. Sensitivity to other cultures which oppress women should be discouraged, not the opposite. It is up to these cultures to conform to the ideals of women's freedom that have been shaped by feminists in our world. It is up to them to change their minds, not up to us to go backwards for fear of . . . what? Hurting their feelings? Where there are anti-woman, anti-feminist, misogynistic beliefs, the people who embrace them are responsible for grasping the present meanings of women's lives. It is they who are expected to learn the wisdom, the morality, the proofs and the incontrovertible claims of women's higher development, demand for resources and individual liberty. If there are any compromises to be made, we determine what these are. They are not imposed on us by primitive ideas and backward cultures.

Political correctness is sycophantish and indicative of mental paralysis. It reduces our ideas and cows us in the face of the challenges of group pressure. We all have to grapple with our own bigotry and smallness and the goal is to grow out of these primitive urges and continue the progression of a just society. This is not done by silencing ourselves in the face of group pressure.

My feminist self is not synonymous with anyone else's race or class. The political thinking of all progressive activism is part of the continuing process of human knowledge. It does not take the place of, nor does it redefine the basic ideas of feminism. It adds to the mix. It continues the evolution.

CHAPTER 4

FAILURE OF NARRATION

When people ask what I'm writing about, I try to respond in a few short sentences that mention the topic and the point of my efforts. I make it as concise as possible -- while they chomp at the bit. They think my every word is their cue to hold forth on the one thing they know about feminism. Everyone wants to speak their mind. They all have one idea and it's usually the wrong thing. Most completely miss the point.

The statements run the gamut from misunderstanding to dread. The former can be attributed to insufficient education and unawareness; the latter to the blowback that blames feminism for anything anybody will listen to. And listen they do.

Feminists are blamed for 9/11, Hurricane Katrina, the decline in morality, education and the birth rate; the "boy crisis," male impotence, the rise in crime and every other calamity that misogynists and their helpmeets can come up with to trash women's independence and regain waning male power. The public disparagements are amplified by what women hear in their personal and social environment: belittlement and lashing out. The negative effect is that they use this trashing and lashing to shape their own opinions, negating their own self-worth and power. Then, not wanting to appear to be completely out of the loop, they glom onto their favorite fragment to appease the blowbag blowback. Here are some examples, along with my response to what's skewed up with each.

All the Wrong Things

Marsha. Young women just aren't interested. It was different in our day.

•Considering her lack of awareness, it is unlikely that Marsha was involved with the women's movement. She just went along for the ride and used it for what it was worth (lots). Every young woman I've spoken to becomes interested in a matter of minutes and wants to know more. The young women Marsha speaks about haven't had enough information or experience to understand the limitations brought on by sexism.

Alia. One thing I know for sure, is that men don't like strong women.

•She's talking about men who must be in control, or those with puny or overblown egos. They prefer weak women. The more self-assured the male, the fewer problems he has with females, period. Strong or powerful does not phase them. My prediction for Alia is that she will give up her own maturation for a relationship with an oppressive or needy man.

Cindy. My brother was on the wrestling team, but it got cut because of Title IX. After that, he started goofing off, getting bad grades and things. It's not fair.

•It is not unfair. Title IX of the Education Amendments, requiring the education system to invest equally in high school and college girls, rectified centuries of discrimination against women in education.   Your brother was involved in a male entitlement program, which should have ended in 1972 when the legislation was passed. Obviously the college he attends was breaking the law until they ruined his life by cancelling wrestling.

Hedda. We got what we wanted. So let it go.

•You got what you wanted. An education and a way to make enough money to live the way you want to. Yours is a narrow vision. Your awareness of others, intellectual acuity, willingness to take a risk, willingness to speak out, have all been limited by your attachment to your own goals.

Bob. You got what you wanted. So let it go.

•Sounds like Hedda, but isn't. Bob is saying, "Women have gone far enough, now stop!" He's defending male social, cultural and historical territory and doesn't want any more infringements. He's unable to see that women, children—and men—who are treated unfairly, are downtrodden, underprivileged and suffering, mainly because women lack development, resources and authority. He also has no idea what he's talking about. He does not know what "we" wanted, nor want, because for him, reality is filtered through penis-centered assumptions.

Elizabeth. The superwoman was a myth. They couldn't handle it. Women are opting out of the job market to stay at home and raise kids.

•One: you're trapped in the "either career or family" polarity. And you're pushing the "sacrifice career for family" agenda. To start with, whoever came up with the superwoman idea was unaware that *everything* around women had to change, as well as she, once women became full participants in the education and job markets. Superwoman is a myth because it's a bad idea, not because women can't handle complicated lives. Two: the facts, with plenty of data to back them up, prove the opposite.[4] Women's careers and families get along perfectly well. What doesn't work is the media angle on this topic. Also not working are the conditions in the work world and the home that would make career and family compatible. This is the need for an advanced society, not the end of superwoman. And why should she sacrifice one aspect of her life for another?

Gene. I grew up in the same neighborhood as Betty Friedan. What a meeskite! That's Yiddish. D'ya know what it means?

•That statement is a rhetorical anvil, used to undermine the conversation. What I'm doing has nothing do with her appearance and a great deal to do with the products of her mind and efforts, which are obviously a threat to you. And as for your cheering section over there in the secretarial, er. . . administrative assistant pool—no, her work is not outmoded. But they obviously haven't been able to figure out why.

Laura. It's too radical for me!

---

[4]For facts on this issue, see the Catalyst or the Family and Work Institute websites. Numerous other sources can be found by searching the internet.

•You're trapped in the "feminist as man-hating-fiend" playlet. There was a radical faction which was suspicious of all things male (government, for instance) and rejected everything in the past as it pertains to gender power. They may still exist, I don't know; my interests lie elsewhere. You need to be more knowledgeable about the overall subject as to how it changed your life.

> In the 1980s feminism was scapegoated by the media, as well as by the right-wing political parties that had been returned to power, as responsible for all kinds of negative social change and moral decay.
>
> Elizabeth Tacey, Contributor
> *Propaganda and Mass Persuasion*

Carly. I want a home and family—the way my mom did it!

•With the exception that you have a college degree and career, right? All feminists I know have homes, most have kids and some are great cooks. Some have never turned their stoves on; some have woeful taste and serve horrible meals. The prefeminist world of homemaking—endless cleaning, laundry, scrubbing, three meals a day, chasing kids, scrimping and enduring a lifetime of paralyzing tedium, is available. I'm sure you can acquire man and brood happy to avail themselves of this kind of devotion. But be careful about hitting the bottle too early in the day. Meanwhile, as you work it all out, take heart in the words of British hottie, mom and cooking diva, Nigella Lawson, who puts it all together:

> ". . . a lot of women, I think, feel illogically that cooking will detract from their intellectual gravitas. And I always thought that was pretty dim. . . . I think cooking helps proper thought. And I've always felt that the feminist's — and I'm a feminist — argument about cooking is weak. If you say all the traditional female roles have no value, what does that say about women?"
> *(Source: Montreal Gazette, 7 October 2006.)*

Now don't you go and get carried away with PDC (public display of cookies) just because Nigella does it. There's a limit to everyone's tolerance for sugar.

Chondra. I never thought I needed it. I come from a family of strong women.

•This country, and all countries, are built on the backs of strong women like your mother and grandmother. The strong woman syndrome creates a mental bubble that pressures you to ignore the underdevelopment, deprivation, sacrifice, heartbreak and inevitable abuse your foremothers experienced, and where it came from. Its cause was sexism, misogyny and the rest of the oppression, subordination package. It's all around us now, just as it was then. The degree to which it affects us personally depends on how we educate ourselves about the subject.

The syndrome creates the comforting idea that you're not affected by it at all. It takes willful understanding to recognize the sexist structure of society as it affects you personally.

Natalie. We live in a matriarchy! I see women all around me lording it over men. Plus, they control vast wealth.

•You're talking about your grandmother. Outside her family and immediate social circle, she lives in the same patriarchal reality that I do. She's protected from this unsavory truth by her privilege and has handed this attitude down to you. Her banker, broker and bishop grovel before her because she's rich, not because she's superior. If she lost it all today, you wouldn't see them for dust.

Susan. I know a few women in business who are feminists. They're much harder than men. The new head of our department is worse than any man I've ever worked with.

•If feminism is seen as a reason for female managers to act worse than men, then they've sorely missed the point. It is meant to enlargen one's perceptions and possibilities in life, not to reduce her to the lowest common denominator. But perhaps her style has nothing to do with feminism. Could it be you, Susan? Using feminism as a cudgel to beat this woman back and get brownie points from your male colleagues?

Dakota. Feminism is for the privileged. It's a rich, white women's idea. Poor women and women-of-color are not part of it. I'm not interested.

•You have bad information and no real knowledge. The journey to equality in this country and around the world was traveled and endured by women of all races and classes; those with the most minimal means and possibilities along with those who not only had their leadership to contribute but also the greatest to lose; in many cases their freedom. But it's a journey you have to take yourself, if you want to speak and be credible. Start looking into it. Read some books.

Ann. I want to get married. I think feminists gave marriage a bad rap and young women suffer for it.

•What it did was present the case for life with a greater scope— and hope. The marriage and mommy trap was exposed for what it was worth—a one-sided affair where women were supposed to be satisfied with the warm and fuzzies of man and child. And after that? I've noticed some positive changes over the years in men's behavior in the marital-family compartment and it appears to be getting better for some women. Meanwhile, most feminists are married. Some would never get married. Some have had multiple marriages; others would never get married again. So look at the institution and male behavior within its context, rather than scapegoating feminism for your lack of bliss.

Willa. I like men! Do you know about Valerie Solanas? She wrote the *S.C.U.M. Manifesto.* Do you kow what it meant? (Pause.) The Society for Cutting Up Men!

•Of course. I read it when it came out. Valerie Solanas was a violent and obsessed nut job. If you've been led to believe she's a feminist heroine, think about it. Women have gone to jail for feminist causes. Mutilating and shooting men because they ignore you isn't one of them. And by the way, I can hardly believe you came up with this one, as your one "wrong thing."

All the wrong things are rhetorical tools of opposition to feminism and exist within the context of patriarchal pressure. Bad knowledge is meant to be overcome. First, one needs some information about basic principles; then one must understand feminism as a philosophical and social movement with a political agenda that serves all women, all people. This causes one to realize the power differential in our professional roles, our social and governmental structures and in our relationships. More important, we discover that the women's movement was not a knockout punch. No one pretended to have all the solutions to all the problems, neatly presented in a pink package. The biggest one remaining, is filling the mental void surrounding that one wrong thing.

On the Wheel

All of this fear, denial and lack of education is par for the course: we have 5,000 years of it behind us. But considering the striking changes to society because of the movement, by now all women should at least have a working knowledge of what the power imbalance means, how we buy into it and how we change it. But this is not so.

Why is all human knowledge cumulative, but not ours? How come we don't put this altogether, and see that it is fundamental to our personal, social, cultural and political lives—and the future? The problem is karmic. What goes around falls apart before the finish line. And then it happens all over again. Here is how I state the problem.

Premise

The women's movement has a cyclical nature. It rises up in the public consciousness, only to disappear within a decade or so and return again later. Because of this pattern, the principals of feminism fail to establish themselves in the culture at large.

The language has not been developed in the common dialogue. As the language is missing, so is the cultural narrative of the significance of women's values, experience, talents and wisdom. This is reflected in the main feature of women's history: a cycle of loss and partial recovery. The failure of the current philosophical and political narration today is similar to the disappearance of women's dialogue in the past.

Why do we keep losing this knowledge? Because feminism is not accessible; not made democratic. It does not get passed on. Does this mean that we do not value the wisdom and brilliance inherent in women alone? Or have we just not found a way to transmit this knowledge as part of our collective culture? These are the issues that motivated me to develop this project.

The premise combines with two practical observations.

Issue #1: Women and the Macro Picture

Onto the topic of advancement, women have reached critical mass in the workforce, are becoming better educated and making the transition from cheap labor toward equal pay and better jobs. Education and jobs are the great divide women crossed as a result of the second wave and it is not necessary to quantify this progress here: statistics abound elsewhere.

There are now many women in positions of importance. At decision-making levels, thousands of women have had a significant impact on certain front line issues in local institutions and environments and geographical pockets. At the elite levels, women are slowly making an impression on certain aspects of society.

It is not apparent, however, that the sensibility of women's vision or women's leadership has reached anything near critical mass. In fact, at the macro level, women's influence is nowhere to be seen. **Nothing has changed at the top:** and that is Issue #1. They have not improved how the world works. The structure of social and cultural reality has not changed, nor has the script. We do not have an equal role in the direction of society. Male control of power remains virtually intact. The power structure does not reflect back women's interests in any generic sense.

Different groups of women have evaluated women's rights to serve their own options, and justly so. This does not, however, make them exemplars for women's roles, now or in the future. The most equal women are elite and this equality does not trickle down. Women got to these positions of leadership by driving forward their own demands and ideas during the crucial days of the women's movement. More often than not, these are women using power in service of the patriarchy. The tools once wielded against women are now being wielded by woman.

The question is, what are we driving at now? The answer is, inclusion in the male power structure. At this level, women's power is concentrated among the elite, where any changes that do occur, do so in the service of the patriarchy. And this means, that in spite of women's advancement, politics has not changed and women at that level are facilitating the imposition of unsuitable models of social organization and cultural progress. This is hostile to women's sovereignty, equality and equity, while pretending that it is not.

Issue #2: Women's Advancement in General

So you now have a scenario about how things do not get changed at the top. And what about the middle: the mainstream?

Every woman in this country has benefitted from the efforts of the feminist movement. Sexism has been exposed to one and all for what it is: crippling and unjust. Yet few are able to describe the reasons or actions that brought about this change. They not only resist the concepts of feminism, they openly argue against it. **Women take advantage of feminism, but will**

not support it: Issue #2.   They think equality is some kind of default position.

Women's elevated social and political development has not been internalized by the majority of women as something of fundamental value. We are not inclined to believe that we have a unique history, or independent political rights and definitions. This indicates there has been no long-term investment in establishing feminism as a topic in the general education of women.   It appears, therefore, that we, ourselves, do not accept this knowledge as an essential intellectual and ideological force in the process of human social and political development—although it has already proven itself to be just that, over and over again.

•

So here you have a picture of a vicious circle. Because the critical mass (#2) does not identify with women's principles (premise), we fail to influence the structure of public life (#1). As our language is missing in the common narrative, our culture and politics do not embody our values, needs and interests as a requisite of women's very participation in society.

There is no question that women voters and women's organizations played a critical part in the results of the 2006 U.S. midterm election. The 110th Congress has 74 women (of 440) in the House of Representatives, 16 (of 100) in the Senate[5] and mother, grandmother and feminist Nancy Pelosi, has broken through the "marble ceiling" to become the first female Speaker of the House in history. Hopes are high that these numbers will result in "change, honesty and cleaning up Washington" as well as a new push for women's equality.

But it takes a lot of energy to run a capitalist superpower. Will these newly elite women change the nature of power and practice of politics into a humane, intelligent organization which legislates and oversees fairness and justice for all women? Will they execute upon the feminist vision and strategy that established the ground that put them there at the table? Or will the existing corruption, co-option and maginalization carry on as usual?

And what of the electorate—us? Will we wake up to our civic, cultural and intellectual responsibilities and the fact that these new legislators have joined a club which has compromised women in favor of their own interests throughout the history?   As citizens, it is our duty to grapple with the conflicts of their privileged interests and our common good. Will we insist

[5]*Source: Congressional Research Service, The Library of Congress.* Figures include Laura Richardson's election (D-CA) to the House, 21 August 2007.

that they challenge the underlying assumptions that have created the unfairness in our social order? Keep the pressure on? Or will we carry on as usual, accepting one execrable decision after another and tolerate lying, bungling and theft as standard operating procedure for social, economic and political action? The jury on that one has yet to be convened.

CHAPTER 5

GETTING OFF THE WHEEL

The subject of new leadership is a serious topic of discussion among younger women and retiring feminist trailblazers. Fortunately, while we're waiting around for it to emerge, there is plenty to do: educate and inspire the potential force from where these voices can emerge. This is to be found in the mainstream, grassroots population.

Since the second wave feminist movement, our range of experience has expanded, the resources of our vocabulary have expanded and we live in a world of a more complex reality, much of it our own making. The question is, then, when does women's essential knowledge begin to take hold? And what do we have to do to get it to do just that. This is not a folksy grassroots idea, but a basic survival one. How do we turn this into something of value at the mainstream level: angle this activism to interest the average woman?

Capturing the imagination of mainstream women regarding the importance of feminist knowledge is a larger concept than women's rights. It is a gestalt—bigger than the sum of its parts. It has been done before and can be done again. There must be movement at the grassroots level plus leadership with the mission to establish feminist principles and ideas in the culture—to make them stick.

> Men and women must be educated, in a great degree, by the opinions and manners of the society they live in.
>
> Mary Wollstonecraft,
> *A Vindication of the Rights of Woman*

The Grassroots

We need to hear the voices of ordinary women: the grassroots voice of common sense, plain speak; clarify ideas and move on. Grassroots is dialogue that takes place outside of "elite" circles, mass media and academia: authentic voices speaking outside of that "special vocabulary" of manipulated and corralled conversation—in places where real conversations and real social progress take place.

The potential power locked in these women is enormous. Millions of women fit the profile and they must be heard if this society is to evolve. We are squandering resources when we miss out on the advantage to be found in these voices. This is the critical mass that feminist thinking—still isolated in academia and with the intellectual set—needs to reach. Preoccupied as we are with our own definitions and lateral solutions, we miss the base. When we marginalize these women, we cut ourselves off from our human responses and sensitivities to ordinary people. Justifiably, they become suspicious and reject the women's rights movement as a source of power and inspiration.

And then there's the other grassroots—the people we fail to see. It is all of our responsibility to acknowledge women who are less fortunate, or not as well socially positioned as some of us. Women whose education and language are deficient to adequately express her life in generally spoken terms. Women whose oppression takes place in private and which they consider personal; within degrading and inhibiting social forces. Women who are shy about disagreeable subjects; and those who suffer from chronic humiliation and helplessness. Women who do not realize that these private, personal problems are issues that feminists address publicly as part of the mandate to protect others from violence, victimhood and shame. Women who are defensive because they feel inferior to other women who have had greater opportunities to acquire knowledge and skills. These women may very well wish they could read a good book, try a new restaurant and go to the theater: or be able to muse upon a metaphor, have a challenging discussion or keep a journal. They may want to be part of the feminist ideal, instead of the feminine leftovers. But they are missing the spark to get the engine going and nobody's giving them the ideological boost.

There are great advantages for women's progress to be found in the class which tradition has dispatched to the "grassroots," which is another name for the repressed. But feminism is not tradition. These women possess a vast and significant territory in our culture, albeit trampled by history and overgrown with the brambles of exploitation.

To make sense of our time—and for average women to make sense of feminism itself—women have to see themselves as part of a larger world; to widen our perceptions to take it all in. Feminism forced the issue and was successful. As individuals, we have to broaden our cognitive skills to cope with it.

The ground where we can do this is at the grassroots level; a comfortable place where women can get to understand each other and where even the hoity-toity like to return now and again. This way, we illuminate things from below and get a real sense of the fundamental sweep of things, instead of waiting for light from some distant future to shine down on our compromised circumstances.

Jargon, Fear and the Problem of Language

I heard bell hooks speak at the New York Public Library around the time of the publication of her book *All About Love: New Visions*. She spoke about her life as a feminist and noted that feminism had failed in its mass appeal. The movement had died, but not feminism itself, she said.

What is wrong with it? Why doesn't it "appeal" to the rest of the population? (Apart from the terror that unleashing quality female power strikes in the heart of man. And woman...)

One of the main problems is jargon—that obnoxious lingo that occurs when the mind is imprisoned by theory and its owner lacks experience. But this jargon is the same quality as any other that makes it into the sonar world—think of all the droning on, and holding forth we hear every day. Why then, is the voice of feminism so grating? How does it differ from any other message? **Because we don't actively want to hear it.** Most of the rest of the world's rhetoric doesn't even register, because of the distance between the ideas and our reality. But this one is about us and it hits home. If we listen to it, we may have to do something about how we've organized our reality and our values.

It's time to wake up. The jargon actually reflects a set of principles that have gone missing in our lives or have never been there in the first place. Feminist principles that don't make it into our hearts and minds means that the message doesn't take. They are still at the jargon stage and we dismiss them, which is the real problem. We fail to discuss the principles of equality in our lives in terms of the common language.

The other problem with the jargon is that it creates **fear of feminism**: fear of hearing, fear of speaking, fear of an unknown power because when we restore our own sense of worth, it is at a cost. Often the price is casting men in an unflattering light and they may not like it! They may retaliate! But men can't have everything.

Ordinary women don't see things in feminist terms. They don't understand them and mostly don't like them. From this vantage, the feminist knowledge conversation is going in the wrong direction. Mainstream women don't discuss it, they have bad information, and/or they don't want to know. This is a major inhibitor of the transmission of knowledge.

While I wrestle with concepts of intellectual and narrative development, millions in the middle and at the edge of the social matrix have no idea what I'm talking about. Worse, they fear that even hearing this stuff will threaten the loss of what they have or believe they are going to get (if they act in a prescribed way, which is arguable). Why would they make an effort for a culture which passes them by, keeps them addled or on the edge of privation, and delivers a state of permanent crisis as a way of life? The language of women who have not found a way to express their knowledge must be nurtured and captured and spread outwards: women speaking as knowledgeable individuals in communities. This is not only the best hope for change, but change itself.

If we're willing to put our foot down and continue fighting for a better life—and to maintain our rights—we're capable of staving off regressive forces. If not, then women's condition starts to collapse into the sink holes of neglect. Whatever is left ends up in the archives and is recycled as theory. Except for the students of women's studies, this does the culture and society very little good. Mainstream people don't like to be bothered by theory and it is indigestible in grassroots reckoning.

Whatever the difficulties, we must give voice to the rationale of the millions who are silent—who need new language. Knee jerk reactions to patriarchal power plays must become a thing of the past. This is not an organizing issue: it is an organized idea to serve an organized mind. The grassroots are permanent. There's a ripple effect in the grassroots. It's where vitality and progress stick to the land.

•

We all must seize the advantage to educate ourselves (that "we") and shape an initiative to fundamentally reorganize education at all levels to reflect women's history, principles and advancement. Every group can draw from the struggles of women's past and the knowledge we have acquired in the present. Everyone can use this to improve the quality of their lives and others' by organizing around knowledge of their own oppression and subsequent advancement. There's nothing new about this; it has been going on since time immemorial. What's different is that we must put an end to having to relearn and reinvent it in every generation of women.

Circling Back

Where is this grassroots thing going? Straight to the top—back to Issue #1: at the macro level, women's influence is nowhere to be seen. Nothing has changed at the top.

The grassroots is the place that raises everyone up if properly nurtured. Part of this process is demanding that women who are elevated into positions of leadership and power are expected—and morally and legally obligated—to ensure that all sectors of society treat women equitably. This is a priority that is not being met. It's obvious that after several decades of putting women into these leadership positions, the pressure to change their old boy habits must come from the base: from mainstream grassroots women.

The superiority of grassroots knowledge—which is conveyed and enlargened by what we say to each other—is that anyone can grasp it.[6] We get to know and understand each other through interdependence, difference, strength and individual qualities. We move in different dimensions at the same time; backwards and forwards, learning how to work things out, all of which is modeled in the workings of feminism and the generation of knowledge. And what we have to remember is that what we learn is also the language of protest against untoward power. We must weave this language into our thoughts and narratives and allow it to guide our actions.

•

Like all movements, feminism, as we knew it, ran out of political steam. It reached a certain point of development which we all wanted to maintain and that is when it began to fall apart. As usual—and historically—we had not escaped the cyclical nature of the movement and so it turned on itself. Having risen in the national consciousness, it was destined to collapse again and call for solution from the inside. The cycle was destined to repeat itself— internal consciousness becomes political will, flames, then relapses into the few heads left who accept the job to guard the flame and try to figure

---

[6] An academic stated that feminist concepts are not plausible to many because their class (read lower) infers that they are incapable of learning them. That is absurd. The social and cultural circumstances that withhold basic education is the problem — not their ability to learn. They are lacking accessibility and development, not potential.

out the same thing all over again, starting out with "revolution from within." Full circle.

Creating a New Perspective

To get off the wheel, we need a new perspective from which to see ourselves in relation to our own culture. At present the culture does not embody, nor reflect, an iota of what women contribute to the world and that has to change. As we personify that culture, the first change has to happen inside ourselves.

First, our attitude about our social construction has to change. This requires us to stake an unbreachable claim to that which is rightfully ours. This is our society, our culture. We own them. We all have to take an active interest in our history and the shaping of our future. We must make a commitment to recover what we have lost and create the language we need to permanently influence the culture in the service of securing our goals. Everything that we see, hear, is recorded, has influence, and is deemed important enough to be part of the cultural context, must reflect women's values, interests, experience, history and wisdom.

Next, we have to change the way we think about ourselves. We need to accept the context we live in and get over our chronic amnesia. Feminist knowledge creates an intellectual framework of common language and ideas, while introducing fundamental concepts to increase our general awareness and shed light on the hidden forces which dominate our thinking and our daily lives as well. This framework allows one to look at herself in relation to the culture and vice versa. Change your mind, change your reality.

The next step is to identify how our individual values, needs, concerns, ideas, experiences, expectations and certainties are misshapen or absent from our conscience altogether. It is then the task to develop coherent descriptions of these gaps. This means turning the reality of women's oppression and subsequent liberation into a personal narrative that people can understand, so that it becomes part of their consciousness, and in turn, part of common cultural dialogue. This is the language that will help future generations of women stand up against male domination and not back down. Clearly, we must develop, at the same time, a practical mind set to be able to weather external forces and our tendency to succumb to excessive emotion. Getting off the wheel means staying on the journey.

From Model to Angle

We can deduce from the cyclical nature of feminism, that as a model, it is here today, gone tomorrow and is unstable over the long haul. So far, it has been a boom-and-bust story. But we have also seen that in a few short decades, it has improved all women's lives and minds immeasurably. Now on the downslide, again, it is taking a beating and the black beast of ignorance and repression is on the offensive.

We are at a different historical moment now. We require important changes in society and in ourselves. We can wait around for the moment to swell up again and yield up a handful of independent and courageous thinkers to provide a vision for the rest of us; but that is unwise. In the first place, the vision of the second wave is about as good as it's going to get in this democracy as we know it. In the second, we should never have lost sight of the vision to begin with. After all, this movement is a product of the 1960s, not the middle ages: and so are we.[7] As the model of the philosophy of feminism has failed to become part of the common dialogue, it would be more advantageous, as a practical measure, to consider feminism as an angle. One doesn't act ideology. One thinks about it and uses it to appraise ideas, information and events.

Understanding life from the angle of feminism puts the universals of the patriarchy in their proper place. Human relations look different when viewed through a feminist lens. And without question, expressing a full-bodied version of your life as a woman will be more interesting, more original and more important personally, socially, politically, culturally—and historically.

---

[7] Yes, things happened before then. But we now live the results of activism. Our autonomy is not restricted to voting for the first time in history, getting jobs in wartime because there are no men around to do the work, or cutting loose from Victorian social morality by bobbing our hair and going out to smoke, dance and have sex in flapper outfits.

PART TWO

☆

THE BIG PICTURE

CHAPTER 6

WHERE WE LIVE

D ecades have passed since the rise of the contemporary feminist and women's rights movements. And although there is not one woman in America whose life has not been improved as a result, the awareness of the issues generated by these struggles has plummeted to the bottom of the public consciousness. What remains are a few pioneer individuals and organizations and young advocates bearing the torch for the rest of us, who, for the most part, are unable to articulate how we achieved our advancement or why we should keep our rights. In light of conservative forces ever-expanding their power, all antennae should be up. Instead, we are greeted by the well-rehearsed chorus of, "I'm certainly not a feminist!"

If the -ism of feminism could not become part of our cultural identity and lodge itself in the common dialogue, then it means that women just weren't buying in—even though these spurners were more than willing to grab the pay offs of the feminist cause. But such is life. We can't sit around waiting for another "whenever decade" for inspiration. So it's time to get off the wheel of waves and movements and approach women's entrenched problems from a different perspective: how we talk about our lives and selves in the first place. **We must address the problem that the language of women's autonomy and independence has not been developed in the common dialogue**. As this language is missing, so is the cultural narrative of the women's world.

In this section, we are constructing a framework of facts and concepts required to get a clear picture of our circumstances and position within them. We will build up a mental picture, element by element, of what it takes to read the hidden forces in the environment effectively. This is knowledge that can be used regardless of the issues and situations in one's life. Consider it vital information to add to everything you already know.

This knowledge is what makes the feminist standpoint, discussed in Part III, relevant. If approached in isolation, these things don't make sense. Together, however, they're dynamic, therefore useful.

WOMEN'S RIGHTS ARE LEGAL CONSTRUCTS.
FEMINISM IS WHAT'S IN YOUR HEAD.

Against What?

Women's rights? What was wrong?

The "struggle for women's rights" means that something was preventing us from having them in the first place. We had to struggle **against** something. That was, and still is, the patriarchy: against the forces of sexism that determine the overall outcome of our lives. To get out from under it was, and is, the whole point.

The Patriarchal Enterprise

Patriarchy is a word like feminism: people are averse to hearing it. Nonetheless, it's unavoidable. Life is relational and this is where we live. If you don't know what the patriarchy implies, then you don't know where you are. And it is always essential to know where you are.

So let's get this over with. Patriarchy means they're men and they rule. As in—it's a man's world! We're born into it, learn to live in it and it has been designed and built by men. It is a honeycomb of theories and systems, history, institutions and traditions, all held together by a central power. This set of beliefs, concealed strategies and greater physical strength—which uphold the alleged superiority of the male—is called **the patriarchy**. It operates on male priorities and assumptions translated into goals, objectives and missions. These are the forces that conceptualize and organize our reality, so it's important to have a clear idea of the nature of this scheme. To do that, we must look below the surface of daily life.

Where the patriarchy dominates, women's coordinates are not part of the picture. Where male norms dictate rationality, women's motives are sidebars. And the patriarchy means men **opposed** to matriarchy. Regardless of the protestations, all women are subordinates in this scheme.

It's not difficult to understand the structure and hidden forces of the patriarchy; but doing so is just an encounter with words. The point is to get a grip on the concepts behind the words and the actual, not just perceived, power they have over our lives. Within this context, we need to develop our observations, interpretations and realizations based on personal experience: questions, thoughts, feelings, and sense of things—and the rewards of the search itself. Somewhere in all of this, our lost knowledge is buried.

•

The patriarchal enterprise—the whole thing—is the megalevel of reality. It is a construction of complexes: overlapping, superimposed and always changing shape. What follows is a sketch of its major elements as observed from a feminist point-of-view.

Brobdingnagian Reality: The System

Life on this level is shaped by a configuration of systems. The main ones are idealistically described in sociological terms, such as the following:

The political system—accommodates conflicts and maintains order in the society;

The economic system—produces and distributes goods and services to fulfill the needs of its members;

The educational system—trains the new generations enabling them to play their roles in the society's activities;

The religious system—deals with emotional crises and enables the society members to maintain a sense of purpose while facing life's hardships;

The family system—entrusted with procreation to replace the dying members of the society. It also plays the role of socializing the new generations to transmit the cultural traits and to preserve the ancestors' traditions.

Source: unknown

Such definitions fail to set forth the negative aspects of these systems, about which women are usually experts. Seldom, if ever, do they equitably represent or intersect with our wants and needs.

Democratic capitalism is a prime example. When political economist, Adam Smith, declared in the *Wealth of Nations* (1776) that a new social doctrine and economic order could be driven by human self-interest, women's self-interest was not what he had in mind. Nor did women's work and contribution to wealth enter the capitalist equation. Nor does it now, unless it is quantifiable according to capitalist measurements.

When you apply the democratic doctrine of Thomas Jefferson ("that all men are created equal, that they are endowed by their creator with certain inalienable rights, that among these are life, liberty and the pursuit of happiness") to the economic system, wouldn't women and children share in the rewards of Smith's self-interest theory like everyone else? No. Because this is a patriarchal capitalist system and it is in men's interests to exclude the rights and daily exigencies of women and children in its structure and perpetuation. It is designed so that they get theirs, and we do not get ours.

Systems result in institutions—the military, law, public education, higher education, low and high culture, technology, and the like—organized facets of society which gain proprietorship over the entire enterprise of your life. These institutions were established while women had no legal rights. As they evolved, men defrauded us of our equity and usurped our authority to regulate social and political power. Sexism is institutionalized in these systems. This is where gender relations are maintained by laws and policies that guarantee the systems survive.

Consider our economic system, which concentrates capital in the hands of the few, and how this affects you today. In the past five decades, women have doubled the workforce and caused unprecedented wealth. Millions of women make millions of economic decisions. But there is no evidence that unprecedented capital is now in the hands of women. In fact, most women are permanently harassed by having to work more, the rising cost of everything, money buying less and the debilitating cost of raising children. This is evidence of sexism in the economic model itself.

Culture: What Makes the Cut?

Culture is a record of what remains of the past—the repository and manifestation of the collective memory. The lofty view of culture refers to fine arts and architecture, music, literature and the accouterments of a rich intellectual and social life. A little more down to earth, however, is one of Webster's definitions:

> The total pattern of human behavior and its products embodied in thought, speech, action, and artifacts and dependent upon man's capacity for learning and

transmitting knowledge to succeeding generations through
the use of tools, language, and systems of abstract thought.

The key word here is "man's," and it does not connote the human
capacity for learning and transmitting knowledge because women are not
known to be essential contributors to said culture, whichever one you're
talking about.   The content of the grand human archive is a masculine
apparatus, authored, curated and sanctioned by men and their points of
reference. The ideas and products of women's consciousness have not made
the cut: we have been disqualified because of our gender. Prejudice against
women is deeply ingrained in our cultural genes. In our day, there is no
feedback from any popular medium about the ingenuity of the women's
movement, for instance. Instead, feminism is an enemy.

The story of Frenchwoman, Emilie du Chatelet (1706-1749), is a good
example of how extreme this is.   Chatelet did early experiments in
photography, foresaw infrared radiation, and showed that the energy of a
moving object is proportional to its mass and the square of its velocity: $E = mv^2$. This knowledge was used by Albert Einstein when he produced his
famous equation $E=mc^2$. He used the two, the square, which Chatelet had
recognized more than a hundred and fifty years before. The year of her death
Chatelet translated Isaac Newton's *Principia Mathematica* into French. In
it she included her derivation, from Newton's principles of mechanics, of the
idea of the conservation of energy. Her translation is still in use today.

Her brilliance and discoveries, however, faded soon after her death: they
did not make it into the culture. As writer David Bodanis, who has revived
her biography and intellectual reputation in his book, *Passionate Minds, The
Great Enlightenment Love Affair*, tells us, "misogyny took over." She
became known only for her liaison with the great French intellectual
Voltaire!

The informational content of the culture is particular to the times we live
in and is transferred from generation to generation. Each of us programs her
brain with this information in tandem with all other influences from the world
outside.   Our beings inhabit this masculine apparatus.   Our thoughts
entertain and our actions interpret it, hidden pathologies and all.

Cultures lack self-criticism and are self-cannibalizing. Civilizations
collapse within the cultural context and regenerate their remnants within the
same scheme. As an example, World War II Germany was the victim of its
own failure (World War I and postwar destruction) and instrument of its own
re-invention (National Socialism and ideological corruption leading to
colossal inhumanity and even worse devastation).

The denial of man's darkness smolders in all cultures. It is a negative which shows up positive—as a void—in both the culture, and the individual, when the going gets rough.   Women are generally exempted from disparagement in these historical breakdowns and justifiably so. Her gender disqualification creates yet another negative, which reflects man's lack of intelligence and solidarity, and which inevitably contributes to the collapse of societies.

•

The following charts the history of grand ideas contributing to significant changes in society and the way we think and behave: and the results for women (compiled from *The Alphabet Versus the Goddess*, by Leonard Shlain).

WORLD CULTURES

"If a woman speaks out against her man, her mouth shall be crushed with a hot brick." — First Mesopotamia written law code, c. 2350 B.C.

Gerda Lerner, *The Creation of Patriarchy*

CULTURES	RESULTS FOR WOMEN
Mesopotamia-Sumerians, 3000 B.C. Between Tigris and Euphrates Rivers. Arrival of agriculture.	God Marduk dismembers the Great Mother and women's rights.
Egypt	Women enjoyed greatest equality. Eventually destroyed by Coptic misogynist Clement of Alexander, 1st century A.D.
Hebrews and Israelites, 1500-1000 B.C. Monotheism.	Repression as we know it begins. Male unigod causes disappearance of the goddess. Men offer up their foreskins; women do not partake in the sacrifice and do not participate in the religion.

Aegeans: same period as Israelites. Greeks	Revision of mytho-history to disempower women. Zeus degrades Demeter, goddess of the earth.
5ᵗʰ century B.C. Greek mythology ejects Hestia, goddess of hearth, family, children from Mt. Olympus. Replaced with Dionysus, god of wine, sexuality and dance.	Male god usurps feminine attributes. Allegory of rise of patriarchy in Greece.
Athens and Sparta	Socrates and Aristotle - blatant misogynists. Severe restrictions on women (Sparta less so).
Indus Valley, 2500-1500 B.C. Advanced cultures	Evolve sati — bride burning; female infanticide; purdah.
Buddhism (Hinduism)	Equates source of all pain with birth, woman's gift to the world.
Taoism Confucianism	Taoism - embracing egalitarian viewpoint from the past is won over by Confucianism which champions male dominance. Epitomized by foot binding, crippling females which excites males sexually.
Macedonians, 338 B.C. Alexander the Great	Women gain near equal status which ends quickly. Alexander defeated by Roman warriors.
Roman Empire, 1ˢᵗ century B.C.	Women's status improved.
Jesus Christ and early Christian movements; Orthodox, Gnosticism, Carolingians, Augustinians, etc.	As Christianity grew in stature, women's rights were curtailed.
Dark Ages begin with sack of Rome. 476 A.D.	Church is dominant institution.
Middle Ages, 500-1500 A.D.	Image of Mary as "divine" (not earthy mother) emerges.
Benedictine Order, 6ᵗʰ century A.D. Profound social movement for next millennia.	Benedict was jilted by his fiancée as a young noble and tormented by this throughout life. Beginning of sterility cult; girls are pledged to convents at birth.

Muslims Mohammed born 569 A.D. in Arabia	Polytheists abandon gender; allegiance to the goddess is ended. Holds acquisition of knowledge as highest ideal and for next 500 years every aspect of Islamic society benefits, except representative art and women's rights
Age of Chivalry, Arthurian legends 8th century	Idealism conceals truth of women's experience. Courtesy conceals thuggery.
Christian Church, 11th century Canon Law, Crusades, Inquisition, Thomas Aquinas and Scholasticism, etc.	Church is the most powerful institution in Europe — men only. Total misogyny.
Renaissance begins in Italy, mid-14th century; mixture of art, war, poetry, treachery, music, science, architecture, pragmatism, sculpture and money. All-powerful popes, clergy, church; Borgias; Armies and war.	Unearthing of lost Greek and Roman treasures. Creed of Humanism — by men, about men, for men — behind all advances in all arts. No input from women — loss of common sense. All-male culture amplifies hunter-killer instincts.
Protestant Reformation begins 1517. Martin Luther, Wittenberg, Germany Begins a century of grim doctrine.	Lumps women with vermin, plague and wild beasts sent by God for Adam's disobedience.
Calvin born in 1509, France. In 1541 founds Geneva as City of God. Most repressive police state in history of religious movements.	Harsh, masculine protestantism. Portrays women as tainted by Eve causing the downfall of man. Any single woman found pregnant was drowned.
Ignatius of Loyola founds Society of Jesus in 1540	Scholars and educators compete with secular society. Offer all students free education except women.
Spanish Inquisition, 1482	Human sacrifice returns
Columbus discovers North America and people, 1492	High degree of gender equality among North American Plains Indians
Henry VIII, 1509 Begins English Protestantism	Divorce and killing of wives legalized. Puritans end imagery of and devotion to Mary.
Discovery and settling of the New World	English begin the slave trade

The Burning Times: Witchcraft ideology. Pope Innocent VIII, 1484 (*Malleus Malificarum*), King James II of England, 1597 (*Daemonology; King James Bible*) and continuing into 17th century.	Witch hunts throughout Europe and British Isles kill women for being women. Women's rights and values plummet to all-time low.
Isaac Newton 1642-1727	Rationality grafted onto all aspects of life. Irrefutable logic proves man is standard — woman a defective version of him.
Ages of Reason, Enlightenment, 18th Century. Untrammeled use of reason. Voltaire, Diderot, Kant, Hume, Locke	Backlash of Romantics -- return to Nature. Rousseau, Keats, Byron, Goethe, Shelley
American culture. Begins with settlements in New England in 16th century	Equalized risk and labor between sexes. Once settled, old gender prejudices returned and reestablished.
Industrial Revolution begins with steam engine, early 1800s.	Radical social implications with serious changes to women's security and rights
Modern Times, 1500 to present (as compared to ancient and medieval and situated in this chronology so we can relate to it). Marked by reconciling political and religious ideology with human experience and new knowledge	Traditional gender structure is barely influenced.
Charles Darwin, 1859 publishes *The Origin of Species*	Survival of the fittest describes dog-eat-dog world where love, nurture and cooperation deemed weakness
Nietzsche, mid 1800s Declares God is dead	Male unigod replaced by god of masculine individualism. Women and children left out again.
Sigmund Freud, 1900	Theories result in new pseudoscientific angle on the inferiority of women Countered by Jung's concept of collective unconscious and grounding of human awareness in animal nature
Albert Einstein — modern physics	Father of modern technology gone mad. No input from women.

Karl Marx and Socialism	Extreme patriarchy. Communism severely oppresses women.
The 1960s and Movement for Social Change. North America and Europe "Second Wave" women's rights movement	Backlash and rise of fundamentalist conservatism. Women's rights are not guaranteed.
Western Culture, 2008	Hunter-killer values now dominate around the world.

•

Modern men have been known to ask why so few women in the last centuries made stellar contributions to the arts and sciences. Most men have never had to fear sticking out from the crowd far enough to elicit the heart-stopping accusation of "Witch!" Ancient female wisdom—medical and otherwise—accumulated painstakingly over eons went up in flames along with the "witches."

Leonard Shlain, *The Alphabet Versus the Goddess*

Patriarchal Naval Gazing: The Great Father

Along the evolutionary way, men realized that the old magic was wearing out so they came up with a new idea: the singular, masculine patriarch. The male unigod! God, Yahweh, Christ, Allah, Buddha, you name it—whatever the unigod spin, they all subordinate women and with disastrous consequences.

The unigod usurped the place of the old female goddesses and pagan gods, which were embodiments of the natural elements. It was the perfect device in which to invest the stakes of patriarchal power. In the process, jealous unigod built a convoluted narrative around the idea of feminine evil to reinforce his power. As women did not reject this slander, the myth set up camp in our hearts, minds and bodies and took hold. The ultimate payoff was in making women feel culpable for male oppression and violence.

The patriarchy has perpetuated a vast array of ideas and practices that have different values and applications of fairness depending on one's gender. They use one set of standards to judge themselves and another set to judge you. A good example is blaming Eve for the downfall of "man" because she picked and gave Adam the apple—not blaming Adam because he took it and ate it. Eve not only takes the rap for picking and giving, but also as middleman causing Adam to act against God.

God. I told you not to do it and you did it anyway.
Adam. But she gave it to me!

Adam's responsibility for his own behavior is thus deflected and even though he secretly knows this, instead of fessing up, the male authority invents guilt. Guilt is sin seen in retrospect—shipped off for a psychological jail term. They then project their own guilt onto Eve (a hidden tactic) and blame her (a public affair) taking the glare off Adam—again. Sin, guilt, blame and shame—all in one little folk tale.

But it's not over. Then they came up with forgiveness; forgiving Eve, that is, upon whom they had piled their corruption and cowardice. Eve, in turn, was expected to forgive them for their corruption and cowardice, which she did.   But the act of perpetrating the fraud upon Eve—over millennia—never comes into question. That part is gummed up somewhere in the lint of patriarchal naval gazing.

Flesh and blood men established themselves as agents of unigod to protect "His" occupancy in that unruly territory known as women's minds and bodies; and in the process, men legitimized their rights to lord it over us. In the Great Father, we have patriarchal fraud operating at a genius level. (I really have to hand it to them.)

The dialectics of God's nature and authenticity vary, depending on who's talking. Even God's existence itself is challenged from time to time, and his popularity takes a bashing. Whenever this happens, male egotists rush in to fill his shoes with a substitute doctrine. The common theme these days is "new man as god" sent to reveal the truth to the masses. These replacement icons, like the cults and pseudo-cultures they spawn, usually collapse as a result of delusions about their own greatness. Nietzsche, Marx, Hitler, Freud, Mao Tse-tung, are examples of these Great Ones (and short, Ethiopian tyrant, Heilie Selassi definitely got some of "the divine right of kings" on him). There are also individualist god-poseurs like writer and master egotist Norman Mailer who pronounced that what God left unsaid, it is up to the novelist, i.e., Mailer, to say. He also bestowed upon us the absurdity that within the psychopathic murderer, lie the makings of new man's, new nervous system, "freed of the inhibitions and blockages imposed by morality and conditioning that prevented the free flow of "life-force." (Take that, all you mothers! They'll be coming out of your uterus.) Mailer died in November 2007, with the reputation of literary lion still clinging to him, but as a god figure, he was typical—just another flash-in-the-pan.

Another type in this category is film maker and alcoholic wingnut Mel Gibson, who claims to have the last word on unigod's truth and makes the movies to prove it (The Passion of Christ). Gibson is bound to crash and burn in hubris any day now—lucky us. But keep an eye out—there are always plenty of contenders waiting in the wings, eager to make an appearance as god. Tom Cruise has made his move as scientology guru and is now being called its "movie messiah." And you can see the up and comers on the screen with regularity: they usually start by playing angels.

Man's need to project his own image onto ultimate reality is a symptom of his lack of self-knowledge and denial of death. In other words, unigod's maleness is his biggest problem. For a more restorative way to assuage the terror of the final moment, they should try contemplation on the wonders of creation and the day-by-day palliation of introspection, self-knowledge and telling the truth. Fiction is an unreliable solution for ethical and moral failure.

God always makes a reappearance, having banked a great deal of residual recognition over the years. The rise of Christian fundamentalism and George W. Bush's claim that "God wants me to be President" are examples of God's bounce. And the 2008 salvation twist? Democratic presidential candidate Barack Obama and his messiah news, "We are the ones we've been waiting for." Praise God and pass the mashed potatoes.

After a hiatus, unigod inevitably rises once more like the phoenix of backwardness, fulfilling the patriarchal promise of inadequacy and narcissism, yet again. With preposterous fantasies of righteousness and salvation, the earth-destroying hunter-killers are bound together in a deadly rampage which instead of making themselves humble in the reflection of their own foolishness, makes them think they're right! Man's struggle with the mysteries of nature and the universe ended long ago. He traded in the wisdom of the search for what we've got now—organized unigod religion with all of its emotional, intellectual, spiritual corruption.

As the enlightened aspects of secular society in the 21st century attempt to acknowledge the scope and extent of gender oppression, the unigod forces push back with all their might. They employ their misogynistic strategies in all aspects of political, social, economic and cultural life. Despite this blatancy, women still buy into the childish fictions of religion en masse. Addressing the logic of their position would be a more reasonable place to center their search for meaning. As churches and religions would not survive without women, women should be eliminating sexism and anti-woman dogma from religious doctrine and practice, not propping it up.

The New Backwardness

In 2004, the government of the Province of Ontario, Canada, sought to recognize Islamic law, "sharia," as part of the Arbitration Act, for the purposes of resolving family disputes. In theory, decisions based on principles of the Islamic religion would have to conform to the Canadian Charter of Rights and Freedoms. (The Charter entrenches and protects basic rights guaranteed to all Canadians, and is part of the *Constitution Act*, 1982.) Tribunal (sharia) decisions would then be recognized by the regular Ontario courts.

Sharia is an inflexible body of medieval rules of law which Muslim scholars claim were laid down by the Prophet Mohamed. It is based on the Koran and Muslims believe it provides divine rules for behavior. It is misogynistic, discriminates against women and for many is a brutal form of totalitarianism. Promoters of Islam in Western countries have been working toward integrating sharia into democratic legislation for years. To further their Ontario agenda, they set up the Islamic Institute of Civil Justice, training arbitrators in sharia and Canadian civil law.

This is a fundamentalist drive. There are over 1250 mosques in the U.S. and Canada. Most of their financial support comes from Saudi Arabia, Libya, and other regimes which assert Islam and Islamic law in its traditional form. This has led to a right-wing, social-conservative movement that does not recognize tolerant versions of Islam.

While the sharia debate was playing itself out, I was present at a speech given by Homa Arjomand, Coordinator of the International Campaign against Sharia Court in Canada, and one of the most vocal opponents of the plan. Born in Iran, she knows about the conditions of living under sharia first hand. She endured it until she escaped her home country and fled to Canada. She now lives in Toronto, where she works with immigrant Muslim women and children in distress.

In her presentation, Ms. Arjomand told the audience why this sharia plan must be defeated and recited a shameful litany of the abuse, imprisonment, violence, deprivation and unthinkable subjugation suffered by women and girls in Toronto. The nosharia.com website describes what life is like for women living under this system. It also describes the actions the organization is taking against sharia, honor killings, polygamy and other life and death issues that Muslim women suffer around the world and here at home. (In 2006, Homa Arjomand was honored as Ontario's Humanist of the Year.)

As for the Canadian Charter of Rights and Freedoms protecting these women, that is pie in the sky. It doesn't now and will not, unless these women escape the tyranny of Islamic law being practiced in their families and communities. And after that? The Charter has no practical application which prevents incidents of repression, oppression and violence against women, whatever their religion or society may be.

Sharia was thrown out in the fall 2005 and in early 2006, Ontario repealed all religious-based tribunals from the Arbitration Act. Said Attorney General Michael Bryant, "When it comes to family law arbitrations in this province, there is only one law and that is Canadian law."

The cockamamie idea to graft Islamic law onto the Canadian justice system owes itself to the Canadian habit of bowing down to the trinity of diversity, tolerance and multiculturalism, which is government cultural policy. In the sharia case, it goes like this: "cultural diversity requires that Muslim law be accorded the same respect as other legal systems." This, in a democracy. The idea is as backward as sharia itself.

> "This is an abuse of multiculturalism. . . . There is a lack of courage [on the part of governments], and also a fear of offending Muslim sensitivities." Alia Hogben, President, Canadian Council of Muslim Women

> "I chose to come to Canada because of multiculturalism. . . . But when I came here, I realized how much damage multiculturalism is doing to women. I'm against it strongly now. It has become a barrier to women's rights." Homa Arjomand

Source: Our Own Correspondence, BBC Radio 4, 26 August 2004

During their push, the Islamic power brokers used another titillating tactic to persuade the politically correct Canadian consciousness. They proposed that Canada would be a good place to work on fourteen hundred years of underdevelopment, as described by a female Muslim academic, anonymously quoted in the same BBC4 news report mentioned above.

> This is a chance for us to develop a progressive and tolerant form of sharia . . . consistent with 21st century notions of gender equality. . . . This will force Canadian Muslims to define who they are. It could even be a Canadian contribution to an Islamic reformation.

No thanks, babe. Go find some other place willing to destroy itself so you can dig your way up out of the pre-medieval hole you've found yourself in. And good luck.

The point of telling this story is to come back to the point of feminist knowledge. It is not only important that we recognize this issue, as it pertains to the oppression of a specific group of women living here and abroad. Or that accepting theocracy into Canada would erode our common democratic values, such as they are. What is equally important is understanding the implications of such a venture, which run far and deep. First of all, success in Ontario would be used as a precedent for political Islam to push its agenda to gain a foothold in the justice systems in the rest of Canada and indeed, around the Western world. Next, is how Canadian women see themselves in the context of this entire issue. I brought up the sharia subject with a variety of mainstream women. They had vague or no interest in it: the it-doesn't-affect-us or it-can't-happen-here syndrome. In fact, they usually seemed perplexed about why I was even brought it up.

Feminist knowledge recognizes that all religions oppress women and that theocracies have the right to control women by law and according to male dictates. That, alone, is sufficient to make anyone fight to keep religion out of government and protect the basic democratic principle of the separation of church and state from collapsing.

There are further implications here. The standard of women's equality that apply here are ones that women have fought for and still do. The levels of oppression that women bring with them from other countries and perpetuate in North American society are not acceptable. Somewhere between the democratic principles of equality and women and girls who stay in the house because they are told they can't go out, give everything they earn to their husbands, marry before they've even developed physically, or walk ten paces, head bowed, behind their husband on the American and Canadian streets is a problem. Regardless of how, why and whence these women have come to live in such circumstances does not change the fact that they live here and reflect upon us. They're "we." They are not only symbols of misogyny and discrimination in the culture, but the real thing. They have a civic responsibility to uphold women's equality and if they don't know this, it's time they learned.

When I first heard about the Islamist power play in the summer of 2004, I wrote a letter to the editors of several newspapers:

> . . . Every foreign woman who enters this country with the intention of settling here should be given a primer on

citizenship the moment she arrives. She should be informed that freedom and justice already have a meaning here and it didn't just arrive in somebody's suitcase. It was fought for and evolved over centuries on this soil.

That here in this democracy, freedom is a different venture for women: that our position in society has not been, nor is it now, equal to that of men because of gender prejudice. That we have had to commit to struggle to obtain and maintain our rights and as a result of doing so, have transformed this society and its laws in ways that could hardly be imagined only fifty years ago.

That submissive roles are not admired and perpetuate a backslide in women's equality that causes damage to our society and the added burden of redefining battles we were already winning. That submissiveness excavates misogyny from depths that this society should long ago have buried and left dead. That obliviousness and denial of this reality and women's sovereignty are not an option here and that we detest the encroachment of any repressive ideologies into our personal, public and political lives.

Then she can go to the motel with her old man and have a lively debate about what it means to live in a free country.

That Thing

We live out the drama of our lives in perpetual tension: our personal existence on one level, external reality on the other. This gives rise to anxieties and perceptions we cannot articulate—pervasive things that defy description. So not surprisingly, while working on this book, I sensed certain inexplicable things that ended up as a pile of indecipherable notes. I had no idea what they were about so I tossed them in a file called "That Thing."

As it turns out, the thing kept eluding me because it is, by nature, illusive. **That Thing is the historical consciousness of the superiority of the male.** This translates into five thousand years of patriarchal dominance, whose strategy—they're right and we're not—is concealed. It is an abstract, psychic phenomenon that colonizes psychic space. And it is the dominant influence in determining the overall outcome of women's lives.

MEN: WE DO IT BECAUSE THIS IS WHAT WE DO.

Bringing the unspeakable That Thing into focus requires, first of all, the intention to deconstruct the wall we're conditioned to smacking into when we try to see our own reality with clarity. Secondly, the effort requires emotional flexibility—like that needed when trying to wrestle a dream into focus and keep it there. Struggling with illusive ideas is a challenge, but worth the effort because we tend to deny the existence of that which we cannot see or do not understand.
So what is it? That Thing?

• **It is the force out there.** You feel it all around you. It is the palpable, depersonalized force of male power and history and its overall influence in determining the definition of society and outlook of the culture. It is the large, sweeping "out there," an amorphous condition which oppresses and haunts us all. It is strong, overwhelming and invisible; the indescribable aspect of walking-around reality; a psychic tide against which no individual has a chance.
It is the quality of reality that defies instinct, integrity, common sense, and the natural flow of energy. It constricts, constrains, stymies and binds us into itself by distorting our self-image and usurping our authority. It is Brogdingnagian reality—the preponderance of power and dominance that controls women. In other disciplines is called hegemony, a word that provides little consolation when you hit the wall and stunned, ask "What the hell's going on here?" It is the hidden menace that flows through everyday life and nature itself: the halt of individual freedom and social evolution. That Thing is a mass of teeming aggressive maleness. It is the law of male proprieties and possession, with no sunset clause.

• **It is inevitability.** No individual has a chance against it. "I can't change it. I can't do anything about it." Bound in the truss of male ideology and operations, that is how we react when we feel its pressure. From the feminist angle, That Thing is not the system of inequity and cockups that men rail against unto their own death, but the inevitability of inexhaustible male imprints of habit and interpretations that catch us up in their fallacious version of reality and its *ad infinitum* extension. Women's endurance is the handmaid to the inevitability of That Thing. And inevitably, this servitude eventually becomes intolerable and rises up within us as rebellion. So far, we have failed to prevail.

• **It is incomprehensible universality.** Universals are cognitions that all humans share but which don't necessarily manifest as mental conceptions. They are the results of reason and apply to the whole species. This is also called human understanding and no one needs description to know what it is.

That Thing is the opposite. It is the specter of unspeakability which intrudes on every aspect of life and which men allude to in code and with covert motives. This code encases and protects its incoherence—disruptive, mind-twisting, illusive—in a psychic space where there is no logic or structure and it is sensed in the negative experiential. As in, "what's wrong with me?!"

The incomprehensible universal is the power of patriarchal totalitarianism, the most powerful of all human schemes, imbued in the kaleidoscope of human consciousness: the ultimate gestalt. It is the assumption of the rationale of hidden male power extracted from gender inequity, founded on lies and nonsense erected as truth and which confers upon men the exclusive right to freedom, the right to appropriate resources and the right to oppress women.

That Thing occupies a position in all space and all time in concert with our own responses to it. Because it is inexpressible, it has remained unthought out. Lacking the dynamics of the language to describe it, we ourselves are powerless in its incomprehensibility. That Thing is what we render unto Caesar and the brutes. As long as we fail to rationalize it, we maintain it as the cornerstone of our own ignorance.

• **It is definitive proportion.** That Thing is the mythic measure of the construction of male power; a magnitude perceived but not apparent. It is the weight of history causing downward pressure on what is supposed to be life's balance, and constructed to conceal the male's disproportional approach to nature and human relations.

Imprinted on its rules, women demonstrate disproportional credibility in this reality which controls us on the scale of micro to macro—from the female egg to the possibility of nuclear annihilation and everything in between. The strength of the scheme relies on being right or wrong, proportionally depending on one's gender.

CHAPTER 7

THE DOMINANT VOICE

From the cradle to the grave we're tuned into a sound track telling us what it is, that is. What life is—past, present and future. This is the sound of the dominant male voice. This power obliterates and invalidates women's take on reality.

The Dominant Voice prepares the ground for what we are to believe. Ergo, women are conditioned to automatically reject feminist ideas by branding them radical and anti-male, therefore dangerous to women. Not only that, it prepares the ground for what women are to think about themselves. The backlash to the women's movement was successful because it was determined worthwhile by the phallocentric point-of-view which controls the cultural narrative.

A recent study about men and women talking in the workplace revealed that in general, men "earn respect" from co-workers while women lose their trust. They did an experiment where a topic was chosen and the male and female participants reversed their gender voice. The men discussed the subject using women's way of speaking; women described the same topic using men's way of speaking. Response in favor of the men's authority did not diminish, regardless of how they said what they were saying. The women had less credibility, regardless of using male language. In other words, it's not women's language or way of speaking that leads to colleagues not trusting them. It's their gender. Controlling is the power of the male voice and the correlative overvaluation of anything male.

. . . His eloquence renders absurdities plausible, and his dogmatic conclusions puzzle, without convincing, those who have not ability to refute them.

Mary Wollstonecraft,
A Vindication of the Rights of Women

The Controlling Narrative

The Dominant Voice creates the narrative for what we tell ourselves, about ourselves. It shapes the message which is broadcast within the communications and social apparatus. It assumes the power to think for you: how to understand things, what has meaning; what's important, how to value. And it regulates behavior: what to do with our bodies, minds, resources. And decides how pure, oblivious and how corrupt we can be, according to mores of the times. (For a slice of life observed from this angle, read Alexandra Jacobs, "Campus Exposure," *New York Times*, 4 March 2007; about behavior, sex magazines and pornography on campus.)

The oracle tells the people its common story in words, sounds, pictures and various forms of cultural expression. It dictates standards of objectivity, rationality and justice. Its message shapes individual minds, societies and nations. The message is sent out, echoed, reflected back. It is the reverberation of unlimited male authority.

The voice carries the ideology of the male view of life. On the basis of male assumptions and attitudes, it prescribes the social vision and acceptability of the humans within it. It reduces history to a string of male events, people to measurements, minds to models, while promoting the ideals of manliness through heroic testimony and drama. This apparatus is the voice that speaks loudest, farthest and longest. It authors the message and filters it down to subordinates.

The male consciousness establishes the content of what we know and why we should know it—the common knowledge. It constrains authentic progress by validating its theoretical scheme. Occasionally, self-motivated individuals contest the "official" story and force their truths into the mainstream. But in the long run, the patriarchal voice spews forth its ideology unperturbed and with minimal protest from women, despite the indignities it embeds in its narrative.

The Worldview

The mouthpiece prescribes the social vision and dominant ideology. Allegedly, the voice of "what's what" operates within a self-correcting system maintained by competing visions and doctrines (e.g., conservative v. liberal; traditionalist v. populist). This is just more male propaganda. Vain and exclusionary like the patriarchy itself, the Dominant Voice evades its own better judgment and thrives on the spoils of intellectual and ethical incontinence and corruption. Negative motives are concealed in the language of ideological pathology.

Take, for example, Marxist ideology and its implementation, competing against the democratic panacea. In this instance, the oracle of this particular package of bad thought and trained ignorance, abject immorality, stupidity and enduring failure, was oblivious to its own inadequate understanding of the facts of life, as was its tenacious opposition, the Western democracies. When the people of Eastern Europe themselves caused the collapse of communism, it took the free world quite by surprise! So much for "vision."

This compulsion of the dominant male to "pursue rationality beyond human practice" and then try to cover up with more bad ideas, could be remedied by heeding the voices of smarter members of their lot. It would be in their interests to listen to others—French philosopher and sociologist Michel Foucault (1926-1984) for instance, author of the quote above, and extrapolator of the impli- and explications of such willful blindness. From their manly positions of pretended superiority, however, they are insulated from evidence and above the lessons of learning. And on that subject on a personal, level: more than fifteen years after the demolition of the Berlin Wall, I have yet to hear any liberal or leftist with Marxist leanings say, "It was a flop—I was wrong."

The situation leading up to World War II is an example how colossal is the failure of one Dominant Voice speaking with another and this scenario is repeated throughout history. It speaks of the chaos that lurks just below the surface of the socio-political artifice and points out, as well, that the real political spectrum is not left to right, but top to bottom. Everything is crooked from the top down.

"I think it is one of the most incredible stories in history," Dorothy sighed, "that a man could sit down and write in advance"—as Hitler had done in *Mein Kampf*—"exactly what he intended to do; and then, step by step, begin to put his plan into operation. And that the statesmen of the world should continue to say to themselves: 'He doesn't really mean it! It doesn't make sense!'"

Peter Kurth, *AMERICAN CASSANDRA,*
The Life of Dorothy Thompson

Powerful patriarchal men are not required to extrapolate meaning from facts, as their truth is what they presume to know. They eliminate what they can't understand and obfuscate what deters them from their personal ambitions. This is censorship from the backside—exclusion with a twist. Toxic masculinity wins again, whatever way you phrase it.

The relevance of the worldview examples related here refer back to Issue #1: women in power aping the oracle and projecting the grand vision of men.

Woman Portrayed

The generic *he* tells women what it's like to be alive. And dead. He tells us the story of our character and experience and creates the framework for our thoughts. Nurtured on the stories, myths, images of the male-centered view of life, we thrive on the language of our own subordination—with bits of flattery thrown in now and then, to keep us pacified.

In the great sweep of time and history, women are written out. While the male projects his own mystique—kings, popes, generals, explorers; dashing, adventurous, virile rogues—by its omission, what is female, is trivial. When we do make an entrance, we are ranked with slaves, barbarians, children and other objects of lower necessity, and worse. We're blamed for the downfall of "Man." We're nothing you'd want to emulate: don't "act like a woman" or be a "girly man." And occasionally we're thrown a bone, as in Freud's hunch about "penis envy!" References like this are in plentiful use today and still discussed with a straight face.

> . . . What effect, one might ask, would these seminal tales have on the psyches of young girls and boys learning them? Would not a young girl's sense of self-worth be diminished by them? Would not they encourage the concept of patriarchy in the minds of young boys? The death throes of the Great Mother can be read between the lines of these sexist credos.
>
> Leonard Shlain, *The Alphabet Versus the Goddess*

The Female Echo

The female echo is the affirmation of the Dominant Voice. Trained in the language of subjugation we are complicit in the erasure of our own truth. In the absence of anything else to turn to, we live out our scripts. We sympathize; we're tender. We use the tried and true arts of our sex to keep things from falling apart. We charm, conciliate, appease and deny ourselves and choke on the antidotes to our humiliation and fear. We hear the voice and we misogynize ourselves. Occasionally a scream of suffering or a rage from the repressed breaks through and the real truth is acknowledged. But it seldom lasts. When we do not challenge the mouthpiece, we thrive on the language of our own subordination.

> There were always some slaves who revolted; there were some women who sought greater development and self-determination. Most records of these actions are not preserved by the dominant culture, making it difficult for the subordinate group to find a supporting tradition and history.
>
> Jean Baker Miller, M.D.,
> *Toward A New Psychology of Women*

> . . . most insidious oppression alienates a group from its own interests as a group and encourages it to identify with the interests of the oppressors, so that political struggles must first awaken a group to its interests and its "experience". . .
>
> Rene Denfield, *The New Victorians:*
> *A Young Woman's Challenge to the Old Feminist Order*

The one story that the mouthpiece keeps under wraps is the story of misogyny itself—not only the thing, but the inescapably distorting effects it has had on man's theories about human nature. The history of "man" is laden with strange doctrine and muddled principles all too tedious, tangential and untenable to be worth examining to see if women fit into it or not. For the purpose of gathering information, one can read it, yes. But to evaluate its content from a feminist point-of-view would be a waste of time, as it is a distortion by nature.

As for female life today, there are fair and realistic expressions—both pro and con. Disruptive voices are heard, imaginative stories are written, injustices against women are exposed. But it's mainly more of the same. While women flourish in the media and communication arts today, the models they work with existed long before they ever came onto the scene. Mainly they perpetuate the same old agenda, with the same old themes, with newer and flashier ways to tell women's stories from a point-of-view acceptable to what men think women want and vice versa.

•

Are we up to turning this off? Is the answer to the misogyny of rap, for instance, "girl power?" Or do we respond to this culturally as a tool of male desperation, phallic showing off, tacky and idiotic language in the service of arrested development, creating low expectations and false values, and elevating inhumanity; and whose pervasive rhetoric preys on weak minds with tragic and even deadly consequences? It's hard to fathom imagery as vile as rap's holding a generation of young women in thrall. But if they don't like being called sluts and whores, whose only use is to fuck and dead is okay, too, then I guess these women should do something about it. Like what? Some, I know are working on it, but they're a long way from reaching critical mass. Meanwhile, guys rule.

CHAPTER 8

GENDER STRATEGY

Patriarchal dominance is not some random development, but a strategy. And contemplating the hidden forces of the patriarchy is not just an encounter with words. The point is to understand the concepts behind the words, and the power they have over our lives.

Gender structure is the central organizing mechanism that drives the engine of male power. Did they hunker down back then and brainstorm until they came out with this in hand? Not likely. People are instinctive and hone their skills as need and opportunity present themselves. This strategy developed to serve men's basic drive: to gain, exercise and maintain power on the basis of sex. It is the original "divide and conquer."

Gender means sex: a set of characteristics of homo sapiens and other living things and male or female is a biological designation. By itself, gender holds no implications of who should have power over whom. If it did, by nature, women would not resist men who try to dominate them. (The fact that they usually cave into the pressure is part of this whole story.)

The practice of gender operates according to a patriarchal plan—goals, objectives, missions—which cohere to male beliefs, are based on male assumptions, and result in a set of compulsory gender performances. Couples, families, communities, regions, nations, NAFTA, globalization—all follow the model of the patriarchal scheme which subordinates women and prevents them from refashioning and redirecting themselves. Gender practice defines how to think, feel, understand; how to BE, wrapping this pig up in a poke called "the greater good."

The Gender Split—Man, Woman: Sexism

Biological truth aside, the gender split divides the human family on the basis of who is male and who is female. The split distinguishes men from women and links them together as the superior creative and moral force from which the female deviates by default. It implies their sex makes them superior to women. This is **sexism**. As the ideological axis for male supremacy, sexism unites belief in male authority and implies that men are entitled to dominate and obstruct women.

This basic situation affects our entire lives. Sexism underpins and informs—and deforms—our identity. Male standards confer our status as inferior. Their values determine our behavior. Sexism prevents us from achieving our higher powers.

Women's tolerance of sexism not only distorts our understanding of reality. It results in men's failure to deal with their negative sexual behavior: aberrant obsessiveness, aggression and violence.

Female-male power relations are asymmetrical. As women's interests are discounted in terms of what is rational, there is no mutuality nor reciprocal basis from which to contradict male constructs. Our take on reality and culture, therefore, is irrational. This goes a long way to explaining women's historical silence (and why women cry a lot when they start arguing). In the asymmetry of sexism, you may take a position, but they have already limited the terms of what is credible. This means that women are unable to assert their authority because they do not have equal credibility.

"YOU MAY NOT AGREE, BUT IT HAS TO BE ON MY TERMS."

The content of what is true is restricted to fit into male norms which eliminate the possibility of losing power. The active operation of this asymmetry is mirrored in the way we think and is preserved in polarities—the either/or trap that keeps both our intellectual hatches and expression deep in the keep. Polarities work by confining the range of rationality. Within the poles, the patriarchy maintains dominance by fudging everything in between. Rational arguments are unlikely when you have no credibility in the first place; and are constricted by the black and white of patriarchal plausibility in the second.

I do not accept the legitimacy of this arrangement and so I turn the tables here. The point of feminist knowledge is to confront this irrationality and establish the ground for women's missing credibility. I use this strategy for my own intents and purposes. The only way to approach That Thing rationally, is from a feminist point-of-view. Feminists' purpose is the process of self-development and unfolding; and not on patriarchal terms.

The Polarity Thicket

Intrinsic to the male-female polarity is the dominance of one side over the other. The scheme proliferates a morass of dualities, hypocrisies, mind-bending contradictions and manipulations. Double standards, double binds, false binaries, polarities, dichotomies, dualisms, doublespeak and all of them intertwining to various degrees and at various times and intersections.

An obvious example of the double bind is the twofold character of American democracy. As citizens, we undertake to live up to the spirit and principles of the thing. At the same time we are denied full participation and our struggles for equality meet with opposition. The Equal Rights Amendment, drafted by suffragist leader Alice Paul, was first introduced in the United States Congress in 1923 but has not yet been passed. Nonetheless, we are bound by tradition and authority to accept the system as it is, even where it does not serve our interests; and worse, where it works against us.

Ranking high in the polarity scam is the classic mind-bender, doublethink, which works something like this. Male authority strategically absents female reality from the culture and prevents those negated aspects from making an appearance. At the same time, they calculate that women are inferior. By doing this, they eliminate all hope of their own evolution and sap the life out of women who must eternally reconstruct humanity and societies after male blunders.

Doublespeak is with us every day, coming at us from all sources, private and public. These are the ritual and literal uses of language for purposes of self-rationalization and cover-up. One level of language tells us what they are talking about. The other is tells us how we're supposed to think about the message. Say one thing, conceal another. Say this, mean that.

The most iconic duality is the Cartesian split. Around 1650, French philosopher, René Descartes proclaimed, "I think therefore I am," thereby establishing himself as the ultimate source of reality. Theoretically, this statement declared his intellectual independence from the strictures of tradition and the past. Practically, this was to be interpreted as Descartes placing his quintessence in the intellectual basket at the expense of his bodily nature. His simple statement was, and still is, used to associate mind and spirit with the male, body and matter with the female. For centuries since, generations have clung to this rendition of male superiority and used it as the mainstay for phallocentric overreaching in philosophy, social and most other theory.

> He thinks, therefore I am.
> Carrie Fisher, *Surrender the Pink*

The Cartesian split is simply a latter day projection of the gender split, a cult started in the fifth century B.C. by the Greek, Pythagorus. No woman with any brains believes her mind is exclusive of her body. Or it can be put another way: when men die the mind goes with them, just like women. And another: without women's body, man has no brain—no life, period.

> This Cartesian "Me," this autonomous little homunculus who sits behind our eyeballs looking out through them in order to pass judgment on the affairs of the world, is just completely ridiculous. This self-appointed little editor of reality is just an impossible fiction that collapses the moment one examines it.
> Robert M. Persig, *Lila*

Being trapped in this psychic and actual polar thicket causes women to come up with statements such as this: "If women ruled the world, there would be no more war," exchanging a vision of moral and ideological perversion with a virtuous promise—but one born of conceptual weakness. One of the objectives of every woman should be to train herself out of the psychological constructions which authenticate our own contributions to the gender split.

> Bohr challenged another scientific shibboleth in 1927 by proposing that opposites were not necessarily *either/or*, as all earlier Western dualistic thinkers had assumed, but rather might be *both/and*. He said that the opposite of a shallow truth is a falsehood, but that the opposite of a profound truth was another profound truth.
> Leonard Shlain, *The Alphabet Versus the Goddess*

(Niels Bohr, won the Nobel Prize in Physics in 1922.)

The problem doesn't stop with sexism. The double binds of gender structure are complicated further by interweaving women's inequality issues with other forms of oppression such as race, class and body aesthetics. Each prejudice has its own character of oppression and purpose in the power equation.   If you're starting to envision this structure—to see the problem—it's the formidable power of an inquiring mind working in tandem with the greatest invention of nature: the female body.

Within the polarity of the gender split lies the pivotal point of the perception of the power and status of male-female inequality. It is the ground of the confusion, fear and violence that arise when women act to redress this imbalance. In women's experience we understand it as "backlash" and so avoid individual actions in favor of feminist principles, independence and our own wholeness; because we believe it will harm our relationships with men who hold the power in the gender thicket.

Women in This Scheme

At this point, a working picture of the patriarchal scheme will have come into view. Now we can look at the implications of living in this system.

The social structure is the level where we fit into the strategy as active members. This is where female-male relationships are built and the status of dominant male and subordinate female are integrated. Here we learn to adhere to the pretended rights of the male and become experts in the practice of gender inequality against ourselves.

The Social Contract

The gender arrangement is interpreted through an unspoken agreement known as the social contract. It sets out what it takes for people to get along on male terms, having sidestepped and distorted the natural laws of community.   An implicit set of inclusions and exclusions determine masculine and feminine behavior. Categories of manliness and womanliness are inculcated and become practice.   "Manners, customs, mores, acknowledgments of details are completely understood by both."

The explicit terms of the social contract are obvious. There are the institutions which determine and implement social control—the U.S. Congress, the justice and legal business, civilian and religious agencies, law enforcement, the National Guard, and the like.   There is also the huge industry invested in promoting its core beliefs: social, economic, political and every other kind of science, theory, government policy. The reigning propaganda says, that "only in the bounds of this tacit agreement can human society survive—without such rules and constraints, society collapses." This is rubbish. The agreement is continually being defrauded, broken, challenged and changed, inevitably in favor of more patriarchal power.

Affirmation of the social contract heightens awareness of male power and privilege and is therefore encouraged of both sexes. In terms of social orientation, however, men all start out even, by definition of gender. Dominant, they maintain social relations in their own image. Women participate in social relations which manifest and express masculine authority.

The social contract is a swindle. This is evident in the fact that our status in society is not equivalent to the contributions women make in all aspects of private and public life. None of the terms, implicit or explicit, have been bargained out by women according to what is valuable and necessary to us. Women live in painful coexistence with this lopsided deal that robs us of our equity and imposes great responsibility with no power (except for tokens, where men concede nothing). This phallocentric deal is not only the underlying cause of all social problems that affect women, but also prevents us from exercising our natural power and legitimate destiny.

CHAPTER 9

FORMING AN IDENTITY
IN THE PATRIARCHY

We are framed as subordinate before we are born. At birth, we are propelled into a mankind which believes males are superior to, and more valuable than, females. We are admired as objects, not equal subjects. Our own interests and impulses are presumed not to exist independently. The male universe is superimposed onto all aspects of our experience.

Our role as subordinate means accepting the idea of ourselves as inferior or secondary. In the process of tamping down and tearing out our own desires and natural skills—and rejecting our advantages—we demonstrate men's definition of our inferiority. (This brings up another false polarity, which is belief (ours) in the idea of male superiority.)

Females are defined as inferior at birth and socialized to enforce our own inequality. As we develop, we learn language and conceive thoughts in patriarchal conceptions. Male images are internalized and we are habituated to ideas of submission: unimportant, weak, minor. We shape our identity according to what is "feminine." We aspire to embody this ideal and study passivity, immaturity, irrationality and obedience. We are often unsuccessful, ergo disappointing.

The experiences we have been denied, we learn to deny ourselves. In female societies we nurture and cultivate our special self-deceptions and fail to develop mature values and language. Naivete and vulnerability claim us—as though we were immune to the lessons of falsehood and deceit. We internalize skills that are critical to survival on men's terms. We learn the rhetoric of challenging male dominance—but only to the point of not doing anything. If we march to the male drummer and "learn to play the game" we're predatory and we "act like a man!"

We conform to the male structure of reality, which is what passes for normal. But double trouble! Conditioned to see the world in male terms, we perceive ourselves to be secondary, so it is impossible to live up to these norms! Our fundamental principles do not relate to reality, nor do those we have cultivated. When we attempt to reconcile with the real world, we stumble over the purposes others have determined for us. So when women describe their specific experience to men, we confront the universal consciousness of male normalcy: That Thing again. And the dominant ideology tells both man, and woman, that he is right!

In Service

Thus, with patriarchal forces in control, we define and transform our drives into the service of their own. The development of our human potential is determined by what the patriarchy considers it needs and wants from us. Our fate as subordinates depends on accommodating and pleasing dominants. We learn how to bow to power and authority and are robbed of the motivation to become adults who will participate fully in managing the affairs of our world.

Then along comes that special guy—wow! Whatever power we had is exchanged for his approval. Whatever boundaries we had are dismantled. Soon, we are giving up more and putting more out. Our self-sufficiency is exchanged for paired incompetence. Then it turns ominous—the shadow appears. If we speak anything but flattery, he considers it a threat: we "get it" and shut up. We begin to make decisions based on values imposed and not our own. Being a woman has gotten to us at last. Finally, we're home, where we're supposed to be.

We project his powerful disdain onto ourselves and fall victim to self-contempt and unwholesomeness. "Even when I do what he wants, I'm doing something wrong . . . " We confuse his acceptance with our acceptance of abuse, having been untaught the language of our own authority and the principles of survival. But we still have faith in our delusions. "If I keep working at it, he'll change!" We are starting to collapse into the quicksand where we've built our hopes. Finally, "I can't do anything about it!" We realize that "it" is impenetrable but don't even know what "it" is. We fail to learn the lessons of women's past.

Crisis: And Then Some

Sooner or later what we have denied makes an appearance. We sense invisible things about ourselves and our relationships in the world and they act on our imagination and our personality. Like ghosts, we doubt them but we are persuaded not to fight them. We are in the grip of an elusive force which insists upon things that are not true. We are the sum totals of our experience—yet culturally seen as only a fraction. In the battle between instinct, knowledge and experience, something comes apart.

By the time we get to this point, we're looking for answers—stocking up on self-help books, running to the shrink or sifting through mythological promises trying to reconcile the ironies of the "universal oneness of humanity." Regardless, we're still translating our motives into the service of others and denying that the living of a life is for ourselves. We have never acknowledged that humanity is a two-way street and we're on it.

> It's given you a great compassion for the miserable and dispossessed, Francis, and that's very fine, so long as you don't let it swamp your common sense . . . immoderate compassion will ruin you quicker than brandy.
>
> Robertson Davies, *Bred in the Bone*

Anxiety sets in. We feel impotent and paralyzed. Emergencies scream at us and we can't act. We bite the skin off our nails and lips; gorge, starve and puke ourselves into paroxysms. We wonder what we are living for, what the hell we're doing here. We subject ourselves to morbid self-examination, searching for what has been denied, cut off, dead.

Before we reach this point is a good place to learn that being fully conscious is also a two-way street. Self-knowledge requires understanding our external world as well as the internal. Knowing what we're up against is as important as knowing who we are.

What We Have Lost

Loss of self in service to the patriarchy is the classic female pathology. It is offset by society honoring our deference and sacrifice. But by failing to act in our own self-interest we have not ennobled ourselves; instead, we have suffered incalculable losses. Our truth and history have been erased. We have lost our self-knowledge and collective heritage. We have lost our individual creativity and the strength of our voices. We have lost our honor.

We have turned away from inquiry and rejected the calls to develop into our higher selves. Loss of the incalculable wealth of women's talents, experience and wisdom causes us to live in a false history and operate with a constrained cultural imagination. We've been dealt out of the stakes of living on this planet. In what way is this noble? When one realizes the full range of damage the patriarchy has done, it can be a source of considerable pain and insult to the ego.[8]

Loss of self leads to self-effacement (or the other extreme, narcissism). In the external world, loss of self deprives us of communal authority and creativity which we give up in favor of diminished roles and oppressive toil. Our prejudice against our female selves fuels the power and capacity of the forces that enchain us.

> . . . By the time a woman understands the dangers of her conditioned immobility, neurological patterns are set—anyone with sufficient psychic or physical strength can overwhelm her.
>
> Unknown

Tied into the male power game as subordinates, our higher faculties are compromised and often shut down altogether. We implicitly agree to understand life at a lower level than we are capable of achieving. Not only do we concede, day by day, because we believe in the inevitability of our plight in life, but we are permanently compromised by the male determination of our inferiority owing to the fact that we are women and therefore lesser than they. This has taken a great toll on our immediate and extended relationships in our lives and in our world.

We exchange self-censored truth and limited vision in our **mother-daughter relationships.** We cannot teach but what we know, and that includes our own self-deception. Our daughters perceive a sense of matriarchal betrayal and we lose the joy and potential of their womanhood.

We lose the **wisdom of our elders**—the great repository of power and ballast for upcoming generations. How can we understand women's wisdom when we subconsciously—and overtly—devalue it?

And we lose the best of what could have been in our **relationships with men**, which are stunted by false values and unnatural expectations and which characteristically spiral out of control, leaving a legacy of more and more divergent behavior. What should be a communion of mature experience and

---

[8] It is women who hide their feelings. The problem is compounded by thinking they're doing the right thing in protecting men from the truth.

understanding turns out to be a wasteland of female-male social and sexual inadequacy.

All this because women's truth has not been spoken. We are not bound by nature to stop short of the full course, but by the impositions of a system which robs us of our distinctive roles and whose point is the restraint of women's knowledge coming to the fore. In this way, we have lost the cultural manifestation of women's investment in humanity.

The Gap

What we have sensed was missing—and now know is lost—must have gone somewhere. As we begin to get an inkling that this fugitive existence might be captured, there are plentiful theories and feel-good gimmicks available when we finally begin to seek. We look to the language of symbols and metaphors—the forgotten language of interpreting myths, fairy tales and religious visions. We search for evidence of our own specters in dreams, nightmares and lost worlds and ancient civilizations in stories, histories and lore. We attempt to stake our reality in old ways of knowing—mysticism, alchemy, Gnosticism and the occult. Any of these will work to varying degrees of entertainment, diversion or satisfaction, but offer little practical advantage for living a life.

Or we turn to psychoanalysis—tutored by others to dwell on our sacrifices and failures. They teach us to excavate the buried sources of our discontent and do battle with them in an inner-outer language to determine, ultimately, where to lay blame. Indeed, there are professionals in the field who are brilliant therapists, analysts and phychiatrists[9]—people who save lives and us from our own self-cannibalization, by laying out frameworks for mental development and methods to escape our own psychic bog. But mostly, these people are strangers who operate at the lowest level of educational and emotional rigor, who are ignorant of the subtleties of the human condition both inside and out, who are often drug-addled themselves and languish for want of genuine interest in life.

Or we seek the time-honored escape into religion. It is never the answer to our problems, but brings a kind of naive comfort by blotting them out. Of all the theology I've soaked up, the one useful idea is the Anglican teaching that one is supposed to enjoy one's life. But it is the state of the human ear not to be attuned to such a message: wretchedness is far more compelling. Whatever the case, most attempts at self-knowledge rely on

---

[9]The late Jean Baker Miller (1927-2006), for instance, quoted several times in these pages.

catching up with our past while we are in the present and going into the future.

In this project, we start beyond that. The challenge is to identify the gap itself—the one between our own underdevelopment and potential wisdom. There's no need to worry about what caused it to go missing, as we've already discussed that in these previous pages.

> I don't like to think about this very much because it is too large
> for me, but sometimes this knowledge falls on me like misery.
> Linda Hogan, *Power*

The Negated Consciousness

While reading Norman O. Brown's classic, *Life Against Death, The Psychoanalytical Meaning of History*, it occurred to me that theories about the collective conscious and unconscious were inadequate concepts *a priori*. Women's reality was not factored into the thinking of people like Jung and Freud, about whom Brown is writing. Only women as objects are a subject of their concern. Their presumptions, therefore, are half-baked.

Considering these useful but semi-invalid ideas, it occurred to me that the gap in women's consciousness is our unuttered knowledge of life and the human condition itself. It is combined with the deprivations this void suggests—sorrow, suffering—in the external world. This is a type of consciousness, but it doesn't exist yet. It is there; buried inside us and inchoate around us. We sense it, intuit it, but women's existential condition precludes this consciousness from making an appearance. The environmental conditions are hostile to it and therefore it has failed to manifest. I call it the negated consciousness. The concept is absent of the assumptions of male dogma, as it occurred to me during the evolution of this project.[10]

The idea of this psychic black hole is invigorating, because it elevates the problems of the subconscious above the slavish concept of repression. The negated consciousness positions itself as a psychic mirror, right in front of us. Its contents will only to be developed or enlightened by the positive forces of intuition and will as a conscious act. In this process, each of us can dig up—and tune up—our lost forces. These forces are like a bad battery, that drain and undermine us; and nag us about being off track or faring

---

[10]A few years after the idea of the negated consciousness popped up, I inquired about it at the Jung Foundation in New York to make sure I hadn't just osmosed it. No one there had ever heard of it.

poorly. The negated consciousness shows up as the symptoms of things we should be able to do but can't; able to realize, but don't.

Drawing on a Zen idea, "the bigger the front, the bigger the back," (or, the more you excavate what's buried, the more you discover what's missing) the negated consciousness is the backside of consciousness. For women, our history having been erased, it contains our innate knowledge, wisdom, creativity and voice, along with the realizations we've locked up because we have not had the wherewithal to put it altogether rationally and manifest our development in daily life in the form of adult experience. It contains what goes in and then some. It is not just a layer in there somewhere, that you need a psychiatric shovel to dig down to. (Then what?) The negated consciousness is a reflection of reality and knowledge of emotion and imagination that has not yet been realized. It contains the untapped power of our human nature.

As active agent of the lock up, the patriarchy keeps in place the fear which prevents us from manifesting the contents of our negated selves. We are afraid of conflict, afraid of thinking, seeing, saying, believing in ourselves. Afraid of doing and afraid of success. Afraid of power. And most of all, we are afraid of expressing the alternative to these fears, meaning we are afraid of language. We are afraid to interpret, clarify, criticize and argue to win.

But the mind knows about the presence of alternative thoughts. The mind is aware that other possibilities have been removed by tyrannical pressure. If men have been the agents of our repression, why do we continue to allow them to be our jailers, keeping us in this semi-cognitive prison? This speechlessness? When we feel in conflict, why should we not **be** in conflict? Conflict useful to us, that is.

> We, as women, have learned and forgotten more than they have
> ever set down in books. . . . We are sustained in our weakness
> by something they have never even heard a whisper of.
> Kay Boyle, *Decision*

This lacuna, this negated consciousness of women's reality is a unique class of information—a category in itself: of unrealized language and unlived existence. But the mind seeks these missing and alternative thoughts. It instigates its own gapology by causing discontent. It is dynamic, confrontational, argumentative and demands creative results. It contains the ingredients of change. Through this faculty, the negated consciousness, we can reclaim ownership of what has been lost. The answers in the gap will bring all the elusive thoughts, ideas and dreams you have into relevance with your life.

So if we are more conscious than we know, what then, is actually our problem? This: we don't SPEAK it. This problem is the negative dynamic of the category. Giving words to what is in the gap is the solution and the essence of power.

•

So what's in it—this gap between ourselves and our life? And why have the forces of history been so vigilant about keeping it under wraps?

In it is our lost knowledge, wisdom, talent experience—the same thing that's missing from the culture. If women were to manifest the unspoken thoughts, insights and truth they have been concealing, instead of swallowing and disgorging male dogma *ad infinitum* and *ad nauseam*, we would expose and cure the basic fallacy upon which men base their claim to power, that they are superior and women are second best.

Higher and more creative ways of thinking lie dormant in all women. We possess a silent, psychic language in common—the one that grasps the substance of things. People intuit what's true and that is why you know that what is being described here is the missing knowledge you have but don't think about. That's what understanding is. If my conclusions didn't ring true, you'd negate them all by yourself. You wouldn't need Freud or Jung to do it for you.

•

In January 2008, America is gearing up for the November election and the parties are getting ready to select the candidates who will run for president. Fascinating, is to listen to women discuss their positions on either Hillary Clinton or Barack Obama.

Who will qualify as the best leader is not the point here, but what young and mainstream women Obama-supporters say about the possibility of electing the first female president in our history. The sense of their own equality is either one of total certainty or not even a concept, depending on who's talking. As a group, women's historical, political and social reality is just a blip on their own singular and narrow horizon.

This kind of denial looks like the female version of That Thing ("the historical consciousness of the superiority of the male," Chapter 6). In this case, the negated consciousness is That Thing — a willful blindness that keeps us from looking into the huge and unexplored world that lies just beneath the surface of what we think about what appears to be.

CHAPTER 10

POWER REALITIES

P atriarchal power is that of all men lumped together. It is constructed on the claims of male superiority. Women are what this male authority sets itself over.

It is held collectively and defended by men in association with one another—both aggressively and passively. This gives each cog in the patriarchal wheel the right to have the upper hand and males learn this early on. From this position, a man who applies pressure to dominate women is implicitly validated. This means they can lord it over us, steal our resources, exploit our activities, censor our language and worse.

Male power is totalitarian in nature. The "power structure" is the organization and system of maintaining that power. It intrudes on every aspect of women's lives and is willing to devise any extreme to keep us shackled to the system. Women put up a struggle now and then, but more often than not, we become resigned to the lopsided arrangement on the outside and to our own fear and confusion on the inside. We perceive what we get out of it to outweigh the damage it does because it looks better than nothing when you have no other options. In other words, women are tied into the male power game as perpetual losers.

The patriarchy is not a self-regenerative system. It cannot generate the tension nor the creativity required to adjust to new realities. It is dumb and cumbersome and thrives on brute force and low-level ideas that make it fall back repeatedly on violence and tyranny as solutions to its own failures.

Feminism expands our knowledge and when we integrate this into our life, we raise our level of independent potential. Men don't like feminism because it causes them to lose power over women and as a consequence, within their own group.

Martha and the Links

In the summer of 2003, Martha Burk, Chair of the National Council of Women's Organizations led a protest against the male-only Augusta National Golf Club, which was hosting the U.S. Open Golf Tournament. When someone asked what I thought about this my response was, "One club full of self-important, semi-ambulatory, high-handicapped, bad-looking rich guys with trophy wives in the steamy, testosterone-infused South? I don't care, actually."

I learned to care and why I should later, when I read an excerpt from Burk's book, *Cult of Power: Sex Discrimination in Corporate America and What Can Be Done About It*. In it she lists the six ways the "power dynamic manifests itself" and how male corporate elites keep women out, which are recapped here.

•Power re-creates itself in its own image. (In the Augusta case—white, male, exclusive club member.)

•Power elites enforce norms and systems that guarantee continued power. (New members are chosen—"trained" in culture, behavior and vital know-how.)

•Power creates a sense of entitlement. (Men have first claim over women in jobs, sports, opportunities.)

•Power creates invulnerability, leading to a flaunting of society's standards. (Surrounded by fawners and yes-people, they dismiss normal standards of conduct and fairness.)

•Loyalty to power overshadows other loyalties, including gender and race. (Power confers power, ergo loyalty to the power pack. Women are not immune to this behavior.)

•Group loyalty combined with power can trump good judgment and override individual moral codes. (Elite masculine values applied to power, dominance, control: corrupt.)

The message here is that for women to influence others and accomplish what we want to do—and to rise in corporate America—you have to understand this environment and be able to play at this level. What happens to one's character on the way, is up to the individual.

•

The enlightened members of the world now accept the reality of gender inequality. But understanding women's situation in terms of "inequality" is a negative. We have yet to accept the implications of the feminist claim to the power to manage and regulate society. (In fact, many essential concepts and realizations developed in the women's movement are still unrecognized by women themselves.)

The positive intentions of feminism go unacknowledged because of the male construction of what is rational—what is taken seriously, that is. Women's interests in the terms of male rationality are still a blank. Therefore, there is no reciprocal basis from which we can contradict the construction of what is fair, unless we can make our case using feminist knowledge.

Our Men

The crux of the feminist matter is **our men**. The ones in our homes and in our beds; at school, at work, the coffee joint, bar, the nabe, the hood. Our men all know about their gender power and practice it. They support the patriarchal agenda because they are supposed to—because they're male. They sense women's vulnerability in the scheme because that is the nature of the thing. Our men are socialized to be antagonistic toward women's equality, like all other men. By the time women get around to challenging this arrangement (if ever) men have already been training since birth to foil their efforts.

When the patriarchy is criticized, women get uncomfortable and throw up "our men" as a barrier to their own higher knowledge. They protest with things like "my father was such a gentle man," or "my brothers treat me like one of them." And "my husband lets me do what I want" and other paeans to the Y chromosomes in close proximity. I have yet to hear them say that these men acknowledge the arrangement of male entitlement and corresponding prejudice and harms this has caused in the lives of "their women." Have their men ever admitted that they assume the mantle of subordinator by accepting the patriarchal package? Highly unlikely.

Another common rejoinder to the subject of male oppression is, "And what about man's cruelty toward man?!" There is a marked difference between the exploitation of women and men. For women, male power comes *a priori*, by way of history, tradition and the social contract. It is universal. Man's struggle against oppression has yet to liberate women and equalize their status as citizens. This is also universal.

The basic mechanism of male power lies in the gender structure. First, they have the power over women that comes with the gonads. Next, they shape their identities and social position by staking themselves off from other groups and classes of men. As power and authority grow, males aim to dominate women and other males as well. Regardless of who is doing what to whom, men and women are not equally oppressed by men.

The other comeback is that feminism is "good for men," too. There is no question that men's participation is necessary for full equality.[11] We do not live on separate planets. Right now, however, we're still at the stage where men condemn women's achievement for their loss of power and manhood; and women have the need to apply the balm of feminist knowledge to men's salvation. Educating ourselves because it is good for men is a misplaced motive. Men's limitations can only be solved by initiatives yet to be defined. Understanding women's authenticity and gender realities can help them get to that point.

All of these reactions by women are fear based. "If I express my authentic self," says Fear, "will it alienate me from men? Will they reject me for speaking the truth?" Don't worry and forget the romantic anxiety. The bond is already ridden with falsehoods and bargains that protect the male superiority deal. The arrangement is constructed to generate the fear that women's independence will destroy the relationship. You're not inventing it; and it's not going away.

•

Personally, I've had plenty of opportunity to observe our men. Friends, family, colleagues, lovers, husbands and among them a roster of ferocious male chauvinists, misogynists, bullies, neanderthals and nobodies. I've known some who believe, without reservation, in equal justice and status for women. Others believe our advancement has somehow harmed them. Whatever their position, I am not stupid enough to believe that any of them would relinquish their power in exchange for a life of reform and commitment to "straighten this gender thing out!" Men have not and will not

---

[11]At a forum on women's literature in New York in 2006, Marilyn French, prominent feminist and author and best known for her novel *The Women's Room,* said it would take another three hundred years.

relinquish their generic power without a struggle. They will, though, claim, "I'm not responsible because I didn't create it." The hidden aspects of male life maintain the power relations that perpetuate their advantaged situation. All men benefit from it and our men do not live outside of this reality.

Loving men has nothing to do with feminist knowledge—which has to do with the best interests of women. By raising our own consciousness, we are, in fact, raising that of the rest of society, which includes our men.

CHAPTER 11

MEDIA

The macro tier not only controls society, but it also tells us what we're supposed to do in it. The mass media conveys the message that the power structure wants to tell us about ourselves. Here images and fantasies about status and identity are put out for universal social approval and to a large extent it works. Whatever the ideological persuasion, the media performs the function of preselecting what the "it" of life is. Media, therefore, performs the construction of the culture itself.

They disseminate their message by broadcasting, print, recording and the internet and the minds of women are one of the main targets. The media monolith creates elements to prey on the minds of females of every age and type—kids, girls, young, medium, old. Media confronts us with an onslaught of new ways to violate our own sense of propriety. Celebrity junk that women lap up, sorry vignettes that pass for issues, the essentials of hot style and fashion in everything, and weird behavior to emulate. All of this is connected to standards created by the chieftains of politics, economics and advertising who tell us how to vote, what to buy, how to look, what to do and how to do it; but mostly how to think and make judgments. The "must be" and "must have" delivered with an excruciating torque: you must keep striving till you get there and you will, they promise—week after year, after decade.

There's a new tune struck up in the last few decades. Women are now highly visible in the media, compared to only a few decades ago. Females display leadership and expertise by rehashing, revamping and lending their insights to the eternal re-invention of the patriarchal strategy to control the cultural narrative of women. Little wonder that the issues of real women's lives are not a political priority. Sexism (not even mentioned in Webster's Third New International Dictionary Unabridged, 1966, which sits on my desk) still permeates every form of media except for *Ms.* magazine and a few webzines, underground periodicals and blogs. Fortunately for us, our culture can now support a roster of significant women writers, broadcasters, journalists, and film and video makers, but seldom do they make it onto the mass media A-list.

On the odd occasion that women's stories do make news, feminism or feminist action is never mentioned as having had anything to do with it. Usually, media-appointed feminists and anti-feminists comment on the state of feminism's vitality, which is inevitably a negative story or a cat fight. If culture is a huge feedback system, it is reasonable, then, that mainstream and young adult women don't know anything about feminism. Why should they relate to something when all they see and hear about it is unappealing? After all, media grooms you for the simplistic and the likeable; not the struggle.

The real life of women goes virtually unreported. Instead we get regular media buzzlets—chain reactions and feeding frenzies whose underlying mission is to keep society off track about women's progress and increasing power. Speaking at the Women and Media Conference at MIT, 1 April 2006, Caryl Rivers, Professor of Journalism at Boston University, described the stories people in the media create about women, while knowing the stories are not true. Some of the topics she mentioned are: miserable career women who don't have children and have lousy sex, women with too much education can't get a man and become infertile, selfish career mothers who neglect their children, killer nannies and bad working mothers who hire them, can't do science and math, girls doing better in school because of evil feminist teachers, men don't like smart women, high IQ women are less likely to marry, women are less desirable if high achievers, feminism is a bust because women are too tired to have sex. And always high on the buzz list is the "opt out revolution" about women chucking their careers and heading back home.[12] Rivers debunks these stories and corrects the record on these fake trends, false links, bogus connections, unsubstantiated generalizations and untruths.

Media misogyny lives on and we will continue to hear such fabrications until we get a grip on our own culture.

---

[12]*Source: Center for New Words and WGBH in association with the Lowell Institute. See* http://forum.wgbh.org/wgbh/forum.php?lecture_id=3047

The Crass Ceiling

The media loves pumping up banalities about women, particularly what is now called "hot!" body, style and fashion perfect, with sex, please. Also known as "girlie" and "do-me," hot describes the nouveau lifestyle of the sexually liberated. The qualities needed to fit into the hot milieu are big boobs, belly button bearing designer threads, expensive workouts and matching looks and if you're a porn-loving, walking orgasm and fellatio gourmande, you've really got it made.

> Because of the feminist movement, women today have staggeringly different opportunities and expectations than our mothers did. . . . We get to go to college and play sports and be secretary of state. But to look around, you'd think all any of us want to do is rip off our clothes and shake it.
>
> Ariel Levy, *Female Chauvinist Pig*

Like the flappers of the Roaring Twenties, the girlie bit is highly perishable. Somewhere in the flash and trash, the point gets lost. Sexual freedom turns into the same old sexist exploitation game—inferiority and domination—and poor girlie has no idea what's happening. Time and people grow tired of girlie and soon she is pushed out of her niche, only to confront ageing, change and other elements of reality. Like all women, girlie meets same shit, different day. Girlie fades away, no one cares and the culture is left with the accouterments of girlie's halcyon days: tawdry images and a bad taste in the mouth. Mature women bowing down to the youth culture is just another face of that underdevelopment.

The media manipulation of women's imagery has a far more serious side to it. "You don't realize what kind of pressure that puts on us," said Margot, a young filmmaker friend. "The media has created this image and if we don't buy into it, we have nowhere to go. You can't get out from under it. It's like a lead cloud hanging over us."

Hearing this, the idea of the "crass ceiling" came to mind. Obtuse image control, insensitive to the mental and moral expression of everything outside its own narrow and exploitative authority, hangs over the heads of the young. Our pop-obsessed society elevates every fad and banality into cultural significance and obliterates all that does not conform. This leaves millions of young women unable to develop a cultural rationale for their own time and generation. A collective identity eludes them, as their values and interests are not reflected back to them as a vital part of our culture by the mass media which controls our imagery, therefore the way we think.

If you're young, female, don't dig crass, and looking for good information to help you negotiate mainstream society, don't look to your culture for it. It isn't there. If you don't act according to cultural "norms," you're nowhere. And if your shape, values and behavior don't match the prescription, you're nobody.

> "The social current is so strong, it's so hard to swim against it.
> . . . I remember feeling isolation, solitude, which I couldn't wholly grasp because I was a happy person. To me, I wanted to be perfect." Sophie Gregoire
>
> Eva Friede, "Sophie's Story,"
> *Montreal Gazette*, 7 November 06

And then there is us: women in media. There are some very talented women working in the media machine, many of whom are leaders in their field. Women in whatever end of the business promoting the patriarchal narrative as news, cultural development, lifestyle requirements and storytelling must develop their own awareness about the effects of their work on others and on themselves. They are responsible for coming up with the answers, just as individually we must discriminate as to what messages we relate to and why.

•

This media problem relates to both Issues #1 and #2 in Chapter 4. Whereas the media could intelligently represent the preponderance of issues critical to women and actually influence change, it does not. For the average mainstream woman, it does not portray her peer society and therefore has the effect of isolating her in a cloud of misinformation and cultural rubbish.

> If there was ever a story that deserved more coverage by the news media, it's the dark persistence of misogyny in America. Sexism in its myriad destructive forms permeates nearly every aspect of American life. For many men, it's the true national pastime, much bigger than baseball or football.
> Bob Herbert, *New York Times*, 15 January 2008

PART THREE

★

THE BETTER IDEA

CHAPTER 12

THE ROAD TO WISDOM

I believe in wisdom, and the journey we all must take to get there. Wisdom is not advice. It is the pursuit of learning from adult life and the creation and use of better ideas; ideas that are superior to the ingrained habits and dogma that prevail in both private and public life. The wise understand the intricacies of human relationships, meaning of judiciousness and the regulation of power. And they understand the necessity of integrating all that women have learned in the recent past into the rest of the world's knowledge.

The concept of women's wisdom barely makes an appearance in the common narrative and when it does, it is usually a pejorative. It is perceived as an exception to the rule, that is to say, the surprising or dubious appearance of female thought or action on the scene of patriarchal operations and opinion. It is found in myths and story books, characterized by the "wise woman," witch or fortune teller—figures who trade in cunning, idealism and fantasy, but seldom sagacity. And in real life, it is preserved for the old grandmother or elder, whose job is to dole out aphorisms and platitudes that are sanctioned within the family circle. If the elder is sharp and articulate and holds a position in the community, she is probably self-censoring; living up to the implicit demand that she should never threaten the male ego, nor undermine other women's complicity in the maintenance of this charade. So filled with fear and self-doubt are we about our own intelligence and higher powers that we accept the status of weak, inferior and muted, rather than make the case for our own superiority in the knowledge and handling of life's affairs.

The definition of wisdom is apparently quite illusive. According to Stephen S. Hall, in "The Older-and-Wiser Hypothesis," *New York Times*, 6

May 2007, psychologists and researchers are trying to figure out not only how to measure wisdom, but to decide what it is in the first place. Hall tells us that the nature of wisdom was first contemplated by Vivian Clayton in the 1960s and 1970s, who was then an undergraduate at Buffalo University and then a graduate student at the University of Southern California. Because of the complexity of the subject, Clayton left academia in 1981. Now a psychologist and beekeeper in Northern California, she wisely reduces the meaning of wisdom to its most elegant form:

> You know, bees have been around for hundreds of millions of years, at least, as living creatures . . . And when you work a hive, and you're there with that hive alone, and you hear how contented the bees are, you just have the sense that they have the pulse of the universe encoded in their genes. And I really feel that the concept of wisdom is like that, too. Somehow, like the bees, we are programmed to understand when someone has been wise. But what wisdom is, and how one learns to be wise, is still somewhat of a mystery.

Wisdom is part of the life force. It starts with life propelling us to understand it, and instilling in us the desire to overcome the limitations it brings with its challenges.

Accepting Life as an Adult

The history of women's submission and subordination is not only the story of oppression, but of our underdevelopment. Each of has a responsibility to transcend our own backwardness and rise to the challenges of mature adulthood. Embarking on this journey means changing the way we think about ourselves. It requires the heightening of consciousness and willingness to overcome the habits of reduced mental functioning and limited ideas of what we should expect of ourselves—and out of life. When you change your mind, your wants and needs change. You place yourself in a different perspective, which in turn changes the nature of your relationship with the outside world. You come to see yourself occupying a stable position and start to live in the context of higher expectations—instead of seeing yourself as a case, in the history of women's chronic underdevelopment.

The passage to wisdom leads to adjustments in our relationships with other people. When we open our minds and create new possibilities, we are able to weigh more variables and our own truth matures as a result. This causes conflict on the outside. How we deal with that conflict—that difference—is a test of our developing wisdom. Some situations and relationships will be maintained on their former plain, but not all.

The first, and perhaps the greatest, challenge on the Road to Wisdom is making an intellectual adjustment to the influence of the male voice. This is not an argument—not an arrangement of issues, into which men are invited, and encouraged to debate; not a niceness game, where we massage the male mystique and play the sympathy card, so men don't feel threatened. The preservation of the male ego in the equality struggle is not women's problem. Our problem is changing ourselves at the fundamental level of rationality—neutralizing or eliminating all dominating male influence, real or imagined, from our functioning. Men will just have to deal with women growing up and out of perpetual girlhood. It may even help them to mature themselves. That's up to them.

> . . . that toy-box history of the world adapted to young ladies
> which made the chief part of her education . . .
>   George Eliot, *Middlemarch*

Because men as a whole (socially, politically, culturally) have no experience with taking women's wisdom seriously, the specter of what will happen when women abandon their girlishness has resulted in a body of bizarre propaganda to the significant detriment of maintaining women's equality. All of these are reflections of the male protecting his position in whatever territory the traditional sexist arrangement gives him the most power. Women's advancement (feminism) is blamed for 9/11, Hurricane Katrina, the impending collapse of the Social Security system because of the demographic crisis caused by abortions, the "decline of boys," the crisis in male sexuality, and every other problem known to man and which men, clinging to the power which they have heretofore used so badly, have not been able to solve. These fictions are summed up in the more polite anti-equality charge: that the changes are "tearing apart the fabric of social life without creating an alternative."

To women who are not able to articulate their position (or defense), such extreme accusations can be intimidating. To the knowledgeable, the charges are absurd and contradicted by the countless improvements that women alone have made in present-day society. The mature woman's mind, therefore, does not buy into false sexist accusations. Women possess generic wisdom that men do not have. First and foremost, women are relational. Connection is the essence of human survival. No man, and no oracle, has to reveal this to any aware woman.

Backlash propaganda is an expression of the male fear that women will declare their posturing and inadequacies as unacceptable and leave them behind. And as usual, it is self-serving and egocentric. If and when such a thing happens, it will be a self-fulfilling prophecy, proving men's resistance to adult development themselves.

Another barrier to mature development is the over-importance placed on youth, the youth culture and the over-importance attributed to statements by the naive and inexperienced, when addressing their own responsibilities toward equality. Most younger, post-second-wave women inhabit the same asymmetrical conditions that the movement struggled against—with the difference that they accept the improvements along with continuing, unfair conditions as the end result. I often talk to young women who describe their work environment as loaded with male executives and female administrators; male managers and female support staff. Some are disgruntled and protest. Others simply backslide and see male-appeasing bromides as the solution to what they do not even know is a serious problem. Two common approaches out of the mouths of these babes are the skirting "we have to find another way to talk about this," and the "moderation" exhortation.

> Sarah says, "I just think it's so crucial to be moderate these days. And realize that you're not just addressing other feminists—you're addressing everyone. To be so radical and militant, I just think it's so harmful."
> Rene Denfield, *The New Victorians*

Both approaches are built on two missing intellectual links. One is the failure to understand the power and efficacy of language and meaning (voice), period. There would be no advancement if the concepts of equality and gender imbalance were described in the language of timidity and cop out. The very idea is meaningless. The other is that "moderation" is exactly what the Dominant Voice of the culture counts on. Moderation is easy to ignore and drown out. First the voices get toned down, then the message gets muzzled, then society tunes out altogether. And this is exactly what has happened to the contemporary women's rights dialogue. The moderation malaise is used as an excuse for young women not to stand and speak up for the higher concepts which are intrinsic to their freedom.

•

Growing up is has its own secret weapon. As we mature into elder women, we become part of a group which is supposed to rise to the top of the cultural hierarchy; it is not some lucky fluke. In our permanent condition of underdevelopment, however, we plummet to the bottom, where old women are cast off and rendered voiceless in society. The elderly embody the judgment, expertise and vision which is the wisdom of the ages and only women who remain hooked on their own immaturity fail to see that. To nourish and honor our own maturity is crucial for the development of individual vitality, a progressive world and succeeding generations.

Emotional Distance

If the mind and emotions have been torn apart, this journey is where we put them back together and refine our sense of ownership of them both. The emotional distortion that arises out of suppressed minds and repressed action is one of the main causes of women's underdevelopment. We deny the importance of our own minds and life experience, and overvalue the emotional aspects of relationships and the feelings and responses of others. We believe that our needs are fulfilled by serving theirs, and do this at the expense of our own authenticity. We further complicate the issue by assuming the contorted belief that if we become effective in our own right, everyone else's emotional experience will suffer. Getting out of these mental and emotional traps is the first priority in adult development. The journey to wisdom requires making the intellectual decision to create the emotional perspective to understand that good judgment and right action has an emotional constituent, but is at its best when it is not emotionally driven.

Creating emotional distance is a decision to step back—to create emotional boundaries in dealing with others. Normal functioning requires a buffer zone, or perceptual space, between your mind, feelings and those of other people. This boundary prevents you from getting sucked into their personalities and their impositions upon your own. Think of it as a mental moat. The drawbridge can be down or taken up, as you will.

Loosening restrictive emotional connections creates space for understanding. It allows you to get to know yourself in an intimate relationship with your own feelings. With this new perspective, you can examine your complicity in the sexist repression that has prevented you from achieving wholeness and in turn, solve the relational problems caused by your own mistaken identity. It allows you to organize your personal life so you can work toward your goals and bring to all relationships, the experience of growth in your life.

Men and children are a major challenge. Both are highly adept at squelching our freedom to make independent evaluations about their priorities (assuming that you don't have any of your own to factor in)—because they can get away with it. One of the biggest drains on women's full exercise of rationality is her role in affirming the manhood in men. Whatever her relationship with the world, her own voice is telling her that she needs to think about what men think about what she's thinking about. When it comes to expressing these thoughts, a whole different level of self-censorship comes to the fore, due to the fear of men's fear of what she might say—particularly if it's the truth. So successful has been the patriarchy in co-opting women and robbing them of their intellectual and vocal freedom that we have adapted the protection of rampant and convoluted emotionalism sufficient to paralyze us, so that we can prevent ourselves from damaging men's idea about what we think about their manhood!

Manhood affirmed, self-expression muted, then comes the next round. That's when men come to women's breasts for intimacy and nurture, sympathy and sex to complete the entitlements of their life package. What a deal! And as far as I can tell, no one is threatening to take it away. However, when women grow up, parts of it may disappear—that's just the way it is. And we should expect to be expected to fix men's problems that result when we solve our own—that's just the way that is.

The Road to Wisdom means valuing your emotions as your own. Emotions are not a squatter's village or a group orgy. What you feel is a personal attribute—not a relative bargain. Other people, including those closest to you, have no right to mute or suppress your impulses or desires. An intimate relationship with your own feelings means knowing yourself. Interaction with others is far more interesting—and satisfying—when you let yourself be your own emotional guide.

"Children, too!?" a friend exclaimed while we were discussing this topic. "Yes, children, too." After giving birth—one of the most consequential actions in human affairs—we bond with our offspring and live with them through their helplessness, weakness and immaturity. Struggling with them through this early development often includes losing our identity in this relationship—or failing to keep it separate—and reinforces the terms we impose on ourselves which restrict adult growth.

By maintaining reasonable emotional distance (the buffer zone) with your children, you are able to bring to the relationship your experience of the growth in your own life—and the evolution of the minds and behavior of the whole family unit. The alternative is a preponderance of immature and overdone adult emotion which is too heavy for children to bear. A step back will make it easier for them to grow up and leave the nest—and easier for you to get over it.

The other great trap women must get out of is being all things to all people. In the age of political correctness in a multi-cultural society, women are particularly put upon by demands for understanding and support. It is a delusion, however, to believe that ethical social behavior means spreading yourself so thin that there is nothing left for your own issues. When we are able to tell our grandchildren and great-grandchildren that we stood up for ourselves as women, and made a difference in the world because we did so, there will be plenty of time left over to engage in every other issue known to man.

Mind: The Better Idea

Some years back, I was spending what seemed like an inordinate amount of energy trying to help people come to better decisions (and to improve my own faculties while doing so; as I recall, it was a misery loves company spell). The ones they were making were seriously affecting whatever crisis each seemed to be in and wanted to talk about. Around that time I met up with my old friend, Dina, and venting my frustration, complained, "I don't know why I bother. I urge them and cheer them on. I build them up and praise their abilities. I make up parables with desirable outcomes. And nothing works. They just stick there, glued to their problems. It's a complete waste of time." And Dina, who had already known me for ten years, said, "Don't stop! You're the person who taught me I could think." I was astonished. It had never occurred to me that people existed without thinking.

> And we talked not about her childhood or about mine but about what we had achieved thus far in our adult lives. She insisted that that was what mattered to people like ourselves. She said that what she felt the day she had had her first adult consciousness was the most magical experience in her life and not some awakening in childhood that so many people went on about.
>
> Peter Taylor, *In the Tennessee Country*

You are what you think, have thought, will think. This project aims to help fill the historical space in the mind that is occupied by doubt and its faithful handmaids—frustration, stress and anxiety—none of which enlighten. We must think about what it means to be a woman living in this world. Our minds are the creators of the better ideas that will make a better world.

The first step on the Road to Wisdom is to lay claim to your own mental life; you must lay aside others' intentions for you. The decision to own your identity will map the movement from your status as unequal member of the patriarchy to that of a mature woman, who will create culture and contribute to the enhancement of the lives of those around you. The Road to Wisdom is a right of passage that is taken, not conferred. Once you take this stand, no one's assumptions should be shaping your mental life unless they are contributive, insightful, important or expanding—and welcome. What goes into your mind contains your future—which should be defined by you. You need to decide what you are looking for, how you will get your information, and how you will handle it; what goes into and out of the mind.

The Search

What are we doing, when we begin to search? What are we trying to find? Most people are looking to escape from psychological and emotional turmoil. We sense things buried inside us and want to bring them to the surface. We pursue a new life so we can leave behind the one we don't like. The search for meaning, for many, is a random one. Often the seeker simply hopes that whichever route she chooses will open an internal door, behind which she will find the solutions to the problems that vex her.

But the Road to Wisdom is not just any old search: the point is to arrive at adult maturity. Casting off immaturity means putting childish things aside and acknowledging whatever it is you've been ignoring, or should know. **The central issue here is why and how men have been able to dominate women throughout history and why we have allowed this.** And how do we create the alternatives for a free and wholesome life, while re-harmonizing the balance between women and men, on the basis of our own rationale.

This is not trading in one set of ways of being for another. We are, instead, pursuing the stuff of lost consciousness, which can only be found through the path of women's generic knowledge. With a set of principles and concepts to ground us on our journey, the task is to discover what in this world, in people and in ourselves, has gone missing. Feminist knowledge gives us the keys to the language of what we have lost, how this language has been distorted, and how it must be rebuilt. With this framework in mind, frustration, stress and anxiety drop off the radar. The path and the goal come into view.

Some people think they can make the journey to wisdom just by learning something new. College courses, fitness programs, assertiveness training, empowerment groups, encounter groups, literary, art and cultural pursuits. All of these add grist to the mill of self-knowledge and development. Others take the feel-good, miracle cure or guru routes, all of which promise that happiness can be found in their platitudes or packages if only you'll believe—and pay. But buyer beware. Putting oneself into the hands of an "authority" on anything is misleading, particularly when we are being channeled by the bias of male superiority. There are many hidden motives under the rocks.

The conventional narrative on the road to an improved life is a male construction, ergo a conclusive argument in favor of male superiority. Psychotherapy is in this category. Albert Ellis, founder of rational-emotive behavior therapy, and named the second-most-influential psychotherapist of the 20th century by the American Psychological Association, believes that people are disturbed because "all humans are out of their fucking minds—every single one of them."[13] If you buy into the authority of people like Ellis, the shrink, any development is worthless to begin with, because all people are lunatics. The best ideas, are often ones that others don't want you to have. Feminism is an obvious example.

Adult women must ignore this chicanery and examine many issues from various angles and move on. The pursuit of wisdom comes in what you already know, what you discover and the belief in the supremacy of your own experience and rational mind. The more fearless your investigation, the more interesting the journey, and you, will be.

When the unknown makes an appearance and starts coming at us, how do we handle this new stuff? On the Road to Wisdom, specters come up out of nowhere and mill about, waiting to be acknowledged. What are these things that lie beneath the surface of a woman's civility, poses, niceness; compromises and losses? What do we do with these amorphous ideas and hidden meanings that well up and stalk our identity? Do we relegate these phantoms to that old robot mind we find so convenient? No. Robotic thinking is not a useful mode when we are pursuing our own wisdom.[14] Nor

---

[13]*Source: Adam Green, "Ageless, Guiltless," New Yorker, 13 October 2003*

[14]We perform automatically all the time; there is nothing odd about it. If we had to think through getting up, showering, getting the kids off to school, what's for dinner, driving the car and getting to work, the mental energy consumed would render us useless for anything else we had to do that day.

will blueprint thinking—"that's how Jane does it; I'll try that, too"—do the trick. These are mental patterns to be improved upon. Automatic responses to new information leave us oblivious to its meaning. And the entire point of feminist knowledge is using it to find meaning—in our lives and in the world.

Of course there are internal pressures and social roles to observe and sort out as we journey on our search for wisdom. But we are not robots and we are not clones. The purpose of new knowledge is to integrate it, change ourselves and readjust our social conditions accordingly—and make it all stick together.

> The banality of evil is evil as unthinking routine; the greatest weapons against it are thought and memory. Good people learn the art of 'silent dialogue between me and myself'—because consciousness is a precondition for conscience, as well as for genuine remembrance.
>
> Richard Polt, "Remembering to Think,"
> *Village Voice,* 5 March 2004

As life is a process, so is our development on the Road to Wisdom. Improving our lives inevitably involves leaving behind old patterns which make us unhappy and feel trapped. While we move forward, our past identification travels with us; so the brain of choice for adult thinking is flexibility.

Open thinking allows us to loosen the strictures, toss off the dead weight and accept a sense of responsibility and confidence in the natural processes of life that reveal themselves to the wise woman. As for bumpy roads, much emotion accompanies anyone who embarks on the journey into the unknown. It is the process of this emotion and the mind, coming in touch with the tongue, that brings it altogether, leveraging ideas with language to get them off the ground and employ them in service of your life and in the outside world.

Knowing the Answers

There are so many complexities interwoven into women's lives; yet the voice of knowledge is the male voice. On the Road to Wisdom, we must disestablish the legitimacy of this voice. This is the back road, on our journey to wholeness. But how do we face this daunting idea? Where do we start?

You know you have instincts and intuitions that tell you things: they point to answers. You instinctively know there is more to life than what has been handed down to you. You are a woman; and whether or not you are a mother, you know how to live with the changing reality of human growth—you've already experienced it. You know what you need to survive. You know how to improve on a bad situation. You reach out with a natural empathy to care for other living beings in need. And even with little experience, you know that a search will bring you answers.

You have a psyche and it is constantly trying to teach you things that will help you become a higher interpretation of yourself. You know you exist in a cycle of growth and self-knowledge. You know you possess the power of creating a better life, after you've severed the bonds of someone else's version of reality. You already sense what the wanting version has left out. And you know when you're on the right track. You can feel it.

> When we can think only in terms given by the dominant culture which does not attend to our own experiences but specifically denies and devalues them, we are left with no way of conceptualizing our lives.
>
> Jean Baker Miller, M.D.,
> *Toward a New Psychology of Women*

On the Road to Wisdom, here are a few things you may have lost sight of, that will make an appearance—complex things you already know:

- that each soul has its own hierarchy of conflicting values and preferences;

- that diversity of beliefs and opinions forms the bedrock of human society;

- that we live in an enormous system of complexities and problems are often elaborate;

- that women have changed and traditional forms of social control don't work any more;

- that there is supposed to be ambiguity in life;

- that childish notions of good and bad belong in folk stories;

- that there is evil in the world and recognizing it is part of being an adult;

- that sometimes there are no answers;

•that sometimes you can solve a problem and no one wants the solution;

•that if society can't accept your change then it will have to adjust to its own discomfort;

•that actions are not words—words are words;

•that as you develop your own wisdom, your ideas will find their common origins with other women;

•that when looking for a model of how to live, the arrangement must be flexible;

•that there are women who will always remain shadows of themselves; they have been too poor, too culturally removed, have children too early; have missed too many opportunities and failed to grasp their own sense of purpose; that they are the victims of unfulfilled dreams and we must care about them.

The Alternative to Being Crazy

People have asked me if I thought women might go crazy when they realize they are living in a semi-cognitive state or when they reflect upon the indescribable losses they have suffered at the hands of male power and the answer is no. Original insights can be painful, but as you have the power to realize these things, you also have the power to create the alternatives to these lifelong drawbacks. The key lies in choosing better ideas—and you carry these ideas within yourself. They are the realizations of that illusive knowledge that has always seemed obtainable and can now be possessed.

In this project, we are collapsing a mental world that is out of whack with our nature; and like hitting a slick on the highway, we have to turn into the direction we are heading, to reestablish control. These better ideas lie in the gap between what we believe and the underlying doctrine that controls our feelings, thoughts and actions. What's in the gap depends entirely upon your own vision. You are the author of the better idea. Allow yourself to fully commit to the wisdom that lies within you.

The strength of the universal sisterhood shares your knowledge and dreams your dreams. It is to be drawn down to help you. The women in this sisterhood are no longer distracted by the slogans of femininity and the wishful thinking that promises to lead us out of the gloom. These have long ago proven empty of thought and devoid of potential.

During any transition we are subject to flurries of data, thoughts and meanings. Your instincts will not abandon you. They are the engines of discrimination. In other words, if you get lost, just stick with your agenda. You'll find your own way back to the path—because you are the map of your own journey and have the emerging women of the human race walking with you.

•

The fundamental idea that motivates the journey on the Road to Wisdom is that a woman has a sovereign right to define herself and share in the design of reality. This is a woman's rite of passage. This decision will map the movement from your status as a subordinate member of the patriarchy to the status of a mature woman who will elevate the entire society around you. This right is taken, not conferred. It will not be recognized like a birth, or a graduation or marriage, receiving the approbation and blessings of society. On the contrary, it will often be seen as a threat to other individuals and society in general.

The will to discover the greater meaning of your life will help all people within your reach to understand the feminine principle—the laws of women's lives which have not yet been established because tradition has kept them in the dark. The lost treasure of women's culture and ideas offer the best hope for the evolution of human society.

CHAPTER 13

THE FEMININE PRINCIPLE

There are those who believe that the will toward the feminine principle is *the* idea whose time has come. Apparently, its force is about to precipitate a dramatic change in the world for the better. Because of this claim (and necessity), I did due diligence trying to find an acceptable definition of this force. Instead, what turned up was a variety of opinions, myths, contrivances and nonsense.

Cosmologically, the feminine principle is the fundamental cosmic life force, and the female deity, which created the world. National mythologies, peoples and religions share this belief—Japan, Native Americans, Hinduism and Buddhism are examples. This is the central idea that motivates contemporary women to seek to reestablish spirituality around the female life force and which has resulted in various pagan, goddess, witchcraft and healing teachings. Christianity, misogynist at the bone, is now using the feminine principle as a device to reveal the "other face of Jesus" and the "humanity" of Mary and Mary (Virgin and Magdalen), as it tries to hold itself together while coming apart at the seams.

In the popular narrative, the feminine principle runs the gamut from the sublime to the ridiculous. It apparently holds the yin-yang polarity together; is said to be the chief sponsor of pleasure and the Romantic poets; is the driver of the right-brain; the essence of fertility, energy and the imagination; and responsible for the masculine principle! And if you believe the book, *Business and the Feminine Principle*, it will even make you money.

After my detour in and out of everyone else's agenda, the feminine principle was still waiting to be made intelligible. And as I did not find a rational interpretation, and having come this far on the Road to Wisdom, I decided to define it myself.

Defined

To start with—ontologically—the feminine principle identifies the primary process of a woman's life as it incorporates the rules and values of natural law. It represents the integrity inherent in human nature fundamental to the body, mind and spirit of human wholeness. At its core, it is the authority of female being, in and of itself—essential and without domination.

The feminine principle is germane to itself and is a concept upon which a philosophy and practical ethics can be built. It is grounded in the collective human experience and the inheritance that all women share; that which all women know in themselves and in one another. Defining the feminine principle translates into a decision to create a place for the self in the whole order of things.

FIRST:
Survival of the self;
and the procreation and protection of life.

At it's simplest, the female principle—as motive force and controlling idea—is survival. Women's natural state embodies the privilege and responsibility of procreation. This fundamental principle of women's existence relies on her individual health and wholeness. Any woman can create a life and women are therefore first and foremost creative. Women create community at its most basic level.

The male rendition of this reality is that the ultimate purpose (teleology) of the female sex is to reproduce—likening us to biological incubators, whose role is to reproduce them. Because this has been the "story of our lives," up to this point in history, we have organized our psyches around the imperative that we exist to bear and serve others. According to this reading, women do not have needs, interests and desires of their own and by extension means that women are non-people. The survival of the self, first, clears up this aberration.

When our survival is threatened, it requires that all normal reservation and social constraints are to be dispensed with immediately. At these times, naivete and passivity are the worst traits a woman can have: duplicity and violence are often required. Your moral obligation is to live and the action that drives the life force is heroic, not shameful.

SECOND:
Fulfillment of human nature;
development of all potential to its highest ability.

The feminine principle operates on the personal and communal level. On the personal level, it requires us to enjoy our lives, use reason freely and avoid suffering. In turn, it requires us to turn our compassion and tolerance toward others. Women have knowledge of the needs of all living things and recognize the essential cooperative nature of human existence. We have a specific, operational wisdom for what one needs in order to thrive.

As Americans, the feminine principle requires us to understand the balance between our beloved individualism and our essential social existence. Generic to women, the feminine principle trumps the so-called "rights of man" idea of society, which was never intended for women.[15]

As a normal part of the interrelatedness of things, all the -isms, -ologies, -arians and theories of all other principles are there to be understood for their prejudices and limitations and rejected except for those parts which recognize and compliment the feminine principle. As women define themselves, we also define the quality and quantity of our concern and sympathy for others and other species, based on reason and proportionality according to the principle of the development of our highest—and not our lowest—abilities. The feminine principle is not tailored to empathize with impotent idealism and the shape of others' grievances where they do not relate to women's common priorities.

THIRD:
Embodiment and will of the principle.

The feminine principle plays out its meaning in our individual lives and our interrelationship with all living things. The will of the feminine principle completes itself in relationships. The moral and political rules of nature are within us and extend themselves in the development and mutuality of all people. It is a precept from which other truths are to be derived and clarified. Embodying one's own humanity, expressing it and manifesting it is the challenge of the will of the feminine principle.

---

[15] *The Rights of Man*, Thomas Paine, 1791. Paine ascribed the origins of rights to nature. Accordingly, "the sole purpose of the government is to protect the irrefutable rights inherent in every human being." Sounds good on paper. Two centuries plus later, women are still waiting to be recognized as equal enough to even get in on the discussion.

The feminine principle has nothing to do with exchanging misunderstanding with understanding. It is beyond cause and effect and removed from polarities. It is not reflective of anything male and does not coexist or exist in tension with male anything, i.e., it is inherently liberated from patriarchal problems. Therefore, it does not trade on the idea that women are morally or ethically different from or superior to men.

The will of the feminine principle is to establish women's values in the culture and reflect them to all people and at all levels of society. Inherent in these values is the expectation and obligation of men to uphold their own responsibilities in the mutuality of human development, the holistic progress of society and culture, the preservation of our natural world and sustaining and caring for our offspring.

Femininity

Femininity is a touchy subject these days. The reactionaries have hurled back that an independent, intelligent life can only be had at the expense of what is "feminine"; that is, making oneself unattractive to men. There are different ways of looking at this subject: as the thing itself and the pseudo-femininity fabrications that purport to qualify that which is inherently female.

Essentially, femininity is a natural property of being female. It is specific to the female gender and marks our character and behavior when we express our creativity and authentic selves. It means being comfortable in our female bodies and spending time maintaining and enhancing ourselves if we so desire: performing women's aesthetics. In equal measure, it entails accenting our attributes, punching up our persona, and impressing our flesh and blood selves—sensuous and sexual—on the humanity around us. Emphasizing one's attributes and putting our best foot forward is not hyperbole, nor distortion, but a creative act.

The way we learn to be feminine and how we display it, is individual and should have nothing to do with men, but of course it does. Femininity is just another item in the long list of women's attributes that have been colonized by the male.

> . . . When one is an object, not a subject, all of one's own
> physical and sexual impulses and interests are presumed not to
> exist independently. They are to be brought into existence only
> by and for others—controlled, defined and used.
>
> Jean Baker Miller, M.D.,
> *Toward a New Psychology of Women*

Two parasites have intertwined themselves with pseudo-femininity: the economic and the social. Femininity, the commodity, exists to satisfy male standards of appearance as defined by the gargantuan enterprise founded on the appearance of women's bodies. In this category are the things they say we need to attract them. Every imaginable accouterment—gunk, goo, thing, activity—promises that if we buy into it, they will come. Consumed by this belief, we keep the commercial masquerade going and men on top. While appearance takes care and resources, the pursuit of extraneous femininity—which inevitably causes time and money problems—distracts us from other issues, including self-development. Getting women sucked into commodity femininity at the early phase (it now starts with four and five-year old girls) predicts your presence later, as well. Later comes the "procedure" phase of the femininity industry, when women present themselves to go under the knife to be plumped up, cut down and implanted with foreign objects so they can appear "more feminine" (which often means just having bigger tits) or as though they have not aged, thereby complying with what is required to meet the requirements of commodity femininity.

The other parasite attached to pseudo-femininity is the sexist, social melodrama played out directly with men. This is femininity prescribed as a single standard of belief and behavior that confines women to superficial performance, passive traits and sexual availability. This is known as the feminine ideal, and is the foundation of women's side in the gender drama. Its other aspect is the feminine mystique, the fabrication that makes us think our profound and sovereign femaleness is only achievable when we can attract that special guy, who will set it free and make it come true.

This femininity means heightening certain physical and behavioral aspects at the expense of maintaining one's own identity and power. It often escalates into toxic femininity—debilitating exaggerations of overdone female appearance and behavior. Most women are not aware of how this is used against them, but there are many aspects of social, cultural, economic and political powers which deem this failing to be maladjusted and sick and which exploit it as such.

Our part as losers in this feminine scenario is masked by the pride of the "women's intuition" package. But don't be fooled. Cultivating a lily-livered, watered down versions of possible selves is not intuitive. Intuition is innate judgment: recognizing the truth or falseness of something according to natural laws—judgment that relates to what it means to be human. Sexist femininity is the survival skill of women operating from a position of weakness. Feminine wiles are developed as a response to the male's exercise of pleasure or displeasure. It results when women are unable to stake out an authentic existence for themselves and are incapable of influencing the reality around them to accept their individual authority.

CHAPTER 14

GENERATIONS: TO FLOW OR NO

When I embarked on my own Road to Wisdom a few years ago, it soon became apparent that I had to bone up on what the next generation was thinking—about themselves in the context of feminism, that is. Within and outside of academia, I found a many-hued, though small, movement of progressive young women, doing different kinds of activism and whose characters and demeanor resonated with the history of all generations of women who have tried to make a better world. I also found many of my own generation making a substantial investment in the mentoring, interning and leadership development of their youngers. But mostly, I found that younger women seemed obsessed with "redefining" or "reclaiming" feminism, as if it had lost its identity or forgotten its purpose; or that it was substandard in some way.

Within the span of one short generation, most women, themselves, took the spotlight off the patriarchal subordination issue and turned it into the negative stereotype of feminism itself. It is as if they were overcome by the power of the word—as though they, and the society, would not be able to contain its meaning. Instead of investigating and thinking through how feminism and the women's rights movement affected their own development, and advantaged their position over that of their mothers or grandmothers, they believe themselves to be in conflict with feminism itself. Their main discourse is centered on topics like: "why so many young women don't identify themselves as feminists" or "are uncomfortable with the F-word." And: "have the goals of the seventies been accomplished?" or "whether feminism is still a source of personal and political power." All the while, this uncertainty is lodged in a sense of antagonism toward those who established

128

feminism as a force in the world—my generation—as if they had been done a disservice.

I have to keep reminding myself that feminism in the world is a recent thing. The drop off in consciousness in one generation, and the tendency to reinvent the wheel in another, is in line with my premise—that women's rights movements themselves are cyclical things and because of this, the facts and principles of women's autonomy and power realities never make it into the cultural narrative. In other words, the majority of the next generation didn't "get it." That said, women in general have become better educated and more aware and should be able to extrapolate, simply from living, that the problems of sexism and misogyny are intrinsic and historic, and not specific to one or another generation.

Along my journey, I randomly picked up a book, *The New Victorians: A Young Woman's Challenge to the Old Feminist Order*, written by Rene Denfield and published in 1995.

As the title, "The New Victorians" suggests, Denfield claims that second wave feminism narrowed its focus down to two causes, rape and pornography, casting Denfield's generation as hapless victims, unwilling and unable to control their own lives. This was news to me; so on the whole, I found the book interesting and informative (also verbose and whiny). Pros and cons aside, it was refreshing to hear the voice of a young, freelance journalist, after slogging through piles of theoretical feminism, which I'd managed to avoid reading the first time round, but which this project made necessary.

To quote Rene Denfield trying to bring Carol Gilligan, American feminist, academic and psychologist, to heel:

> There is little acknowledgment that, having grown up after the birth of feminism, younger women often have dramatically different views on gender than older women do . . . By ignoring these differences and presenting all women as alike—right down to how we perceive reality—implicitly dismisses social factors and ends up presenting supposed gender differences as immutable. Women who don't fit her sweeping generalizations are left feeling like aberrations instead of variations.

Carol Gilligan speaks for herself. What interested me in the statement were these "different views" and what was "dramatic" about them.

Around this time (2002), I heard a Brian Lehrer Show on WNYC Radio, New York, which echoed the generational gist of Denfield's book. The focus of the show was an article by Kay Hymowitz, "The End of Herstory," and Lehrer invited callers to weigh in on Hymowitz' premise: "Feminism is over because most women want to have a husband and family." I was all ears. The statement smacked of the same strain of inanity as the one that rekindled my interest in feminist advocacy—a BBC news item in 2001 where some "authority" pronounced that "women have gone too far." That was it for me! I began to develop this book and seminar project.[16]

Lehrer's show comprised the typical range of voices. One took the high ground: "It's far from over. If we stop now, we're left in a place that's very uncomfortable." The middle ground was heard from: "Feminism is about making the choices we want," and "It's about being strong and embracing where you are." There was the defeatist retro: "Feminism became equated with hating men." And there was the myopic, male-identified, ventriloquist who said, "The vision of feminism is fulfilled!" This New York law school student went on to say, "I have never felt discriminated against. I would know if I was being discriminated against." And Lehrer wrapped it up with, "Maybe it's a nonissue." My edification got a slow start: balanced broadcasting—not different, not dramatic.

> ... Stereotypes with negative connotations about the abilities of women may influence a woman's behavior even if she repudiates the stereotype or feels herself to be immune from its damage.
>
> Linda Babcock and Sara Laschever,
> *Nice Girls Don't Ask*

Then things started to heat up. A richer sampling of generational thinking was to be had in academia, where women's studies programs started up in the 1970s to examine the women's movement, women's history and women's lives.

---

[16] Bookend: six years later. In the winter of 2007, a man said to me, "The pendulum has swung too far." He was not talking about clocks but blaming feminists for the "boy crisis." This is a predictable male-chauvinist polarism. It assumes that the advancement of women and girls has been at the expense of males, when in fact, males have failed to develop at their own expense. According to this person, however, women are supposed to assume the losses. For a reasonable approach to the topic, see website boysadrift.com and the book, *"Boys Adrift: The Five Factors Driving the Growing Epidemic of Unmotivated Boys and Underachieving Young Men,"* by physician and psychologist Leonard Sax.

> Our generation has grown up with the delusion that we no
> longer need feminism. The feminist movement of the 1960s
> and 70s may have dismantled the infrastructure of sexism, but
> it didn't destroy it. It merely forced gender discrimination to go
> underground. In its unstructured form, it may be even more
> dangerous. It's hard to fight something when it's unrecognized,
> unsaid or even unconscious.
>
> Sarah Merriman, *Yale Daily News*
> 8 February 2001

And women's studies programs, themselves, became interesting. After decades of struggle and instability, many took root in and of themselves. In other cases, they mutated into gender and sexuality studies and in some, women as the primary focus had disappeared altogether. As Yale describes it, women's studies "moved beyond the feminist-centered experimental program." Harvard describes the co-option of women's studies perfectly, in its misery-loves-company on-line program description:

> cultural and historical differences in femininities and
> masculinities, transnational sexualities, women writers,
> gender and media studies, lesbian/gay/bisexual studies,
> transnational feminisms, gender and environmental
> movements, philosophies of embodiment, queer theory,
> women's history, transgender studies, gender and religion,
> the political economy of gender, feminist theory,
> race/class/gender politics, technology and gender, gender
> and science, and masculinity studies are just a few of the
> areas of study.

As the above indicates, virtually any group that invents itself and alleges to have a claim on women's advancement, has managed to nestle its intellectual and political gripes in the women's studies package. This is different. My generation was trying to get the boots off our necks, the drone out of our brains and the malespeak off our tongues. Just because we were part of the movement for social change, did not mean the door was open to anyone who paid a call and wanted to get some for themselves. The challenge to curb the ongoing impulse to give it all away was part of the general conversation. These were categorical imperatives being born of instinct and insight, and not ideology. Male-metaphorically, this kind of phenomenon is known as "don't shoot yourself in the foot."

And it gets more different. At Yale, brothers Larry '57 and Arthur Kramer '49, donated $1 million to promote gay and lesbian studies, which project established its academic home in the Women's & Gender Studies Program. "The ambition is very clear," says Jonathan Katz, hired as Executive Director of the "Larry Kramer Initiative" (no changing that name). "It's to set up the epicenter for queer studies in the United States here."[17] Here we have a national phallocentric institution establishing itself in a women's studies department that has barely taken root.

Does anybody around there understand that this is a male agenda? Larry Kramer is not only a well-known and successful writer and militant political activist; he is an aggressive male and his macho energy is backed up by a huge and wealthy cultural force. Kramer is hardly a match for a class of female undergraduates worried about boyfriends, and who still think their mission in life is to please everyone and do what they ask. "But its *lesbian* and gay!" comes the chant. Sure, sure, lesbians too. Does anyone really believe that Larry Kramer could care less about muff-diving or who gets to have the baby? So it's comforting to know that some things never change: in keeping with tradition, the women of Yale's women's studies have created the nest that will house and sustain Kramer's next big event. But the failure to defend women's common interests as the top priority in our own heap? Definitely different from my generation. And historically, it's the same old female submissiveness.

The more diverse it got—the more interesting it got. Take the following attitude toward basic survival in the Denfield generation: definitely different.

> Tonight I am going to cook dinner for my friends. This might not seem so remarkable to you, but let me add this little tidbit—I am a feminist. Do I contradict myself? I think not, but it seems that there are some who seem to think that as a feminist, I would automatically decry any woman participating in traditionally "girly" activities such as cooking.
>
> Josie Rodberg, *Yale Daily News*
> 1 November 2002

Finding it necessary to defend herself for cooking food and entertaining people? At what point between generations did it turn out that feminists weren't supposed to cook food and eat it? By some weird ideological twist, the activism that sprung women from life sentences in the kitchen, had

---

[17]*Source: Yale Daily News, 19 November 2002.*

morphed into apologizing for enjoying food and the company of others around the dinner table.

If young women think they have to defend feminism with the claim that one has the "choice" to cook or not, conveying the point of the revolution has been sorely mishandled. In fact, the 1960s and 1970s was when America learned how to eat. In real life that means learning how to cook. Personally, after years of honing my own culinary skills, I moved to an apartment with no dining room because my dinner party habit had gotten completely out-of-hand.

Now here's different: the incident of the Janet Jackson flashing and what young women think about power. Discussing this, Carol Lin at CNN said (paraphrasing) "young feminists today say that if they show off their bodies to get attention and gain power that way, it's an okay thing to do." I was dumbfounded when I heard that. Imagine showing your tit at Super Bowl 2004 to "get power." Lin said nothing about appropriating the women's rights vocabulary to rationalize sexual exhibitionism. But then, most girlies don't, either.

> Like most American women, I've succumbed to tokenism . . . Worse still, I've been seduced by bubble gum-flavored "girl power" disguised as legitimate empowerment . . . The intersection of annoyingly pathetic emotional vulnerability and career success? Ally McBeal! Skanky tube tops and self-aware confidence? Britney Spears! Beneath all this pink-colored fluff are the problems that necessitated the feminist movement in the first place. Gender inequity hasn't disappeared—except for from our national consciousness.
>
> Sarah Merriman, *Yale Daily News*
> 8 February 2001

Here's one that's definitely different. At McGill University, in Montreal, the McGill Women's Union changed its name to the Union for Gender Empowerment "to become trans-inclusive," complete with a new vocabulary. Example. Non-transwoman: a person who has been assigned a female gender identity at birth and someone who identifies as being a woman. ("Yo—listen up! Any non-transwomen in the crowd?" I can hear the roar of solidarity.) These people went off on an incredible tangent and ended up on Io. That's metaphorical. Literally, it's ridiculous.

There was another incident in Montreal; different. I attended a seminar at a university women's center and took part in a colloquy with a few students. I mentioned to a young woman (YW) that I (MC) was amazed to return to scene after twenty-some years and find that nobody mentioned the word feminism.

> *YW*: If you say you're a feminist, people think of hairy armpits and—
>
> *MC*: Pul-eeze! If I hear that hairy armpit bit one more time I'll throw up. The reason you won't say you're a feminist is because you think that if you do, *men won't like you.*
>
> *YW*: Well, it's true!
>
> Firebrand Frenchie (FF) across the cheese table jumps in.
>
> *FF*: Well, zen—may-bee you should sink about za cal-ee-bear of men you are a-so-see-a-ting weez.
>
> *MC*: Let me put it into a different perspective . . . What happens to everything else you are when you say that you're a feminist? From what you say, it's all negated. Everything else you are falls away. Your personality, your energy, experience, talents, intelligence; your sexuality, your beauty. You and your entire exchange with this other person gets reduced to one word.
>
> *YW*: (Blank stare; no response.)
>
> *MC*: And what happens when you think this way is not only an example of the negative impact of your own fear—it is also evidence of how powerful feminism is, in and of itself.

It is also an indication of the power of fear that has no recourse.

•

> There has been a huge backlash against any idea of a women's movement, which our generation grew up with. And thanks to the media and to cultural attitudes, people buy into a very

negative stereotype of feminism before they see what it means for themselves.

Chelsea Purvis '06, *Yale Daily News*

This experience is the same: the twenty-something son of lifelong friends recently tied the knot with his fiancee, the lovely Krista. Krista is doing an M.A. and works full-time in a New York media company, where she has been the subject of sexual harassment on the job, which has been devastating for her and of serious concern for the whole family.[18] Unfortunately, she has not been schooled in the skills and language required to nip that kind of thing in the bud. Sexually harassing women is the same old power trip, and not knowing how to stop it is the same old victim trip. Whatever mind set and language we developed in our generation to deal with this, has obviously not been passed down to Krista. And none of this is different.

•

In discounting the role that men play in women's lives, the women's movement today has made a serious mistake.

Rene Denfield, *The New Victorians*

How did she come up with this idea—discounting the role that men play in women's lives—and this disdainful voice?

Scanning my mental roster, it occurred to me that virtually everyone I know involved in the women's movement is married, has been married or has had long and enduring relationships with men. None of us are strangers to the misery and bliss of connubial affairs. We solved their problems, made homes, made families and loved them to distraction. We tolerated them, kicked them out, wanted to kill them and buried them. We cut our feminist teeth dealing with serious sexism and obnoxious male behavior—including the episodes in the bedroom. Working things out with men has been as much a part of the problem, as a part of the solution. And individual friendships with men have been as important in our lives as friendships with women. And dealing with male antics and aggression and the distortions of the male ego has become a matter of fact. Virtually all of these women have children

---

[18]Interestingly, it was not Krista who told me about this but her new father-in-law, my friend. "And," he said, "there's nothing anybody can do about it." In a related incident, another friend told me about his daughter being sexually aggressed by a mechanic in a car repair shop. She picked up a tire iron, brandished it at him and ran away. Her dad said to me, "What am I supposed to do? Go over there and break his arm?"

and most have grandchildren. So accusations of "discounting men" amongst my lot would be met with a laugh in the face.

But where does this thinking come from? I found a clue in the *City Journal*, Summer 2002 (a publication of the conservative Manhattan Institute), buried in the subtext of Kay Hymowitz' tract.

Her article, "The End of Herstory," caught the attention of the circuit (e.g., Lehrer's show, previously mentioned) by taking a right-wing stand against the women's movement. Using motherhood as her emotional lynchpin, Hymowitz is able to drum the entire catalogue of anti-feminist rhetoric in aid of reducing feminist goals to their narrowest possible reading. (This deprecating tactic is mimicked in Denfield's work, with a different result.)

Hymowitz' argument is mired in two mutually-reinforcing fallacies. One, is that she is an authority on life and feminism; the other that her position is right and there is no other position. Both get attention and throw people off track. On examination, however, these both turn out to be not striking observations, but evidence of her own intellectual quagmire.

The first thing that bogs her down mentally is belonging to the "voice of the inner circle" (people who refer to themselves as elites, experts and—goddess help us—pundits, and are part of the celebrity package). In the early days of second wave feminism, big-city, East Coast writer and academic types staked the claim to articulate the wants and needs of women in general. Hymowitz obviously claims rights in this territory—from across the rio. And so she may do. The problem with the towering, cultural and political writer-and-academic-state-of-mind, is that after its initial outburst, it seldom absorbs or reflects anything relevant to life in the country in general.[19] In the end, these voices go out to themselves. Their message has nowhere to land, take root and evolve through time and experience. They become entombed in their own rhetoric and can only attempt a comeback by announcing one or the other's demise. Their desperate forays then glint off the surface of the media, blinding the curious, captivating the naive.

The other mental bog is her self-entrapping political position. As a conservative, she's compelled to take the opposite side of feminism, period. Her entire argument is made in polar opposites. To her, career is the

---

[19]The women she glorifies for their "return" to Mom Valley, left jobs like: Legal Aid lawyer, lawyer with the Maryland secretary of state, CEO of Ivillage; and Karen Hughes who left her job as presidential aide in the Bush administration. Hughes neither "left"—she was available to Bush at any time—nor did she leave her "career". She was back in D.C. in March 2005 as Bush's arch spinner. How women actually deal with the issues of balancing family and work is obviously irrelevant to Hymowitz. The subject does not fit into her agenda.

opposite of motherhood: "for feminists, motherhood is the ten-ton boulder in the path of genuine liberation" and "feminism today represents not liberation but its opposite: a life that must be lived according to a strict, severe ideology." Ping. Pong. The classic male paradigm.

Hymowitz holds forth, at length, in defense of an argument most rational women in America have outgrown. Her simple method declares that it's either feminism—or not feminism. "Feminism is not simply suffering from a P.R. problem. It's just over. As in finished." That's what Nietzsche said about God. Wouldn't he be surprised to see what's happening today? God is definitely back and people are bludgeoning each other all over the world to prove it.

Frankly, I could work up a more interesting discussion than Hymowitz' with any *compos mentis* red neck woman[20] any place in America. While "experts," like Hymowitz get their take on topics such as "life on the minimum wage" from other writers—Barbara Ehrenreich's *Nickle and Dimed*, for instance—for people living in these conditions, it is life, period. Not a role, not a book, not a story.

Hymowitz goes on about "feminism denied biological realities," "the feminine personal" (that's a new one on me) "liberated motherhood: dropping the baby off at the day-care center for 50 hours a week," etc. If you buy what's she's saying, you'd think the message of the women's movement was to deny the possibilities of a full life so you could turn into a clitorisentric, lobotomized, workaholic robot, living on a babyless planet, with a total distaste for men. *Caveat emptor.*

By creating a fake showdown to argue terms that have already sailed into the sunset, what then is the Hymowitz motive? The answer is, to indoctrinate young women with her reactionary rhetoric. What she's really pounding through is her "family values" subtext. Those are the values that have nothing to do with maintaining the processes of life in an ethical society and a safe and secure home. The "family values" slogan is a rhetorical bludgeon suggesting the return to male dominance, female subordination and the suppression of women's knowledge. Using feminism as a goat, Hymowitz is advancing one of the fundamental principles of conservative ideology: the subjugation of women.

This is an unattractive situation. By thumping on about "barren careerists" and "lesbians"; and dumb things feminists have said and done, Hymowitz belies the deep moral and intellectual convictions that drive women in the feminist movement to work to improve all of our lives. What

---

[20]"Red necks are people who make do with what they have." Gretchen Wilson, country and western singer.

is particularly cynical, is that her message means to limit young women where it should (read moral imperative) be encouraging them to develop themselves as far as they possibly can. If this is construed to mean "don't have babies," then the construer should examine her own bias. But Hymowitz knows that. If she were to discuss the broad range of positive influence that the feminist movement has had, and continues to have, on women's lives, she'd have to drop her conservative mask—and that won't happen. Her intention is to help the patriarchs and their helpmeets bring young women to heel. The majority of young women are neither practically trained, nor influenced by our culture, to defend their own interests; and patriarchal forces would prefer to keep it that way. Enhancing young women's lives is the farthest thing from their minds. Controlling them is their objective.

•

> . . . while older people have prospered, my generation has "fallen of a cliff."
>
> Rene Denfield, *The New Victorians*

Denfield's statement above is important on two counts. First, it provides an opportunity to point out to younger generations that people who have already fought the battles and won, do not do it over again. Most mature people do not go back behind barriers they've already dismantled. But it is also an important echo across from Denfield's side. From across the generations, she pinpoints the gap where the connection is lost, signaling the end of continuity in women's road to the future and their own wisdom. Detour: go around till next time. So little connection between old and young, so little responsibility for maintaining mutual interests, so little communication, and so little desire to unearth the language of our common knowledge that it's a tragedy. And that, is dramatic.

The central issue in the movement is the amelioration of women's persistent underdevelopment. To that end, the political, psychological, spiritual and experiential expression is the subject, the substance, and the motive of feminism. It is about women, for women and speaks even on behalf of women who oppose it. Where there is feminism—and because what goes on in women's lives is different from men's—by definition, it is working in opposition of patriarchal domination.

There must be a will to generational reciprocity to solve the problems of the disruptions in the course of women's advancement. Our job is to inspire the passions of young women to participate in the world—this is what men within their own gender have always understood. And young women must get hip to the fact that they don't have to reinvent the subject, after the generation before them has been reduced to dust on the patriarchal wheel. The ultimate goal is the expansion of women's knowledge and the feminist continuum. And each generation must put forth its contributions in aid of the next.

CHAPTER 15

TAKING A STAND

W hile boning up on some feminist theory, I came upon the idea of "standpoint feminism." In academia, standpoint feminism is a type of critical theory—built out of Marx's understanding of experience and confronting oppression in the power structure. As theory will inevitably do, it reduces life and its boundless possibilities to narrow perceptions, described in turgid prose, none of which goes anywhere but the confines of academic publishing and archives.

But I saw it had great potential. So I have recast standpoint feminism into its most solid, most practical and most potential conception and use it as a pivotal element in feminist knowledge.

Standpoint Feminism

"This is where I stand as a sovereign woman with an independent mind and a free will."
Philosophical and Intellectual Framework
Anchored in Feminist Knowledge and the Feminine Principle
From Which to Assess and Apply Your Own Values

The idea of confronting oppression according to Marxist say-so is bewildering, to put it mildly. It's hard to imagine women overthrowing the patriarchy, given its history, power, depth and breadth. Besides, all of our personal and material resources are tied up in it—albeit devalued by a kind of intellectual and spiritual paricitism, from which we must all purge ourselves. This condition, however, does not avert the struggle.

In the definition here, standpoint feminism is anchored in feminist knowledge and the feminine principle. The central idea is to create a philosophical and intellectual framework from which to assess your own values and proceed with them accordingly. The point of assuming this position is to resolve the crisis of our habitual inequality—and extricate ourselves from the never-ending negotiation of gender status. Standpoint feminism establishes your position in reality; and identifies your position in the patriarchal power structure. In order to hold your ground, you have to know that it's yours.

Out of this concept—this spot at the center of your psyche—all views, convictions, judgments and opinions flow—augmenting everything you already know. It is the ground for self-confidence and the bedrock of free expression; and the establishment of point-of-view.

•

The first time you "take a stand" in life is the first life decision you get to make autonomously. It is often a radical (or "irrational") act, where you escape the trappings of your personal history, or fictionalized version of yourself. You activate your body to manifest what's inside you. Such an event will usually change your outlook on the rest of your life.

I feel right every time I do the right thing.
Protester, Republican National Convention,
New York City, 29 August 2004

On the other hand, maybe you've just been standing there, never committing to anything; insulating yourself with illusions and language to avoid both the evidence and logic of unjust or intolerable situations. But take heart; you are not alone. We can all recall occasions where we've walked away from our psychic and historic catastrophe, only to face it again, over and over again in the future. Establishing a personal standpoint based on feminist values and the feminine principle resolves the habitual crisis which already exists.

Standpoint feminism embodies the idea that our power base is internal and emanates outward. This ideal is brought to life in juxtapositions, connections, dynamics and aspects not previously considered. From the experience of speaking our own truth, we can discover and acknowledge our commonalities as women. Within these grassroots developments, we can perceive and further our own cultural strategy and advance the transformative force that the women's agenda has already proven itself to be. It offers hope in the face of the impoverished worldviews and deceptive ideologies, whose burdens are crushing us all.

Decision: Internal

You have a supreme right to yourself—to your own mind and body—and to keep it that way. This view is personal and taking a stand is a decision you make internally.

The perspective here is different from trying to conduct your life according to a body of feminist ideology. In this scenario, you are assuming the authority of your own will, to establish a set of predetermined concepts and values which are to be adapted to clarify your own. It is a way to settle the variety of minds we have about ourselves and our womanhood, and to stabilize ourselves against succumbing to the regressive positions that are affected both by us, and upon us.

It begins with whom you feel yourself to be as a woman—and based on that knowledge, how you perceive yourself in relationship to society. It clears up the confusion about where we are supposed to stand in the turmoil of life—because when we take this position, we already know that. It directs you away from self-inflicted prejudices based on gender inequality.

Your standpoint is like a compass at the core of your own autonomy. It unlocks a psychic passageway that seeks to discover connections between your internal coherence and the external contradictions of your own reality. It will inform internal resources that have been dormant, because until now, you have not had a position from which to tap them. It's like hitching yourself to a train that pulls you into the world on the track of healthy growth, allowing you to see clearly what to accept, what to reject and what to reorganize. It will serve you for your whole life; not just an incident, or an issue here and there.

Process: External

Who am I? What do I want? How do I expect to be treated by society? As a woman with strength and integrity? Or as a scapegoat for the resentments and failures of the human condition? A feminist standpoint means you determine your life choices as a woman—not a man, not girl and not a child. It is a conceptual tool that serves as an internal anchor to keep you centered and create a solid base for actions. You can rely on it in the process of living your life. It establishes a motive to overcome intrapsychic and interpersonal obstacles which are a regular part of our reality and which have led us to fear our strengths. When you know where you stand, the confidence you need to negotiate the challenges and dynamics of an authentic life is developed at the core.

Inherent in a standpoint is a state of readiness to stand fast regardless of what values are called upon. In the incredible complex of our internal and external reality, no matter what the context, array of issues, or changing situations you may face, being a woman in the world of your own authority is central to where you stand.

The basis for most of our actions has been developed within our situation located in dominant male hierarchies—and results from theories about where women belong in such constructions.   Thus, we tend to compromise in advance—and to make compromises on behalf of our opponents, i.e., those who oppose our autonomy. A feminist standpoint will help to determine what you choose and what you reject. It will anchor the power of your own being. With a clear position of where you stand internally, you hold your ground because it's yours. Wisdom, its traveling companion, tells us to compromise when we must; and guides our transcendence beyond the habits and effects of the immaturities we are discussing.

A feminist standpoint presumes position, point-of-view. It renders you free to speak and escape the paralysis of feeling inferior. It provides an angle, which allows you to exchange information with others about you in the world; to speak explicitly from the source against all that is unacceptable in the gender arrangement. It keeps you tethered to the common sense of your own gender; ergo, your own priorities.

Taking a stand for equality means finding solutions to satisfactorily live our lives. This requires open attack on patriarchal hierarchies and the ongoing disestablishment of the Dominant Voice. As long as the validity of women's needs are subordinated in any context, women will have to create the conflict necessary to reject these constraints—regardless of the authority that imposes them and subverts our needs. A feminist standpoint illuminates the authority to act on our own behalf in the external world as well as within us.

> And so she bought the potion . . . And of course she felt betrayed when the potion did not change her and furious at herself for that bottomless capacity to believe and let herself be swindled.
>
> Ursula Hegi, *Stones from the River*

Implications

As a concept, a feminist standpoint sets you in a new relation within the dominant group: it will change the way you deal with men. It is a structure that constrains and enables, gives rise to autonomous perceptions of your own physical reality, human invention, new ways of life and spiritual being. It is a bypass around the gender argument. You are positioned to hold your ground, regardless of past assumptions or present misunderstandings. It will not be altered by rules, or mood, but by a critical appreciation of one's own experience. It is a giver of meaning—life according to yourself, determining the nature of human ties on your terms.

The standpoint perspective is different from the ideological feminism. Ours is an existential stance that has political effect in and of itself: it evades the preoccupation with how individuals affect the patriarchy. The political effect is a bi-product of the feminist standpoint and reflects the nature of the transformative force which feminism has already proven itself to be. It also causes political awareness to bubble up where women didn't even know they had it.

Historically, dominant groups do not allow conflict, as it calls into question the legitimacy of the larger enterprise. Thus, women who use their power directly in the service of their own interests are bound to elicit a negative response from men. When this happens, women tend to renegotiate the arrangements to perpetuate the unconditional attachments between the sexes and reconcile the conflicts to preserve the status quo.

But blanche not. It is entirely appropriate to throw out these tactics when you are in the process of establishing the framework for your own stand in life. The stand is against the patriarchy. To maintain your old conciliatory behavior is pointless. Think about ending a monarchy: you are no longer a subject of the king.

> Jean-Paul Sartre's distinction between the rebel and the revolutionary is useful . . . For him, the rebel is secretly complicit with the order he revolts against.
> Simon Reynolds and Joy Press,
> *The Sex Revolts: Gender, Rebellion and Rock 'n' Roll*

A feminist standpoint is a gift to the world.

•It allows us to advance the absorption of the feminine principle in our culture.

•It will contribute to the growth of others who have been denied an essential part of life—the ability to acquire self-understanding as a sovereign woman.

•We will be passing on a model for our daughters who will face the struggles of creating a solid base upon which to build their own identities.

•It will help you to guide men in their own quests for growth—except now you tell them, you don't nurse them.

•And it will help all of us to recognize that human evolution is a gift of nature, whose bounty is meant for us all.

Change Your Mind, Change Your Reality

Thinking about the results of the second wave women's rights movement, one is able to perceive the power and activity that created one of the most significant changes in the everyday reality of our world. Each of us carries within us the same potential to affect the reality around us for the better.

Transition

The decision to take a stand means leaving a complacent state and entering a period of transition. This is a challenge to the feint-hearted and sturdy individuals alike. You are on the search for what you've lost, while preparing for acceptance of the self who will be claiming this newfound knowledge. Along the way is uncertainty, risk, and displacement, while you integrate new ideas and defamiliarize some of your most cherished beliefs. Transitional periods are often unsettling times, brought on by new knowledge and being caught at the end of one period in a life and the beginning of another. It is the natural process of individual growth. At the same time, it means passing on the knowledge and truth that we acquire on the journey.

Why is this so tough? What is the point of it all?

Meaning

The present has an intractable nature. In order to change it, we have to create meaning, which is the action of feminist activism itself. As women's knowledge has not become an integral part of our culture—much less part of the philosophical canon—then fundamental to the process is establishing the bottom line. What it means to be a woman, is the subject. Feminist knowledge is the form of understanding—meaning—that will create the altered reality.

In grassroots terms, meaning is the basic sense of what you have in mind. It manifests itself from your intention, or purpose, as it relates to the personal: who you are, as the instrument of your own speech. Meaning is also created in the relational: to whom you are speaking—and for what, and who, the news is meant. The relational are men, and their helpmates, or society and its mouthpieces—those who dominate communication, and who, by preemption, control the limits and boundaries of rationality, i.e., what has meaning. What has meaning is where your newfound understanding, your transition into the person you want to become, and the point you are intending to make, all go into training. You are creating a new reality about the quality, relations and the possibilities of life.

By this time you get to this point on the Road to Wisdom, your words are wafting out into a reality of intellectual and emotional gender asymmetry. As a woman, your meaning corresponds to your position in this arrangement, which is weighted in men's favor.   How you reveal your meaning—in speaking, writing, telling—and how you identify with this imbalance and your criticism of it, can transcend the limits of the Dominant Voice. In order for this to happen, you must fix your starting point beyond their limitations and maintain your rationality, so that it is comprehensible: by them. (You are already anchored in the feminist standpoint strategy.) This then, will put you in a position to be understood on your own terms.   Once you take the plunge, however, there is no assurance you will find equality on the other side.   The point is to establish yourself as fully present in any aspect of reality that presents itself. Life will take over from there.

From polarities to expanding consciousness

Expressing what is missing in the universal perception of women is, by definition, opposing what men presume a woman to be. By this time, your new valuations are undermining patriarchal formulations: you are making the transition from polarities to expanding consciousness; from being a giver of praise and authority, to a giver of meaning. In this process, context is being rearranged. Your meaning transitions from a second-hand contrivance, to an experience in defining and coping with reality.

This attitude represents a change in your value system, in many ways. When you gain the experience of reflecting critically on the dominant theories, institutions and principles that influence women's lives, you are no longer just "working with" men (helpmate), but seizing control.   You are redirecting the process with new metaphors, new similes, new language, new propositions and new sequences of events and facts.   While de-familiarizing your own old patterns, you are also de-familiarizing the patterns of the dominant narrative, which means, affecting the patriarchal rationale.

On the Road to Wisdom, you gain an inner awareness and understanding of the properties and operations of sexism.   As you go about life—and SPEAK—this inner coherence influences your outer reality and the worldview of others: creating reality.   This is the alternative approach to the notion that it is a feminist's job is to challenge men on their every act of sexism—and then have to deal with their every reaction.   You'd never have time to sleep.

·

To be known, our meanings have to be told into the culture directly, authentically; and with a spirit of concrete relationship to the hearer, whether they like it or not.   What you think, write, and tell of an event, idea or experience will eventually become a fact, record, anecdote, reference, or a story.   By speaking your own mind, you develop your own thought processes.   At the same time, you discover the best means of expressing your meaning: by argument or exposition, storytelling or instruction.   And, of course, by gossiping and just plain talking to fellow members of the human race.   Story is everybody's business.   Even the most paltry rendition of events is capable of transmitting value into the culture.   Once the subjects of our lives become conversations—stories—they become common knowledge, which is something people can always discuss on an equal level.

We are all partners with reality.   As human beings, we grow as we struggle to find meaning.   In turn, our reality alters as a result of our attempts to understand ourselves and how we relate to the world.   Changing reality happens incrementally.   Think of the women's movement as a model of the transformative power of human action.   Looking at women's lives in the past forty years, we notice that perspectives changed bit by bit.   Problems and confusions began dissolving, and we could see farther ahead as we got on with the program.   Feminism was the vehicle, and for women's lives, it was the right one.   Whether you embrace it or shun it, all American women are part of the feminist concept and its consequences.   And for those who embrace it—remember there is nothing as therapeutic as an act of courage. Take a stand!   It can change your life.   It can start a revolution.

> Large systemic problems can be changed by ordinary people
> doing simple things.
>
> Mahatma Ghandi

Equity

Equity is justice according to natural law and the essentials of maintaining human society; and is discernable by right reasoning. It is a fundamentally important legal concept to grasp. It means, "I am autonomous, free of dominance and have a natural right to my share of resources."

The concept of equity is the bedrock upon which the feminist standpoint is built. Equity is the bridge between what is essential to my interests and what the external world declares I need to construct my own reality. Exacting equity in life, or out of society, is a manifestation of the concept that the individual is a free and responsible agent, determining her own development and the terms thereof. Equity is not relative, is conferred by no power, and has prior validity to institutional law, whose standards have not evolved according to women's needs and values.

The feminine principle and equity coexist in all considerations and expressions of human existence. Together they underpin our internal and individual power to expect and demand what is right. Equity is not only justice, but is women's investment in humanity.

Claiming equity is a break with the past. Justice and the earth's resources have been our birthright from the beginning of time, and we have failed to claim them both as our own. The claim on equity is a disjunction from the social contract that has not worked; and symbolizes the will to restore our rightful resources in this society. It ignores the deceptive ideas of unity and harmony which have been driven into our heads and which we have accepted because of lack of confidence in ourselves and in the feminine principle.

•

> This is the country that . . . declares it, the only one that has
> made it official, the only one that has made it constitutional, to
> be—yourself!
>
> Frank Lloyd Wright

Equity is interesting seen from the angle of American democracy, where the tradition of equality has meant equal rights among free male subjects.

In spite of recent improvements, we nevertheless function under a set of legal, social and economic protocols which impose restraints on our claim to equality. Justice as a man-made institution is different from natural justice: it is a servant of politics. Thomas Jefferson said that property rights emanate from society, and not from nature (tell that to the Natives). The apparent "emanation" of these rights occurred while women had no status as citizens. Along with their daughters, women were considered the property of husbands and fathers.

Our right to address issues of importance to women is restricted. Thus, gains are inevitably made by contorting our rationale to pander to the concept that the dominant perspective is sexually neutral and that our demands, or criticisms, are pleadings for some sort of special dispensation! The idea of true equality causes alarm about "where it could lead." Chaos and anarchy are predicted as the outcome, while fearmongering directs attention away from the hypocrisies that are embedded in the perpetration of the so-called American dream.

In the American experience, freedom and equality are political principles intended to bring both justice and effectiveness to the relationships of ruling and being ruled. This high-mindedness has deteriorated into mindlessness and unawareness, lacking coherence, and serving to extend male entitlement and the appropriation of women's prerogatives and resources. The tension that once made the American struggle for justice seem rational, has deteriorated into a slack and contemptible scenario of megalomaniacal power, a distinctly totalitarian lack of debate and unfettered greed, combined with the compulsion of individuals to debase themselves. Why fight for a position in that? Why struggle to be equal in a society where what is good is corrupted by authoritarianism, and fundamentalist doctrine and what's bad is so completely over the top that it eludes recognition. Why struggle against ideologies, sociologies and psychologies whose legitimacies are still cemented in place by sexist and misogynistic attitudes?

> In Wright's architecture of democracy, *you* are at the center; you are *always* at the center. It is the essence of democracy that everyone is at the center.
>
> Jonathan Hale, *The Old Way of Seeing*

We fight for position because we don't live in the land of the free for nothing. There is no point talking about democracy if you're not conducting yourself as a citizen of a free state. The opportunity to live free from encroachments on our liberty and persons is there to be taken. But unless we claim our equity, and state the ground of our opposition to the dominant opinion, our subordination will prevail. The concepts of equity and assuming a feminist standpoint are qualified sources of nonconforming principles which have already proven their superior right to be enlarged, as evidenced by the positive transformations they have already had on society.

Equality means the elimination of discrimination against women and restoration of our rightful resources in this society. The question is, do we continue to countenance ignorance and blindness about the injustice of our situation and its corrupt motives, or do we simply claim our equity—never to be relinquished again in accordance with the principles of our own position? Do we continue our musings about fake utopias, or do we just decide to rule our own world? After all is said and done, it is our right, to claim what is our right.

Developing a Position

Let's say that you did want to rule the world. What would you present as your platform to inspire confidence in your leadership? If you were to look for precedents in the women's chronicles of social progress, you would find scattershot protests, piecemeal involvement and ambivalence on this or that moral or political position; even about our own freedom.[21] Being subordinate, women have been denied authority in the direction of society, because we are positioned outside the action of our own time and generation.

You can turn this pyramid on its head by developing a personal standpoint that alleviates the implications of gender discrimination, first and foremost in your own mind. From this position, you can develop the power to cut through the tyranny of competing male dogma and pursue a body of knowledge from a reliable perspective, whose base is the feminine principle. This perspective intertwines your emotional and intellectual development with the quest for truth required to set your world right; matching what's in your head with what's going on outside. The personal and political aspects of your own personality need no longer battle for your attention. You have positioned yourself to become an independent thinker, able to resist the sway of subordinating forces, which have used women's weak responses to authority to further their own gain.

---

[21]The work of Margaret Sanger (1879-1966), birth control activist and founder of what eventually became Planned Parenthood, is still challenged by both men and women today.

A Self-critical Assessment

What's solid, what's underdeveloped, where's the potential?

What does being a woman mean to you? Perhaps you don't really know, which is not unusual. To this point, our individual identity has usually arisen as a result of figuring out where we fit in (or don't fit in) to the foundation of society which was here before we arrived. It, therefore, determines the ground from which we fashion ourselves; or don't. In this predicament, we are forced to invent our own psychological structures (which we must be able to adapt) in order to survive the vagaries of dominating social, political and economic forces.

This flexibility could be commended as a virtue, was it not for the fact that it results from reactionary underdevelopment and is not the result of organic growth. The compromises and underestimations that characterize this flexibility reflect women's innate survival mechanism, not the ability to develop their potential and act on their strengths. It characterizes our inability to plan and shape our society and culture. The local knowledge and experience we have translated into female social forms have more to do with how to maintain our status as subordinates, rather than develop our minds and talents and claim our rightful place. Developing a standpoint allows us to examine and improve these characteristics from a solid position—strictly female—instead of an open-ended speculation about how we fit into men's versions of whom and how we are supposed to be.

Personal considerations

What am I capable of?

Fundamental to individual advancement is looking at our own personal lives in light of the positive results that the recent feminist movement has left behind. What are the post-second wave rewards that you have garnered as a consequence of being alive in this country, at this particular time? And how's it going, vis-a-vis the relational, social, economic, spiritual, legal, political and other opportunities for gain or oppression that contemporary reality is offering up? What is your experience with solving the problems that ensue? Have you stood up for yourself and your integrity as a woman? Or have you lapsed back into prefeminist behavior, because you have not yet learned to use your life activity in the service of building an authentic image of yourself based on whom you are and what you do? The conflicts on this level of consciousness—new thoughts being challenged by old repressive habits—is where a standpoint comes into play.

Social considerations

How do I relate to risk?

When we appreciate the ramifications of adopting a feminist standpoint for ourselves, we can stop questioning ourselves and start questioning society. No longer limiting ourselves personally, we no longer have to accept the limitations of the many spheres of influence that society imposes on us. We can expect more from it, and more from our relationships. What could be better than a greater ability to cultivate our relationships with others? To observe them, to be with them, to love them in all their vitality and uniqueness, their triviality and stagnation—all there to teach us about our journey with them through life—and to teach us about ourselves.

The point of the feminist standpoint is to develop feminist insights in personal, biological, political and philosophical terms. You begin with recognizing patriarchal harms; learn why you should keep emotional distance; create boundaries after a history of not having any; and in the process, realign yourself outside the hypocrisies of culture and politics. It is the mainstay in the struggle for authenticity while you blaze the trails of effective action for your own life. Developing a standpoint is learning to maintain your ground, while enlarging your conception of life and your circle of interaction with the outside world. It means you intend to liberate yourself from traditional constraints and take a progressive position and become a part of the whole—participating in the mutual cooperation and confrontation that is life.

> Feminism . . . the world view, the philosophy rests on a most empirical base: staking your life on the trustworthiness of your own body as a source of knowledge. . . . to transform the way one experiences one's own life . . .
>
> Marilyn Frye

Conflict

What battles are worth fighting?

Most of all, assuming a feminist standpoint means confronting one of the most serious deprivations of our inadequacy, which is the inability to deal with the nature of conflict as regards women. Change alters meaning. By acting on your own behalf and refusing to obey the dictates of any dominant force, conflict will occur. But you are not creating it; you are exposing conflict that already exists. Whatever the displeasure or discomfort (or whosoever's), you have a right to act in your own interests. When you start to resolve these issues, you enhance, rather than diminish, your potential. The likely result is that the binds that held the conflict together in the first place are no longer essential to you, personally or socially. What were important needs and desires evaporate because you took a stand and are moving onto bigger and better things. Understanding conflict is an opportunity to enlarge our mental capacity to refuse to be forced into unacceptable positions. And the priceless social bi-product of doing so illuminates the way for others.

> You cannot liberate me. I can only liberate myself.
>
> Dalai Lama

The stronger your sense of your own position about where you stand in life, society, and anywhere else, the more leeway you have on everything else. This too, is The Better Idea.

"Empowerment" or Power?

When women think about power, it is generally in terms of men manipulating the masses, stealing from under our noses, and clubbing people over the head with impunity. In light of society recognizing our powerlessness in the big picture, the "empowerment" trend has become the answer for addressing our disadvantage. Psychologically, "empowerment" is contained in a package of encouraging rhetoric and enhancing imagery, which acts upon the will to stand up for yourself in situations where you have here-or-theretofore failed. It promises a life on track and an element of control in the circumstances around you. In other words, it will give you power over those who have already made your world what it is—and all within a few hours or a weekend. The "empowerment" approach may succeed to a degree, in certain situations. But there is no indication that it works for women as a pursuit to be reckoned with and relied upon.

The problem with the empowerment formula is that it promotes the idea that hapless infirmity can be remedied with piecemeal measures. It is an open-ended idea with no boundaries or grounding. There is no common interest and no principles for inner direction that everyone can relate to. Because of our history of being controlled—and of nurturing our detractors and executioners—the probability of being sucked back down into the maw is high, if one is relying on the "empowerment" fix for liberation.

With the feminist standpoint as a central organizing concept, power has a different meaning. The general power strategy is to occupy particular aspects of oneself—identity and self-confidence—and learn to maintain them in the interests of having influence. You are addressing the whole problem of female power, not just a segment. This translates into a self-organizing force able to subvert the strength of the dominant situation by a personal combination of intellect, intuition and action. Open opposition to the will of others is carried out from the point of principle—not from hope of gaining a position.

People in every aspect of life try to control women and keep them in their place when they have the power to do so. This is the bedrock of "man's world." If power is perceived by women as something to be gained, rather than something they already possess and intend to keep, any dominant person will seize his advantage to destroy your mission. It's the way things work, at least for now. On the other hand, if power is a trait embedded in your identity, to be used for survival and the enhancement of life, then it can have profound personal and political effects. Every act can build on the potential that women's authority has to offer in all areas of life.

The feminist standpoint connects us to the push and pull of our femaleness in the arrangement of a new context: women's potential set against patriarchal formulations. Based on the feminine principle as the basis for reasoning—personal survival combined with the reality of outside forces—the contradictions are illuminated and are there to be argued and fought out. Meanings are legitimated as they are shaped by the articulation of our priorities. From a feminist standpoint, you are setting the social machine in motion—and in a new direction.

Engagement With It

How strong is my commitment?

Power is intimately linked with the venture of self-determination and there is evidence of this laying dormant all around us. Someone told me a story about a woman with a history of being goaded into buying cars that her husband approved of—instead of the ones she wanted. She did not defend her choices, nor did she follow her own heart and mind and purchase the cars she liked. After a few of these experiences, she complained to him that she had bought the cars she thought he expected her to buy. When she told him this, he thought she was foolish! He could not understand why she had to have his approval to do what she was certain was right.

In another example, a friend had planned a trip abroad and as an afterthought, decided she would like to extend her stay by a few days in the European capital where she was born. She asked her husband if this was all right and he told her she was degrading herself by asking for his permission, rather than just doing it, because that is what she wanted to do.

Although these examples may sound trivial, they were quite significant for the women whose identities were involved. For the men in both cases, such decisions would have meant business as usual—going ahead and doing what they wanted to do. But to each of the women, it would have meant a different kind of engagement with the men who were the authorities in their lives. Both of these women could improve their situation by boning up on The Better Idea! As my old friend and English professor emeritus, John Harrop, said, "Living with powerful women is a LOT easier than living with the powerless."

Having a standpoint assumes engagement with outside forces: discussion, debate, negotiation, settlement; skirmish, retreat, battle, war; disengagement! It requires the wherewithal to occupy your individual position and back it up with the confidence to sort out whatever problems come up and threaten you off your mark. Through action and speaking, you bring new forces to act on meaning, understanding; bringing experience not only into your own life but into a situation. It provides the motive to enlarge or expand one's sense of the original thought, reading, writing, conversation, conflict. You are opposing or altering a personal or social arrangement. And whether the situation you want to influence is imaginary or real, you will learn to read the character of the resistance you are up against, be it external or internal.

Engagement means participation in a verbal game where your external and internal reality become dynamic. Connection, influence, affirmation on the outside; insight, emotions, evaluative changes on the inside. It is a learned and pleasurable skill, with levels of high excitement—particularly when your own values and vulnerabilities come under attack!

The wonder of human communication is the pay off for the willing engagement with the human race to make yourself known. Intention and tactics, morals and meaning. These are the things that drive the culture to rethink itself—about who women are and what we're doing here. To put it simply, women talking, like adults, have a great impact on everything around them. Once you get into it, instead of trying to occupy particular, or narrow aspects of yourself and maintain them in the interests of having influence, by occupying a standpoint you become a self-organizing force. From this position you are able to subvert the strength of the dominant situation by a personal combination of intellect, intuition and action. You're addressing the whole problem, instead of just a segment.

Power Everything: Claiming Our Culture

What are the stakes; and what am I passing on?

There is a recurring question in the dialogue about women's power: how much do we compromise our principles, in order to gain a position of comparable power in man's world, so we can get things done? In this framework, we are buying into the typical male model: power for oneself or power over others. For women, this is a regressive construct; caving into another patriarchal priority. Nonetheless, it is important to understand that engagement—getting attention and influencing external forces—is hardly easy. The present is always ruled by the absolutes of self-preservation: logic. This assures that the solutions are already in place and don't require what the outside has to offer. Absolute answers require little, if any, thinking.

With a feminist standpoint, you do not relinquish one kind of power in exchange for another brand. It's not a barter. You have no need to give up your hold on integrity. The motive of this power is intrinsic. It is central to your personality. It extends your potential to advance understanding and change the culture for the better. But you don't give up your principles in the bargain. Who would make that deal?

There is much unfinished business for women to take care of, and the roles we have to play in our own liberation are multifarious and difficult. There are many tough questions to be sorted out while claiming our place in the paternalistic system, which only pretends to be democratic. What are the material conditions that enable us to exercise our citizen rights? Monopolized air waves, for instance, reduce our rights to cultural and political expression. How do we get the embrace of women who have formed alliances with the "winners,"—women whose power and pride often have fraudulent origins and whose male-identification perpetuates sexism? What has to change in the system so that men make full contributions to home and family—instead of turning up at compline, just in time to read a story to the children before they go to bed? How do we cure ourselves of the delusion that while liberating ourselves, it is also feminism's duty to make men free?

"It doesn't matter. I don't even look at the draw. It's just another person to compete against." Yvette Gondo, Olympic medalist in Tae Kwan Do—when asked who her next opponent was.

CBC Radio, 26 August 2004

Credibility

Am I willing to declare myself and fight for what I believe in?

American women are in a strong position to further women's interests, and drive our culture and society in a favorable direction. It is imperative for our survival, and the survival of our democracies, that we bring this potential into the open and get it working to our benefit. In this process, we must voice our principles and articulate our intentions and arguments. There is no advantage in rehashing the rights and wrongs that perpetuate the patriarchal story.

We are claiming our position as intellectual and social equals to the men around us, with our own ideas, based on the feminine principle at the core, and which are not formulated around the stereotypical messages of caring and community. We are not inviting a debate. It's more basic than that. This is the articulation of an ideological proposition—the feminist standpoint and the feminine principle. Regardless, the debate is sure to arise, once we have competently and rationally established our position. As for the future, the ideological deductions from taking this stand will work themselves out. It is a process, not an equation.

It is important that older women either renew their feminist spirit or acquire it. Elders act out of belief and can say things others cannot say with certainty. Whatever the generation, women must establish a culture of credibility. We must present credible resistance to the forces which undermine and overpower us, including the ones we manufacture ourselves. Credibility is the great force that will propel us out of the world of our own limitations.

We cannot mistake words for power. This is not magic realism. Running around shouting guerrilla rhetoric was useful in the seventies and served its purpose. At this point, it only grates on people's nerves—everyone's nerves. We cannot be ridiculous: an educator told me about immigrant women in Yonkers—in burkas—calling themselves feminists because they were learning how to read. And we cannot be posers: like celebrities presenting themselves as symbols of liberation wisdom. Nobody buys in. None of this is credible. Not only that, it has the detrimental effect of reinforcing the stereotype of women who do not take power and position seriously

Credibility means fighting your own battles and living up to what you expect of yourself. It is the great force that will propel us out of the world of our own limitations. This brings us back to our day-to-day relationships with men. All men have common points in their history that deals with controlling and limiting women. They all have the experience of resisting female authority on the basis of sexist prejudgment. All men have first hand experience with exploiting women's situation of marginality. They have all had the experience of shifting the focus on meaning to something other than what we intend. All men harbor a learned resistance to prevent women's true determination from seeing the light of day.

It is staying power and holding our position that will break down this learned resistance. This—the reality of men—is where our personal credibility is on the line. We are working against the preservation of male authority, patriarchal continuity, extricating ourselves from their mistakes about our lives. The threat this presents can be expected to give rise to altered readings of our true intention—again. And how we restore our meaning will, again, bring our credibility into play.

There are plenty of honorable and cooperative men around. They like to get along and be a part of the flow. With the accretion of experience and time, they reap the same rewards from relationships as women do. That is, until women refuse to make concessions in the interests of men's arguments. This is the moment when men expect to be able to save face.

To women, "saving face" is a stupid kind of negotiation. We tend to work things out—explain them, solve them, or dispose of them; while men operate on a win-loss proposition based on ego protection. They exchange face-saving concessions, in lieu of actually solving problems. Using this mechanism, they leave the problem festering behind the mask. There is always serious reckoning when you try to change the world. In all of this, women must stand their ground, stay centered, and remain credible at all costs.

Your position is grounded and your argument is constructed with reference to your identity as a woman. This is your place in the world—inner and outer. Based on the feminine principle, you stand as a woman on your own behalf, and your terms work on behalf of all people. It is here that you are centered—and remain credible.

> There is a solid bottom everywhere.
> Henry David Thoreau

CHAPTER 16

TALKING THE WALK

I've got plenty of anger in me now and it gets my ass out of bed
in the morning. That's the only way you get anything done.
This country was built by pissed-off people.
Tom McGuane, *Nothing But Blue Skies*

What is the point, one asks, of about feminist knowledge? The point
is to undermine and collapse the dominant male as maker of life's
true narrative. Vote him out. Create our own narrative. Here's
how it works.

Disestablishing the Dominant Voice

Speaking as myself and as a "woman-in-general" to every man I know,
and don't, let me level with you. Every important relationship is shaped and
supported by intelligence and verbal skills. Therefore, we all have ongoing
dialectical issues.

I have provided the stimulus for many of you to accept me—woman—as
an equal partner in our journey on this planet. There has been conflict. Its
roots lie in the rules of interaction, which you expect to govern; as well your
questions about my right to speak, period. The my-archy. I have expected
each of you to take it like a man. Instead what I usually find are angry
defeatists, struggling for one-upmanship, staged from weak positions. Thus,
I've gone ahead and created fake harmonies when necessary or worth my
bother.

When I speak my own truth, out of my own knowledge and intellect, the content is generally funneled into meaning as you choose to understand it. Then the dialogue shifts from what is my intention to what you deem important or allowable; narrowing down, whatever it is I'm saying, into the scope of male tunnel vision. When what I say harkens to your ego, or your emotions, you call your own masculinity into question, and then apply the pressures of the prototypical sexist arrangement. At this point, I may very well begin to self-censor. Old formulae die hard.

I've seen a few changes over the years. A few acknowledgments have been admitted and the odd man has turned up who never expected submission from women in the first place. And it's always comforting to come up against unapologetic sexists, whose intransigence I use to affirm where I stand. They solidify my ground for reservations about the progress men are making with the idea of women's equality.

The problem, generally speaking, is that you men don't grasp what it is that I am un-telling you. I am dismissing what the dominant narrative has told both of us is the "real story." You are unable to meet the contents of my mind, which you can't imagine exists without your approbation and which, of course, you haven't given. "Provocative," you call it. Or, "you certainly have a way with words, Ms. Whoever-you-are!" Trapped behind the door of your own superiority fiction, it's not surprising, then, that when I change the narrative as written, most of you go into shock, or worse. And so do women. That, however, does not deter me from ignoring your prohibitions and rewriting your stale and unrealized scenarios. All we have is ourselves and each other, so get used to it. The days of extolling your virtues every time I exhibit my own, are over.

Malespeak is a universal, self-perpetuating fallacy of massive strength and consequence. Having acquired the experience to transcend the bewilderment of the female upbringing, I've shut the oracle off. So do not mistake my intention. The objective is to subvert the linguistic system we have inherited and to disestablish the dominance of the male voice.

Some would argue that the male-univocal power structure leaves no room for the emergence of the feminine worldview. I would argue that women have the advantage of the dynamics of feminist knowledge to aid in the task of dismantling male power; and the obligation to do so, in the face of the suppression of female authority. The point of this project is to realize that power, so as to influence and improve the order of things in our favor.

It's hard to imagine disestablishing the Dominant Voice. Not only has it created, or at a minimum, shaped, the soundtrack of our minds, but it is the one we hear every day: public figures, frontrunners, writers, broadcasters, authority figures, who are the centers of the social, cultural and political life of the nation, reinforcing what we individuals allegedly want to hear. Add to that the manipulative language that preys on our emotions by stirring up buried feelings and generates conscious connections with repressive messages: fascism, backlash, witch hunt, pogrom, genocide. These things don't just appear out of nowhere. They're cultivated by language.

Not My Metaphor

> Woman in ancient society was the truth sayer, the one who strips away hypocrisy, the keeper of the collective conscience. Her presence inhibited the puffing of others' vanities. If that means saying the emperor has no clothes, so be it.
> Miriam Horn, *Rebels in White Gloves*

The Emperor Has No Clothes? What's the point of that? Everybody's pretending about a guy who's pretending; kowtowing to a totally deluded megalomaniac. This is a story about a metaphor—told as a metaphor. Which is a good metaphor about the historical relationship between women and men. The problem is, that since women have discovered that they have their own minds and stories, the standards for metaphor no longer apply.

But we're still caught in the myth of the surface of the male character. We're explicitly told—and we implicitly understand—that we're supposed to pretend that we don't know what you can't face about yourselves. We convey our fake blindness in acceptable affirmations, told in acceptable styles, in acceptable discussions. So merrily we go along, making you feel at home with your inadequacies and limitations, to keep some kind of alleged civility going. No clothes? Save face? There's not even an emperor!

As women are changing their attitudes about ourselves, we are not translating this into reducing the power and influence of the male tale. We're still in the subordinate mode, acting as if men think we don't have the right to increased influence. As though it would be wrong to approach the entire topic from our own angle.

The male metaphor, in its sexist construction, protects the authority of the Dominant Voice. Its purpose—or value—is to prevent the shape and constitution of men's vision from shifting. There is a change in the volume of a certain aspect of content, however. Women are now weighting the story in terms of what is done to us by men, but little progress has been made in dismantling the iconic male stereotype. All we get in this era of more massive, mass media is a greater sampling of bigger and better socio-and-psychopaths which is simply a logical increase in the quantity of bad quality.

I saw a short film recently—*Montreal vu par...*, by Denys Arcand—which exemplifies the rules of male metaphor. A man and woman are in a crowded arena at a hockey game, during which she announces she is leaving him, after forty-six years of marriage. She walks out of the rink, and though reluctant to tear himself away from the action on the ice, he follows her to get an explanation. She tells him, that after a lifetime of servitude and pain caused by his indifference, her decision to leave has been precipitated by his insistence upon jumping on her bones, a week after she has returned home from the hospital after an operation for cancer. "I don't know much about women's things," is his excuse. The subtext implies that in the time she has left to live, she's opting to rejoin the human race. In solitude or community, whatever life brings, it will be an improvement over living with the burden of a chronic case of male failure and obtuseness.

When are men going to finish this scenario? The question mark is the metaphor. The unfinished or unexplored scenario is the issue inside the question mark. Let me restate this theme: men tell the human race about their own values and emotions and how they think women perceive them, in light of why they don't want to talk about any of it.

It's not that I don't understand these male peculiarities. Indeed, they are not without features of compelling interest. It's that I find them ultimately stupid and unacceptable. No impulse to move on characterizes the dominant male narrative, which is, of course, what makes it a lie. There is always an impulse to speak the truth; ergo I do not accept this muteness. I don't accept the hypocrisy—your face is no more important than mine. I don't accept the smallness of your self-awareness. Admitting your resistance to self-knowledge would open up a whole new world. Should you make the leap, don't use storytelling formula 101, and forget the "boy struggles with adversity and is transformed" bit. Actually, forget boys, period.

And I don't accept that women have to take up the slack in the male character and embody it as her own. Go ahead, tell me about your ego problems. But as for more chicanery, couched in the language of psycho- or any other -logy, forget it. Fess up. Come clean. Get real. You are not reflecting back the perceptions of your own changed reality. Yes, women's liberation has had an effect on you. Instead of grappling with it, you remain cocooned in your own self-aggrandizing mythology.

I want to know what this dork at the hockey game knows about himself, and what the storyteller is concealing, and why. It's not good enough to say "I don't understand women." Why not? What's your problem? Push the envelope. If there's nothing there, say so—but in the context of reality, which means living life in a world with women. Then tell me how you got this nothing and how you managed to pawn it off in exchange for forty-six years of a woman's life. Then tell me fellas, exactly what is it that you're protecting, inside your metaphors within metaphors. Which are not my metaphors. But don't tell me the emperor has no clothes.

Ah yes, the emperor. . . . So here you have a metaphor for self-aggrandizing men, buried in the metaphor of public approbation, transforming itself into a myth that allows us to claim the moral high ground, by setting up imaginary camp in the courageous metaphorical fellow who has the balls to say, "Dude, you're not wearing anything." This story is part and parcel of the arch-myth called the male mystique—that incredible delusion about male invincibility. Which is not my mystery.

Traversing the realm of myth into the real of actuality, I disabuse myself of the fictions of male magic. I distinguish between what is universal and what is personal. The universal is That Thing (the historical consciousness of the superiority of the male), which everybody senses but can't quite put their finger on. The personal is you, fella; your fraudulent "male legitimacy," that everybody knows about and is afraid to talk about.

What I define as the interweaving double bind of patriarchal ideology and practice, is to men, the guardians of the mystique, their implicit but unsubstantiated relationship to power, which explicitly shows up as the male establishment and its assumptions which, valid or not, exist as pressure. You exert it. I feel it.

My Half Way

Not my narrative, my metaphor, nor my mystery. It must be obvious that I do not accept the superiority of the male on any level. And you, guy, must be interested in where I stand and what I have to tell you—which is what I decide to tell you. My intention is to analyze the asymmetry at each point in our conjunction at the level of my own interests. Truths, half truths, whatever the situation, I am engaged in transcending the distortions in my own life, which have arisen because of a lifetime of contact with individual natures such as each of yours. Which brings me to the subject of your struggles with feminism.

Having brought it to your attention that we do not want the phallocentric world, you have responded with predictable scorn and aggression. And manly evasions like, "my struggle with feminism" and "as he responds to the tension of the times . . . ." And of course, there are the regular eruptions of authoritarianism, pride and violence.

All of this is characteristic of a group losing power which it is unwilling to relinquish, and so the narrative goes. I have yet to hear any of you, however, challenge your own assumptions about the innate right to control women's lives. Don't look for help. It's not my job to cleanse the culture of your mistaken presumptions. It is my job to counter these with rational intelligence. Do your own housekeeping.

There's plenty you can do, to come up to the challenge of women's drive for equality, instead of doing what you are doing—which is sitting in the front row watching. This reminds me of the story about the generals sitting in the front row on the opening night of Alban Berg's *Wozzeck* (1925), clapping enthusiastically for a play which has just revealed their own failure as human beings. But back here in the real world, the situation is not entertaining. The cultural preoccupation with the denial of male shortcomings is by now tedious, at best.

Having shown little sign of getting a grip on the situation, even though it's been going on for decades, you are obviously in need of direction. I would suggest you engage your mental powers in the contemplation of feminist topics. It means you will have to consider women's lives more broadly—even when the women closest to you, fail to do it themselves. Feminism is an entire worldview and far more interesting than stupefaction or alibis, even though it does make you mad.

> . . . We are a language-animal, and it is this one endowment which, more than any other, makes bearable and fruitful our ephemeral state. The evolution of human speech . . . has defined and safeguarded our humanity.
>
> George Steiner, *Errata*

Instead of showing some enthusiasm for new ideas, here's the type of things that show up in your narrative:

•Always worth mentioning, is one of the hallmarks of ridiculousness—Jerry Falwell (fundamentalist preacher who left the planet, May 2007) blaming feminists for 9/11.

•There's that old standby—feminists are responsible for men's wives leaving them.

•And here's a new one—irritable male syndrome, "IMS", a new medical condition which is bad feelings about being devalued in society because women have bla bla bla; a metaphor for the sting men feel about no longer being the measure for all things human. It's not a medical condition, for chrissakes—it's a male thing!

•Then this pearl from the addled brains of the Columbia Christians for Life: Hurricane Katrina "is God's way of punishing Lousiana for having 10 abortion clinics . . . the [satellite] image of the hurricane looks like a fetus . . ." *Source: Salon.com, August 2005*

•And don't forget the men's movement, masculinism and "seeking a deeper maleness!" Well, do forget it, actually.

•Muteness, ignorance, denial, evasion, you name it, you've got it.

Feedback like this shows you grappling with your own issues in traditional fashion—by blaming and at the same time exploiting women. Actual honesty would force you to acknowledge that patriarchal privilege is a power-laden fiction and your entitlements have come at women's expense. Even the most simple insights would implicate you; and your own life story would be stripped of its illusion of superiority.

When males assert these bogus messages, women typically rush to the rescue, in order to stop the boat from rocking. Instead of forcing you to confront the failure of your own social forms as the source of the problem, we get co-opted into your dominance agenda—again. The rapprochement begins. The pathological praising is resumed as we suppress the necessity to grapple with our own destiny—again. This is because women fear that you will not be able to prevail in the solution of the problems that you, yourselves, have created and will either flip out or cop out. We fight weakness with weakness. Bathos with pathos. Neither inner nor outer world is improved. And so it goes.

Unfortunately, there is a serious side effect of this condition. When you blame feminists for your problems, your strategy is intended for your complaints to fall on women's weakened ears; and they do. With a lifetime of thinking men's thoughts behind us, women glom onto this one as well. Denying the positive effects that the actions and ideas of feminism have had in improving their lives, they internalize your negativity into a generalized antagonism toward the concept of women's rights speech and activism. Overall, I find this a pretty ugly picture which indicates that critical women's issues are not going to be solved any time soon.

> . . . As long as he is dumb we can tell ourselves his desires are
> dark to us, and continue to use him as we wish.
>
> J.M. Coetzee, *Foe*

For a few words on how you got this play book, let's go back to the beginning. You began life with a deep attachment to the women around you and were quickly encouraged to move out of this state and pursue the male identity; to develop other aspects of yourselves—skills, powers—that would displace the importance of affiliations and responsiveness to the needs of others. As you went through your manhood apprenticeship, during the process you were recognized by some amorphous social authority and implicitly inherited the rewards of male entitlement, which gave you credentials in "man's world." Meanwhile, you were intimately aware that this mystique concealed your weaknesses, which have since been, and will continue to be, catered to by women.

In this odd, male, three-card monte, you were positioned superior to woman, and sooner or later you would lose your promise of status in man's world. The price you paid in this bargain is that you accepted domination from your own kind. You justified and accepted the legitimacy of your own domination and have been prepared historically to answer this indignity with violence, when the impulse or need occurs.

Women are there, behind the scenes, to reorder things in a way that makes you feel manly if you succeed, and manly if you don't. Or so goes the scenario. Your narrative contains a strong expression of what can go wrong if she fails to deliver the magic prescription for wounds suffered from your own lot, in man's world. Your cruelty is always in the shadows of our tolerance. Violence may be a moral failure, but in the sexist setup, it is also a power play that keeps That Thing and male legitimacy going.

The script says men will behave like threatened animals when women don't go their way. Her failure to buckle under can lead to the abusive, murderous, out-of-control, real or stereotype male. She backs off. You resume your workaday manly role and do it all over again, having avoided facing up to your own issues of delusion, impotence and fear, because women have been complicit in your avoidance of responsible adult behavior. We're both playing out this scene.

The idea of unity is a good one. It is invested with the qualities of peace and harmony and only a fool would not want those things. And I definitely look forward to them after I've occupied my rightful position in the world, which is the starting point of the journey to meeting you half way. It's called the feminist standpoint. But don't worry! I'll still keep talking to you. And you can still buy me dinner.

Speak! The Grassroots Language of Feminism

> We humanize what is going on in the world and in ourselves only by speaking of it and in the course of speaking of it we learn to be human.
>
> Hannah Arendt

Arendt's statement gives us incentive to speak the narrative of women's autonomy, freedom of expression, and from oppression. The power of our own wisdom and truth must counter the subordinating patriarchal myths and mysteries that inhibit the truth about the human condition.

The Imperative

We must make it easier for ourselves to speak. A feminist standpoint as the basis for what we say and do will help to accomplish that. A strong position is essential for anybody to develop practical conversational skills that serve as a medium to take you where you want to go. The point is to illustrate how we can begin to establish such a position. The articulation of new ideas is a learned activity, made difficult by old assumptions and the male paradigm for significant meaning, neither of which is going away any time soon.

We lack experience in defending our conversational selves because we habitually interpret a challenge as an attack on our person or credibility. Such is the natural response of the subordinated individual.   With a standpoint, however, you're grounded. There is nothing to back off from, or fall down off, or feel bad about. Dialogue that deteriorates can be put back together when you stand on solid ground. When you've mulled it over and are ready, you reassert your meaning, working outward and upward until it hangs together.

Meaning is created by talking about the intricacies of your thinking. You have a vision of what you want to say and you say it. You talk to sort out your meaning or to persuade others about what is important to you. Extemporaneous, rehearsed, in rehearsal, or make a list. If people can use talking points in board meetings and public appearances to further their agenda, so can you. But however you manage, it matters what you say, how you say it and that you say it. Silence is not only bad for you, but for others. If you don't talk, others don't have the words to find out what you're getting at.

<u>Get Real</u>

Women's voices will have equal power when our experience is firm ground for interpretation of all of life's values and processes. To have an impact on the culture, the female narrative will evolve through the conversations of whole women, living whole lives and those seeking that wholeness and interpreting this quest.

When you start to give voice to the autobiography of the self you didn't know, the immediate benefit is an increased feeling of authenticity. You get real. You're starting to inhabit the truth of your own voice. You are describing your intellectual search, realizations and the experience of that process. You describe it in the context of a world that is useful, usable and available. You relieve yourself of doubts about your point-of-view while doing so. Not only do you ascertain your own uniqueness and meaning, but when you speak out in the world, you connect the points of universality that are of value to all of us as human beings.

And the world talks back to you. It responds unpredictably—with recognition, curiosity, empathy, argument and the urge to stifle your intention. Or it argues the reasons why you should strangle your voice, in aid of subservience and obsequious values. Or that women just don't need feminism and you should "take it out!" In the crucial and potentially unpopular task of free expression, one must keep in mind why we don't have it in the first place, which is the subtext of any argument you are making.

As with most rational causes, the language becomes calmer, and the voice smoother, as you proceed. Speaking the grassroots language of feminism is questing after a common language that embodies the force of women's principles and values which can be carried into the culture and handed over to the future. It will find opposition, which is grist for your mill—not something to shy away from. The credibility of the entire human story is in question and we all have to share in coming up with the answers.

•

While discussing feminism with a friend who is a geneticist and teacher, I mentioned that when speaking in class, women students tend to suppress their intellectuality and creativity if there are men in the room. He answered, "One." "One what?" I asked. He told me that a fellow professor had plenty of experience with this phenomenon. His colleague said that only one man in class was required for the female students to self-censor and dumb down.

If we are that constricted at the college level, what are the chances that these women will express themselves freely when they get out into the world?

Subject-In-Waiting

The subject we are pursuing is life. The legitimacy of the story of life is recognized by the male society as theirs—ours "compares" to it. Men hear women's topics as inadequate at best, ridiculous at worst. They speak as authorities and we feed off the crumbs of language they toss in our direction. We are inured to the greater significance of their topics and complicit in the manufacture of our own self-doubt. But don't be put off. Nothing in our experience is worthless, including 5,000 years of our own misgivings.

Women's narration of reality will give expression to intense dissatisfaction and sources of pain. It will give meaning to the "daily treadmills of material survival, child bearing and rearing . . . ." It will give context to women who resist and lash back, as well as to those who will be carried along with us, as they have been in the past. There will be levels of disproportion all the time.

But by definition, the grassroots are home to us all. And that includes those who exist as they do because of lack of choice and those who have no self-defenses because they have never had a chance to tell their story to hearing ears. All women need a framework within which to develop their repression into communicable ideas—even those who resist the opportunity. We must speak up for ourselves and for those who are excluded from the councils that decide the important things in life.

When we get used to standing up for our own voice, we are positioned to attend to the voices of others and rationalize, rather than absorb and reflect, their points of view. We must organize the world first for ourselves and deal with the freedoms we caution ourselves against; after which we can deal with "other." But the time for abject selflessness is over.

First Line of Defense

. . . feelings are always involved as soon as a
woman sets foot in a room.
                                 Roy Blount Jr., *Be Sweet*

Right. Back to you guys.

To you, feelings are things that happen to you. When they make an entrance they have a quaintness about them, like servile attendants that show up now and then to exasperate the more important pursuits which occupy your life. And they are always accompanied by surprise!

My situation, however, is considerably different. My important pursuits are stranded in the forgotten recesses of my life, while your values and ideas and emotional stuntedness have persistently blundered in from the wings to upstage my own drama; and to which I, as audience to myself, have reacted with feelings about the unspeakability of it all. Well, no longer. To the rescue: a set of guidelines to help stay the ground and ward off the perils of a lifetime of conditioning.

Guidelines and Rules

Pogo Rule. "I have seen the enemy and he is us." The Pogo Rule harkens back to the lessons of the feminine principle—the fulfillment of human nature and development of all potential to its highest ability. I acknowledge and accept my previous complicity in my own oppression. Except, of course, when men talk or act like an enemy, then it's you who is on the pogo schtick. Any hint, subtext, innuendo, rumor, pejorative, deception that smells like enemy? You. Male chauvinist pig boosters and blusterers? Same.

Not in Service. I don't care if you are not communicative and can't express your feelings. I do not have, nor do I want to know about, a template for what men can or will not do. All I care is that you get the point that I'm making a point and acknowledge it—even an inkling will do.

Owned and Paid For. I own my identity. I have a supreme right to my own body and the construction and candid expression of my mind. No one can tell me what my life is supposed to be or might have been. I am unique. I am not positioned against a "control group" that represents men's preferences for docility.

The Subject I. I am re-framing the entire conversation. I will talk about what it is like to live as a woman on this planet. I will not be chained to the male narrative. I will expose the mechanics of the grip the male mystique has had on my life in the past and attempts to maintain in the present.

Try me. I initiate intelligent dialogic conflict. I have the responsibility and therefore the authority to speak. I expect to be part of a conversational feedback system with my peers; that all crises will pass and equal understanding will evolve. Too late for reproach; and not time for rapprochement.

News to you. I will speak of what people don't see. I will not justify what I reveal until—and if—the possibility of rational discussion is present.

Not My Glove. Do not blame me personally, or women collectively, for your problems. That includes my failure to live up to anything on this list or if any of this goes awry. Blame yourselves. This is not a ping pong game and I hit the ball off the table. You do not have a monopoly on logic. This is not illogic, it is different logic. You'll get used to it.

The Bottom Line. The feminine principle is my lynchpin. I will oppose that which does not enhance or advance my life and anyone else's. There is one obvious exclusion. I will not protect grown men from their own special brand of self-destruction and depredation toward each other. In other words, take your own bullets.

Body on the Line. I will embody my own values. I will remember what's important. I will keep the conversation focused. I will relate to what's going on in the daily conversation of life. I will attempt to understand what it means; how serious is it and why and how to judge it. I will discover new meanings. I will make sense of things that have unprecedented resonance in my mind and memories. I will remember and reconfigure the joys and pains of the past. I will integrate the unknown into reflections on the present.

Can't Win, Don't Play. I will not negotiate anything that is not in my interests or threatens to take me off course. If I do cave in, or get sucked in, I will . . . (see next).

Resume After Lunch. No matter how difficult or vexing a situation, I have endless creative layers to employ on behalf of my own position. I will keep talking sense. I will practice flow versus rigidity; I will faithfully contradict the Dominant Voice as it pounds on about its own incompetent pursuits.

Homage to Incrementalism. I will rely on process over calculation. I will continue to develop my internal sense of order which leads me to the conclusions of my higher intelligence and heart's desire; my point, that is.

Life Follows Wisdom. I will not turn every conversation into a debate about women's subordination and this defect in history. My mission is the positive interpretation of life as a realization of the feminine principle and my own knowledge of women's laws of existence as experienced and understood by me and my peers.

We're in Round Two. The rational argument will generally, but not necessarily, trump the emotional. It's easier to recover from a lost argument than a wounded constitution. But I plan to keep both options open.

Screw Your Wars. I expect results. I intend to change reality. I will stay my course whatever the opposition. I will be diplomatic. I will persuade people to listen to what they don't want to hear; to yield up their hidden intentions to disadvantage other people.

•

Be Wary, Women. Be Aware

We have to train ourselves to recognize things that happen in conversations; to see them in front of us and guard against them. Here are a few reminders.

•When we discuss topics of interest to both women and men, we follow the style of men, rendering a one-sided discussion.

•For men, listening to women frames them as subordinates: if not ego-challenged, they are usually patronizing. Except of course, when they are surreptitiously draining all our knowledge out of us for their own purposes.

•We are trained to listen to others' voices of ourselves; we know in advance what they expect us to say and say it. This ranges from, "if I say this, he'll think I'm trying to do such and such to him," to "if I say such and such, he'll think so and so and I'll miss whatever point I'm trying to get to because it's more valuable to protect his ego-manhood than to create my own reality."

•When we make authoritative statements, men will try to sidetrack or derail our point-of-view. Men claim knowledge on all subjects and fake knowledge about complicated things. We compliment this by turning to them for fake help and then display gratitude for his incompetence or totally wrecking whatever project we're working on.

•When you rationalize your position, someone is bound to jump up and say "but 80% of communication is non-verbal." Nice try. Ignore it and keep talking.

•Men argue that women's ideas are inconceivable, impractical, when they are too lazy to deliberate them.

•Men feign misunderstanding when you give voice to your discoveries and disguise this deceit by blaming women's "emotionalism." Often your ideas will be met with silence. But take heart—what emerges from the depths of your consciousness may not have a matching reality in his head anyway.

•Men will claim disinterest. Your truth, desires and life will lose color before their obsessions and sense of superiority and egomaniacal preoccupations.

•Fallacious arguments from both sexes will meet comments about feminism and the patriarchal agenda. Both will attack words and defend their own ignorance instead of discussing ideas.

•Men will barge, insult, clam up, filibuster, rage when they do not hear things their way or don't want to listen to what they're hearing. Nonetheless, don't hesitate to offer inchoate ideas and partial discoveries. Eventually, they'll get used to it. Besides, it's good practice.

The Mainstream Connection

"Why should I buy into this? Besides, it's scary." This is the voice of fear and scorn and a hundred million reasons to reject feminism altogether; and which live in the hearts and minds of the audience I'm trying to engage. My job is to connect to these women on points of mutuality and persuade

First, I reverse the hundred million negatives and use them as a symbol—MM[22]—for the underdevelopment and subordination we all carry within us. Then I look to my own limitations for insight.

When I started this project in 2001, it began with a severe case of outrage and excruciating annoyance. Someone said, "Women have gone too far," and I flipped. My reaction, and the reality of the situation drew me back into activism, after a hiatus of more than twenty years.

I began by sorting out and stating my premise. I followed that with a flurry of new and improved overstatements, slogans and exaggerations that would stand in for ideas until I figured mine out. I knew my premise was right and I was willing to stand on it. I reversed an idiom to come up with the title, *TALKING THE WALK*, to describe my challenge to the hundred million who reaped the benefits of feminism, but were unwilling to claim it as the source. The "Grassroots Language of Feminism" came later and described the solution I was advancing to deal with the issues. Together they carried the message that the precepts of women's equity and experience must be permanently embedded and reflected in the culture. And considering the lessons of history, this can only happen from the ground up.

What I was up against was discovering language that would be effective against my own resistance to independence and liberation, due to my past conditioning as a subordinate. Despite being a committed feminist, there I was with no way to explain it—or myself—in language that ordinary people would want to listen to. All of the friendship, joy, pain and experience I'd shared with women throughout my life provided nothing in the beginning stages. I had to learn how to talk to women as they live in the whole world, not just in mine. I had no idea what I was going to say, only that I had to say it.

Through words, ideas, insights, I began to build on information from the past. I searched, learned, racked my brain, struggled to find arguments, connections that described the truth which proved that I stood where I did. Rhythm, drama, anecdotes, voices. Eurekas! Ceaseless, random reading and coming upon the quotes, throughout this book, that gave me ballast. Dark hours of the morning, suspended in the vague unknown and suddenly, snap—a revelation! Structure, organizing, blizzards of notes ebbing and flowing. Writing. Outlines being reworked until yesterday. Rewriting—tossing the bulk of entire drafts! Words, meaning; words'

---

[22] One hundred million in Greek numbers.

meaning. Self-doubt, fear of attack and losing, of all things! My meaning, period. Finding stability, credibility, comprehensibility and the stomach to tell people what is. Putting myself out there, accepted or not: this is my contribution to the demands of my culture, this time round. Tedium, anxiety, heart palpitations, hangovers and the desire to escape so profound it could only be checked by the stronger need to live up to my own challenge and put this thing behind me. All this—just to say what I want.

As it turns out, this book is the manifestation of innate knowledge that I didn't know I knew. I sensed it—and anchored it in a few intellectual points upon which I built it up, through compulsion and necessity. The resistance was there because I didn't have the language of my own understanding of feminism. It was also there because only a handful of people in the world would discuss it. I had to transcend my—and their—underdevelopment, and move on. So I invented it by having this book help me write itself. But I digress.

Moving onto the issue of connecting with MM, I appeal to each individual on the level of the superficial glaze we see in each other's eyes which shrouds the fossilized, fictionalized and exploited reality of marginalized expectations, behind which resonate the intricacies of the mind. Back there the battle rages each time we want to say something and can't, and don't say something when we should. We glaze over the MM issues that are essential to us or grip our hearts and souls. This is anti-feminism in its silencing mode and it serves the status quo perfectly in the totally negative sense. It signifies that the story of the world does not want you telling it—that the critical elements of MM lives are of no importance in this society. With no women's narrative, and no context to harbor them, society can and does neglect your experience, thoughts and insights. Eventually it all turns into random details that even you, yourself, forget.

The question is, then, considering the things you wanted to say and couldn't and things you know you should have said and didn't, where—at what point—does feminism intersect with your life and your issues. It does have answers. It is there to help you, not hinder you. This, then, is the connection. This, then, is your cue.

Only Connect

What is the language that describes the connection between the problems of MM and my central idea? And how can I introduce them to feminism and the feminine principle so they can use these concepts to their benefit?

First, to restate: feminism is the practice or advocacy of political, economic and social equality for women. The feminine principle is 1) survival of self; and the procreation and protection of life; 2) fulfillment of human nature; development of all potential to its highest ability; and 3) embodiment and will of the principle.

For wieldability, I separate MM into three groups: 1) those not brainwashed by traditional masculinity; 2) those hooked into it; and 3) those who primarily identify with traditional femininity. In a group by themselves are older women.

Group 1 is personified by women who have taken the career track, leaving the confines of the past behind. They have joined the other gender in the pursuit of independence, status and material gain. These women achieve considerable success and then, more often than not, hit the wall and have no idea what has happened.

In the 2005 documentary film, *Her Brilliant Career*,[23] it isn't the wall they hit, nor is it the glass ceiling. According to Laura Liswood, Council of Women World Leaders and Senior Advisor, Goldman Sachs:, "It's really just a thick layer of men." The focus of the film is a group of women having problems with advancement and who participate in a program for women executives to tone down their aggressive manner ("bully broads' school").

One of the women profiled in the film, Jayleen, an IT specialist in Silicon Valley, returns to work after taking time off to have a baby. The first day back on the job, her boss tells her that her management style is a source of conflict with her co-workers and cannot continue; in other words, shape up or ship out. Devastated, and supporting a household with an unemployed husband and small children, she goes through the behavior modification program in order to keep her job.

Particularly interesting is that after doing so, this woman, who started out able and willing to compete in the climb up the executive ladder, ends up chastened, demoralized and disowning the ambition that motivated her to achieve significant advancement before she hit the wall.

The film states that the main reason these women find themselves in this rut, is that while they are busy plying their MBA skills to keep a lid on the chaos and things moving along in the workplace, men are off somewhere else doing the male politics of business, i.e., handling the schmooze. Where, therefore is the connection for this group with the dialectics of feminism?

First I clarify my principles; feminism and the feminine principle. Next I would suggest that they bone up on political concepts like the Equal Rights Amendment, whose purpose is to eliminate sexual discrimination and

---

[23]Producers Patricia Gabel and Ian McLaren, Productions Grand Nord.

segregation below that thick layer of men. The ERA passed Congress in 1972 but failed to be ratified in three states by the deadline in 1982. The Amendment was reintroduced in Congress in 2005 by Congresswoman Carolyn Maloney of New York and Senator Edward Kennedy. It is now referred to as the Women's Equality Amendment.

There is a reason for persisting with this goal and it's not a frivolous one. The ERA is feminist action, whose purpose is to level the playing field because the conditions of the terrain are not fair. The glass ceiling and the predominantly or exclusively male walls we run into are perfectly normal. This is because the patriarchy is the official hierarchy, *a priori*. To disabuse ourselves of the notion that they'd just "let us" rise to equality without a fight, we can take advantage of the rational concepts and knowledge base that feminism has constructed. The glass ceiling is not as subtle as it pretends. Feminism eliminates the glinty illusion and reveals the thick layer of men—and its intentions—in practical, concrete terms.

Then there are less obvious connections to be made. If the problem is that aggressive behavior is not the way to deal with the thick layer of men and their politics (some call bully broads school, "asshole school") then the connection is with #2 of the feminine principle: the fulfillment of human nature; development of all potential to its highest ability.

I am not on the hook to provide answers, but strive to articulate the wherewithal of finding them for oneself. Nonetheless, I will make two points. The feminine principle cannot and does not mean that the acquisition of material wealth is the driving force that creates balance in a woman's life. This is the field of energy where the Jayleens of this group get hurt (often at the core) and feminism can help to explain the source of some of this pain.

The success of our capitalist democracy would *not* have evolved without the subordination and exploitation of women and appropriation of our rightful resources and inheritance. It doesn't take Marxism or anti-globalization forces to point up that women have been bearing the social costs of capitalism since it began. All you need to do is look back in your own family. Women are the bedrock of capitalism's proletariat.

And not only then, now. The enormous increase in material wealth in this country in the last few decades would not have happened but for the millions of women entering the workforce and making unquantifiable contributions to the economy. But there are negative twists here, intertwining and working against everything we are trying to do. Women are sucked into the fallacies of the "fairness" of competition in a system that started out unfair and stays that way. It's not just the system. What's fair about no day care policy, for instance? Instead of disdaining feminism as a marginalized, outdated hasbeen, it would be wiser to appreciate it as a means of understanding the conditions you're trying to survive in. It's way ahead of its detractors.

The other point is that rational aggression is a natural human attribute. The last thing women should be listening to is anti-aggression advice. What they should be doing is improving their knowledge, ergo, their arguments, about equal status. This is highly attainable by adopting a feminist standpoint. Instead of caving in when you're accused of being not passive enough, feminism motivates the skills you need to win on your terms—in a game that was rigged against you long before you got there. To whatever degree any of us has transplanted our psyche and body into the male paradigm, feminism can help to spring you from the trap. It's there for the taking.

In the immediate and near future, two megatrends are likely occur. One is the transformation of every field in every sector to reduce the effects of climate change. "They" have finally gotten the message, circa 2007, that if this does not happen, we're destined for self-obliteration. The other is the redesign and reconstruction of the world wide web: the top echelons of power want control over that wild west, jerryrigged, grewliketopsy, free invention called the internet. As it stands, they don't think it's a good way to run a railroad—or a government, or global economies, and the like. The thought then arises: are women going to engineer their demands and impress their wisdom into these new developments and structures; or will we allow business as usual to go on? This is an important question for women in Group 1.

Group 2 are women bound by traditional masculinity, who are locked into rigid stereotypes and keep men locked in theirs. They are "wives and mothers," "mothers with small children," "come from a line of strong women," and "there's nothing wrong, so why would I want to change anything?" One thing Group 2 has in common is that they unfailingly rush to defend men. The "my father, husband, would never . . ." and "he lets me do what I want" set. We all know men who are sensitive and wonderful and isn't this is a beautiful thing. But seldom do we see them realigning things on their side of the gender fence.

Group 2 make "family" a substitute for life and suppress their own autonomy. They cocoon themselves in motherhood and lose the ability to focus as adults. Independence is swallowed up in childish things, ending up in depression and despair. Or they are the complacent ones, preferring the numbness of their misery, to the frightening challenge of disturbing their mental order. These women depend on men for survival. Their status and authority is vested in masculine prestige—and they tend to keep it that way.

Where is the connection for this group, when their minds glaze over and repressed issues resonate in their silence?

To open things up a peek, Group 2 can connect by looking at what is interesting about the world outside, and how their lives have changed in the last forty years in this context. The equal rights, civil rights and human rights movements of our time indicate that women don't just occupy domestic space anymore. Women add a whole different cause to the evolutionary mix—if it sticks, that is, which until now, it hasn't. In 5,000 years of recorded history, every movement to relieve humans from their bondage to lesser selves has resulted in new and reinvented ways to oppress women in the process. Fear of feminism is fear of the liberty that women have achieved this time round.

As conservative forces swell, there is incremental evidence (and historical precedent) that women will suffer in its wake. When we adhere to the traditional masculine narrative, we collaborate in the dismantling of women's equality and in silencing the promise of women's voices in the world. Group 2 puts their survival in the hands of men, while their autonomy lurks in the background with their personal discontent, hoping to make an appearance. We all know this. But they stick to their guns. This is the way men want it and this is the way men discuss it.

With Group 2, I would connect on the feminine principle, human potential angle. In and of itself, it challenges conservative thinking. When women in Group 2 defend their position, it seemingly has no holes in it. Traditionalists assume a lock on knowledge of subjects important to women—which is not only implausible, but impossible, as women had no part in establishing the principles of conservative thinking. They followed.

Faith in such absolutism is morally delusional. Worse, it implies the application of principles without allowing for circumstances, i.e., ignorance and indifference to other people's pain and constraints. These are people, as writer Mary Gordon puts it, who "know everything important that is to be known." To soften this rigidity, and increase empathy for women's individuality, feminism can provide the rationale.

I would also connect on the subject of the male tendency to overreach—on just about everything. This tangential pattern inevitably involves Group 2 following their partners into areas which bring them into conflict with themselves. (Or not. Some are so confident they never waver.) But by then the mental skills needed to resolve these issues are nowhere to be found.

Dogmatic and theoretical overreaching is myopic, irrational, power mongering and easy; and is a common tactic to avoid dealing with intellectual and moral risks.   Cartesianism, scientific determination, reductionism, theoretical feminism, political ideologies, religious and secular philosophies and intellectualism itself, all take deduction and extrapolation to extremes that thwart insight and the common knowledge. Dogmatism becomes the instrument of loss—of what we could have been and in many cases, of what we already had. Certainly women's knowledge is a casualty. So was the Greek discovery of the principles of the steam engine 2,000 years before the industrial revolution.

Group 2 are women who believe too much in the overvaluation of the patriarchy. Unfortunately for the rest of us, they have great influence in how most of our real life struggles are defined.

> The most important thing they knew was that they
> were always right. . . .
> Mary Gordon, *The Shadow Man*

The following anecdote illustrates my case. An acquaintance (a friendly and intelligent person I'd met on a train) said she wanted to talk about her views and I said I was listening. This pleased her, because apparently (it later occurred to me), liberal women usually weren't interested in what she had to say. She started by explaining that she wouldn't go so far as a friend of hers, voting for George Bush because "he is the only real pro-life candidate." I realized, at this point, that she wanted to talk abortion and so she did.

I had just attended a seminar given by Holocaust survivor, Judy Weissenberg Cohen, which I had summarized for the *McGill Centre for Research and Teaching on Women Newsletter*, December 2004, an excerpt of which follows.

> In her talk, Judy Cohen emphasized the fact that the implications of being female during the Holocaust only surfaced after decades of documentation about the genocide. Finally, gender violence was added to the unspeakable list of the horrors of the Holocaust. In this war, and for the first time in history, women were not treated as spoils of war but as undesirable carriers of the next generation of Jews. Women were specific targets in

the "Final Solution to the Jewish Problem" and killed *because* they were Jewish women.

Ms. Cohen told her audience that women, in constant fear of imminent death, had to live out a gender hell on top of other denigrations. Daily existence was one of filth and the humiliation of public elimination and menstruation. Women aborted themselves and each other from pregnancies caused by rape, sex slavery and sex with prisoners. There were incidents of women tearing fetuses out of their wombs with their hands and binding swollen breasts because visible pregnancy meant certain death. Women who were pregnant when they arrived in the campus endured induced labor and the killing of their babies.

Ms. Cohen recalled a human catastrophe it would seem inconceivable to survive—but by a strange miracle called the will to live, some did. And Ms. Cohen was among them. Moral absolutists and right-to-lifers would be wise to meditate on her experience.

I told my friend this story and her response, in so many words, was that she would not budge on her so-called "pro-life" position. I was amazed by her response then, and I still am.

In retrospect, I would connect with her on both feminism and the feminine principle of survival. Both imply that a serious life means dealing with the life and death questions we all face and have to cope with; that fathoming the suffering of the human condition is part and parcel of the job of living. It doesn't go one way. We take risks to escape the tragic dimension and deal with the consequences, however hard they are to bear. So purporting to "know everything about all the important things" is a self-deception that feminism and the feminine principle go a long way to remedy.

Group 3, the traditionally feminine woman group, is replete with the lovesick, negative female stereotypes, feminine hyperboles and women who think that simply being female in the 21st century automatically confers "power" on the individual. These women cling to their tormenters and let obsessive love fill in for the missing parts of their lives. For the many, femininity is a way of life that brings with it passive behavior, excessive demands on time and resources concerning appearance and carries with it the seeds of victimization. Challenging issues are beyond discussion and verbalization is limited to mundane details, sentimentalities, complaints and emotional outbursts. Also stranded in this group are women who start out on an equal footing with men, but conditioned on overcompensating female values, end up becoming servants to masculinity.

The common meeting ground with Group 3 are feelings of failure and lack of purpose. The projections of themselves as overtly feminine is not only traditional behavior, but self-protection against the forces of change in women's lives. Young women fall into this group, the "who needs feminism? we're here and we're having fun" types. But the bottom always drops out of empty optimism. As one youngwoman said, "loyalties are betrayed, promises are broken, everything you thought was important doesn't matter to anyone else." For this group, the message of this project should be seen and used as the foundation for a new life structure; more suitable for the self and more viable in the world.

•

Of particular importance to connect with, and in a group by themselves, are older women. Having born the brunt of a lifetime of cultural neglect and denigration, the voices of older women are the most stifled of all, which is a great tragedy. The connection is that the women's liberation narrative should be seen as a focal point for older women, to add another dimension to the time they have left. All of the personal histories and suppressed knowledge and feelings can find a purpose for expression in the feminist mandate.

When the silence of the elders is broken, women will finally be able to establish perspective within the male narrative. If we continue to neglect our elders, the perspective of women's reality will continue to be skewed to male values. If this wisdom is to be preserved, we need to provide a way for elders to talk of something other than nostalgia for the past. Encouraging an interest in the present condition of women—through the long lens of elder wisdom—could mine great cultural resources that we are about to lose.

The Promise of Language

We all think about alternative lives—how things would be if we did such-and-such. We dream up images of ways to satisfy our yearnings and escape our haunting thoughts—balm for our anxiety and relief from our regrets. Sometimes we fulfill them, or parts of them. But mostly we let them pass by because we don't really know what kind of life we want for ourselves. We slip on somebody else's for a moment, then let it go. "The Skins of Possible Lives," as poet Renée Gregorio calls it, in her book of the same name. (Blinking Yellow Books, Taos, NM, 1996)

Desiderata: things lacking, but needed or desired. Things buried within us that we have not given names —- because they are inconceivable until you know what they are. How can you say something when you don't even know what it is; or say things you didn't know you knew? The promise of language contains the solution to this riddle. Language is the experience that sets our world in motion. It is the reservoir and the tool of wisdom.

Words carry power and meaning. They are dynamic. They contain energy. They are the seeds of thought which open the mind, shape our perceptions and construct and manifest the life we desire. Each word is the carrier of ideas and implement of higher thoughts. Language molds our way of thinking about ourselves, others, actions and everything around us. It helps us overcome our fear and allows us a little more room to breathe because it helps us make sense of anxiety. And each word gives us a little more confidence, because through language, we develop our knowledge and increase our power to stand up for ourselves and stake out our ground in the world.

•

Women come from a long social history of not being taken seriously, ergo, not taking ourselves seriously. We don't trust ourselves. We don't really believe in our beliefs and this is men's ace in the hole. Most of our thinking has been done in isolation; and piecemeal. Because of our situation, we have been unable to rely on the external world for cues that would lead us onto higher roads of development. As a result, we seldom trust our vision. Not that we don't want to, but because life has already leached out our will to do so.

We are acutely conscious of our voices being overheard by men and what they expect when women speak. In competitive environments, we hold back what we know in fear of offending them. Where we are experts, we surmise they have more knowledge than we do and play down our power. We accommodate the extremes of their puffed-up personalities by self-deprecation—promoting harmony at the cost of our own integrity. And we have been socialized to find our submissive methods agreeable.

> A historical voice tells women how to exist in the marginal universe. It carries this message from generation to generation through our culture. Contradictions and alternatives are generally confined to literature; being silent, the written version is acceptable. The spoken truth of women's issues is incompatible with the decorum and harmony of our subordination, and has therefore been suppressed. So we are fortunate to be living in the dawn of that undoing; maybe. Their earnest candor has been, finally, the source of their great resilience.
>
> Miriam Horn, *Rebels in White Gloves*

We have all been well-rehearsed. In our cultural background, we are good girls. In families we do not speak our minds. We are trained to fear disagreement, develop the feminine characteristics of flattery and servility and we are vested with the desire to be liked by everyone for being what they want us to be. As a means of perceiving significance, our emotional truths are inferior compared to male logic; and we are punished for talking too much, or in the wrong way.

We let our personal experience stand in for our whole selves, disowning our influence in the outside world. Me in here; the world out there. We're still constructing our own fairyland, instead of establishing a beachhead to challenge the structure of patriarchal reality.

Developing Knowledge into Language

Language carries with it great leverage and is the pivotal idea upon which this project is conceived. It is the medium we use to bridge what is buried inside us with what we expect out of life. Language is contact: the connection where all inner and outer things meet. When you know where you stand and say so, you are developing knowledge into language.

As women, we hold the linguistic ace in the hole because nature, our mother, provides us with instruction that begins the day we are born and magnifies it the day we give birth. While we may not have the vocabulary on the tip of our tongues at all times, language is, nonetheless, with us, waiting to be spoken. We find it by thinking about our lives and what we have held back; figuring out what has to change so we can release it.

Through the conduit of language, our buried wisdom is what floods into the gap when we decide to separate from our subordinate identity. We begin to behave like powerful human beings. It comes to the fore when we act independently with the outer world to improve things, which is achieved by thought, speech and action. All of this is embodied and made potent through language.

The articulation of what is rational and what has meaning—in the bedroom, in the kitchen, with our family, on the job and in the world—is what we are driving at. In the interests of the vitality of society and culture, we are obligated to using language that breaks down the perceptions that estrange us from our organic mesh with reality. Language allows our intellect to calculate effect; it calls upon our will to carry it out and our instincts about how to do it. All these things are of a natural order and meant to be used to introduce new knowledge into the common narrative. And we've been unable to get a grip on this for about 5,000 years.

The lines of our lives are running through our language. We use it to push through chaos, confusion and lies to get to the truth, and as we do so, it reveals our intentions to ourselves and to the world which learns about what we value. Through language we learn to perceive our own wholeness and the universe we carry with us. It is how we learn about the width and depth of our existence.

The F word

How many times have you been in a discussion where you start to feel overwhelmed and realize you're going to have to back off from your pursuit? Stymied! The logic, images, and ideas coming at you have just enough truth, so that to challenge them would mean speaking against your own assertions in the process. Separating out the points, arguing the truths and the fictions, exposing the hidden agenda—all become insurmountable. Suddenly, silence. Retreat. Unhappy. Angry. The oracle has spoken and whether right or wrong, is irrelevant. What matters is that what has been said has been spoken with the weight of male voice.

In these situations we are affirming male bias and acting upon biases we have against ourselves. The defeating comments are measured by his authority. Under scrutiny, they may collapse, but you have already caved in. If there was a common ground to be found, it did not happen, because you left the scene too early. This is the way many women respond to the F word—feminism. Male bias reinforces your own bias, so you fold up your tent and abandon site, leaving your stakes behind you.

Our challenge is to know more about where we stand as women, not less. Being schooled in the desirability of lesser knowledge is one of the reasons we have to fight for women's rights in the first place. When we consider feminism in terms of language and dialogue, we are doing so through intellectual and conceptual angles to underpin its purpose. Grassroots feminism is a product of natural and moral philosophy which relates specifically to women. (Humanism, an amenable concept for men, never mentions women.) **To talk about feminism is to speak against the fear women have about openly expressing their own power.**

When you grasp the significance of feminism and the feminine principle, you will see that they are much simpler and much smarter than the tangle of ideological confusions that reinforce the male agenda. Feminism is clear, moral and strong, and brings relief from a lifetime of contradictions and delusions. It does not pretend to be a panacea. We've all come too far to be conned into thinking that absolutes are the answers to human problems, although millions of ideologues would disagree.

Feminism is the baseline which addresses problem number one. First of all, you are a woman. Women's claim to solidarity with all other causes undercuts our power and disperses focus and energy. But if you can get a grip on women's fundamental issues, and make their solution a normal part of life, then there is no limit to what you can do to help others. As for the feminine principle, the concept serves to heighten your sense of self—not through what you believe, but what you know. It is the bedrock of innate morality. Feminine: woman. First things first.

We are mentally and emotionally multifaceted, accomplish a vast array of tasks on any given day and play out life on a variety of levels. Feminism is no less talented in serving all of the dimensions of our personal and public lives. It is generic. It is self-organizing; intellectual, philosophical and political. It boosts the energy for the exponential possibility in each of us. It has changed the hearts, minds and lives of every woman who has ever embraced its wisdom. And it is without question, one of the most interesting subjects of our time. Feminism. It's The Better Idea!

General patterns of cultural thought are absorbed in all places in life, including the edge of the social matrix and the fringes of privation. The people who live there deserve the knowledge that we, of more privileged sectors, have been lucky enough to acquire. In this project, the language of feminist ideology and history is employed as the springboard to free speech and equal status for all women. From whatever position in the hierarchy, real or imagined, each narration is equal in importance to the next, as long as it's the truth. The self-interested voices of women from all walks of life must be added to correct the ingredients of the cultural mix.

Hopi legend tells us that Spider Woman sang the world into existence one word at a time. This is a beautiful metaphor for creating the feminist principle in our lives. One word at a time, each having its source in the privacy of our own mind, speaking it into the existence of women's world and history.

So what are we getting at, here?

What do we want to say? one asks; which is exactly the issue. When we live with an underdeveloped consciousness, we live out our years neglecting our urges, not feeling the feelings and not thinking the thoughts that would describe what it is we sense we're missing out on. So we end up not saying much of anything. Everything just sits there, in a negated lump.

When we think about the reasons why we should be thoughtful—like having a brain in the first place—we begin to heighten our own awareness of where to look if we are to understand what we want to express and how to say it. You don't end up some place just because you think you want to go there. You get there by starting. Raising the consciousness is an organic journey. It starts with a decision about yourself as a woman, that only you can make.

Women have great experience thinking contextually. We think in a web of interrelated factors. Seeing, knowing and thinking all at once and rearranging things constantly: the whole thing, not just the units. In this sense we operate holistically. The way we juggle all of this, day-to-day in the small picture, is the way we should assess our potential in terms of the big picture. What keeps us from making the leap to a higher level, is that we get locked into the small picture and swamped under life's incremental necessities. These are the confines of traditional women's role.

In framing our ideas so that we can develop our knowledge into language, we emphasize intellectual priorities as they relate to our personal, vocational and social efforts. It starts with a closer look at daily life and appreciating it for what it is. Everything there is connected in another dimension by meaning. What is happening has a basic sense that relates to the larger implications of our own reality: context. With this in mind things begin to flow outward and what you want to say becomes dialogue.

Every topic contains an inherent inventory of ideas which gives rise to new expression. We form our ideas in the midst of expressing them. Through dialogue, we sensitize our intellect to arrive at a more enlightened understanding of our own truth and we use its kaleidoscopic possibilities to see our way clear. The English language "fills the niche in the honeycomb of potential perceptions and interpretations. It articulates a construct of values, meanings, and suppositions which no other language exactly matches or supersedes." In other words, language, itself, finds expression for what you don't know is missing. It is the means to redeem our lost sense of self and establish our rightful place, wherever we are. By daring to articulate our imagination, it reveals itself as the source of the greatest of all secrets: self-knowledge.

CHAPTER 17

AT STAKE, AT RISK

No woman engaged in the fierce personal and public battles for women's rights because she had nothing else to do. The struggles constituted a *claim*: the demand for recognition, the correction of social imbalances, a right to the privileges and protections of society and the assertion of equity in the ownership of resources and potential of our citizenship. But it appears that women, generally, fail to appreciate this. Whatever benefits that accrue to them, they take. But they are disconnected from the seriousness of it all.

It must be stated that movements in the past were constrained by women's imagination and limited by the demands of a country in the making. But small steps paved the way to huge strides in the present. In recent times, our consciousness and potential have gone far beyond that of our activist predecessors. But many of the gains are sliding backwards. So the question is this. Will we come up to the challenge of what we can be; or will we abandon the mission, as usual?

Since the second wave, we are already behind a generation. Our goals have been obscured by trivialization, red herrings and the conservative backlash, as well as by the neglect of women themselves, on issues both large and small. We did not get into feminism and the politicization of the personal to lose, but to improve ourselves and become full partners in society. But the cycle of the rise and fall of women's rights movements has repeated itself again.

The immediate crisis is obvious and has been described in this book in a variety of ways. But there are larger implications. A free society relies on people who are capable of commitment and who understand and accept the responsibilities of civic life. The proud concept of women's natural leanings toward community does not just relate to home and neighborhood, but to the human collective, which includes the uninspired, the undereducated, the ignorant—and extends to the waves of misogynists who arrive on our shores and will eventually become our fellow and sister citizens.

Stakes

The first thing at stake is our identity: we have to get better at being ourselves. Our individual and collective identity must reflect the integrity of women who have made significant achievements in all fields and endeavors because of their demands.   The persistence, struggle and will to that achievement is the real story of the women's movement; not the job, the money, the pay off.   The real story of our new identity lies in the fundamental change of women's motives: how and why we do what we do.

Without absorbing that knowledge in our culture, we succumb to images of weakness and subordination which are pulling us under—again.   The specter of negated female power will go back to where it came from and "the problem that has no name" which confused Freud but not Friedan, will go into hiding, waiting to rise again sometime in the future, as though no one had ever heard of it before.   While we're waiting, we'll call it stress.

The highest stakes reside in women's consciousness.   We have discovered that there is a genuinely democratic colloquy in all of us struggling to know what, where, and how the tension is caused.   The little voice in our head, our instinct, our intuition, the hunch, the unspoken drives— all of these impulses sense the injustice and stupidity in front of us. Yet there is still a question as to whether or not we will be able to rise, articulate, discuss and settle these things ourselves, i.e., manifest our own truth.   The potential is in all of us, ready to fight for our claim, *if* we are willing to give it a voice.   This book is about that voice—the creative stakes of self-discovery and growth; the ability to shape our own accounts in our own words and establish the key facts that are ours, and not some hackneyed version of them.

•

We live in the information age, with daily exposure to useful language, concepts, methods and ideas; elements we can use to help us think.   Every day we arrive at important insights by connecting our mundane problems with innate metaphysical and philosophical distinctions.   But because we live in a culture disinterested in our ideas, they go down the tube of rhetorical inexperience and discouraged potential.

We are open to these impressions, simply because of the times we live in. Add to them the changes in opportunity and social freedom and the notion of inferiority appears to become a nonissue. But we ignore the dark underbelly of this development at our peril. Men fear the implications of our vision and patriarchal opposition is in full force, as usual. Women's influence on social, economic and political institutions is not an established fact and we have not gained the foothold to guarantee anything. The stakes in the feminist mandate—securing a permanent and equitable interest in our own society—are high; and still up for grabs.

There is massive social potential in women that remains untapped. Most women in positions of power have emerged through the conduits of affluence and higher education and are largely buffered from environments of repression, exploitation, harassment and violence. Others successful in their fields commonly underestimate their actual disadvantage and do not organize collectively to leverage change. And generally, the traditional assignment of women to the maintenance of daily life, wage labor and women's informal economy is unrecognized and undervalued. Women provide the physical, intellectual, and emotional labor which manifest the preconditions of society: we have the babies and bring up the children! This has never been acknowledged as a critical cultural, economic or political component. All of this is happening in grassroots territory and must play its part in the story of women's significance in the world.

Savvy, well-positioned women have the platform to clearly articulate and broadcast their issues, but the rest of us barely have a voice. At stake is the telling of the living meaning and measure of our unique culture; the words, the principles and the expectations and goals we're obliged to declare as keepers of our society and culture. Our job is to contradict and challenge the fallacies of paternalism so we can propagate and absorb our own philosophy.

The strength of second wave feminism is that so many women have come to it by different routes. Some had read de Beauvoir and Friedan. Some were shocked into consciousness by being caught up in the antiwar and civil rights movements. Some were inspired by the sexual revolution. In some, feminism welled up right out of their core. Others were just sick and tired of the sexism. And millions got with the program just by following the news. Together they have left an astonishing complex of emotional, psychological and intellectual riches in which we can stake the claim of our own equity. But the writing is on the wall. If it doesn't "take" at the grassroots level, it will go the way of all constructs, shunted off into an experiential airlock. Without a living continuum, it will be unsustainable.

A new consciousness is a laborious thing.
Sheila Rowbotham,
Woman's Consciousness, Man's World

Risk

Women who seek to expand their minds and enhance their lives are inherently risking their status quo for something they feel is missing. One can assume this means that their world is no longer enough for them; that they must move on. To what? Freedom of mind and spirit; to realize their wisdom, exercise judgment; to develop the strength of their moral and intellectual character.

Attempting to establish our own authenticity is now in our history. We all have a memory of the clear and direct risk women took by flying in the face of prescribed ways of living and risking the displeasure of others. For many, then as now, there have been dire repercussions. This risk was the essential psychological step in women's liberation. Without it, we would be nowhere. If we had been afraid to take this risk, the women's movement would have been zilch.

Fear plays a major role in the mind of the risk averse. Fear tricks you into believing that if you speak or act the way you want to, something bad will happen. Causing fear is a patriarchal method so ingrained that we can scarcely believe it. And we play hostess to its self-perpetuation. If we relinquish the territory we have gained, we become, again, the victims of fear. This is the major values issue that women must sort out. Do we hang onto our victim identity or take the initiative to control our own lives? And then there is always the lingering question: if we are losers ourselves, do we expect those who follow to live with the same odds?

We have a choice. We can deny our responsibility for our own development or face the dynamics of change and fight to get the deals we want—for keeps. It's hard to believe this, but the hazard threshold is less dangerous than we've been made to believe. In the process of change, we discover our strengths. The more experienced we become, the more risk we can look in the face. (Think of rock climbing, downhill racing, martial arts, or anything else worth doing.) Managing fear and accepting risk is all part of the mastery. Better judgment decides the risks you can afford to take and the ones you should avoid. As an added bonus, hazarding the unknown brings euphoria as well as danger. We are not doomed to founder. The universe makes allowances for people who move on.

There is no question that the drive for universal equality sets the stage for a cultural paradox. The solutions to that riddle lie in the future. Right now, what we do know, is that the paradox between what we contribute to the world, and what we get in return, is inequitable and intolerable.

•

And now back to the interminable, nagging doubt. **If we express our authenticity, will it alienate us from men?** Do we dare put ourselves in a position where men reject us for speaking the truth? Is that what the dithering is all about? If it is, take consolation in the fact that it's too late for that. Every argument, disagreement, dislike, standoff, fracture, chasm we experience with men is opposition. You won't be inventing it, and it isn't going away. The difference is, that from a feminist standpoint, the conflicts are put into proper perspective.

Let us consider men as objects for the last time. What is at stake at this level of interaction is psychic—mental and perceptual power—not your appeal to men. If you turn it to your advantage, you'll probably meet up with some fabulous men! Reality is no longer happening to you. You are shaping it. Your intersect with men will probably keep up at the same rate it has done up till now. But whether or not you confer upon men an equal standing, is something to decide for yourself. Some of us will continue to respond to the terms men set. Some will preserve conventional options. Some will embrace men as feminists. Some will become lesbians. Some will become celibate or promiscuous. Some will create great relationships.

Whatever the case, as students of life and as feminists, we learn through our experiences with men about their nature. And if we're grown up enough, we do not desire to escape our knowledge of male tyranny and revert to our cherished naivete. The current generation of young feminists is naive to think that their male age peers are acting in these women's best interests. More than likely, they are co-opting women's power.

Men are morally and emotionally primitive. They will glom onto the properties of women's thinking and use this to their advantage. They are atavistic and will revert to their own collective ways wherever and as soon as possible. Men are throwbacks at the first chance to exploit women.

Men are not essential to the production of women's knowledge, nor are their norms essential to the establishment of our intellectual, political and economic agenda. Men author the dominant narrative to their own advantage and cast women to play out subservient roles. Men do not like women's public persona of success, or being eclipsed. Men do not change because we believe in fairness. Men are dedicated to men's virtues—entitlement, power, the defense of their egos and the control of women. And they will revert to traditional male behavior easily and quickly.

> "I realized I'd made a deal that nobody else was party to, that I had given up several things that were important to me—my independence, my career—and in exchange I expected Irwin to be there for me whenever I needed him for whatever I needed. He didn't make that deal." Ann Sherwood Sentilles, Wellesley '69
>
> Miriam Horn, *Rebels in White Gloves*

The patriarchy is what it is and any woman deluded into basing their feminism or activism on what men might be, or what they wish the patriarchy to be, should promptly disabuse herself of any such illusion. When we sell ourselves out, men do not say, "I'll make restitution." They take what they can get and they keep it.

Despite countless inequalities and unfairness, woman-man relationships are inseparable and will always be. The bond is rife with falsehoods that generate the fear that women's independence will somehow destroy our obviously natural gender affiliations. It is patriarchal propaganda that to have one level of human growth, we must sacrifice the other—a nasty idea from which we must untangle.

The relationship between the sexes has long ago been disconnected in damaging ways: that is the meaning and result of sexism. In spite of this millennial insult and injustice, women have maintained their natural superiority in the conduct of human relations. While carrying on, the male has adopted the comforting idea that individuality and independence are incompatible with community, which amounts to the inability to spit and chew gum at the same time. This philosophy and its mythologies and psychology, that lead away from unity, is just another marker in the rubble wherein women's troubled relationship to reality is moored. It is this kind of male distortion that is unacceptable in the female-male relationship, not the thing itself.

So the "togetherness-slash-feminism thing" is not the answer to fairness, nor is it flexible. It is just another example of women being torn into all things for all people. Worse, it calls for marked limitations on women's identity and control of our own affairs. It is bad judgment and inviting hierarchy, with men controlling the ladder. If they weren't, they wouldn't be there.

The weakest argument women make in their own defense is that what's good for them about their liberation "is good for men, too!" I don't need proof whether this is, or is not, correct; women's rapprochement with men is up to the individual, or the group. That feminism is good for men is certainly not a requirement of feminist thought or women's rights activism. If this dismissal evokes fear of "man bashing" it should be converted into positive energy: create new language about this phenomenon in favor of understanding women's narrative, not in fear of it. Men don't need any more mothers than they already have.

•

As our identities as feminists ricochet around the private and public reality, it's a good time to look at ourselves in relation to women in other countries, to see how we're doing in perspective. We have seen Afghan women organizing their election, ditto for Iraqi women in 2005; Wangari Maathai winning the Nobel Peace Prize and African village women educating against AIDS and genital mutilation. There are models of women's activism in every developing country addressing issues and solving problems sometimes in the smallest possible ways, but taking the kind of action they do because they are women working to solve women's problems—feminists. They do not hide from their uniqueness as women. Nor do they fear the name, feminist, in politics. They do not shy away from socializing women to feminist activism and they do not shirk the obligations to reform their own and other women's lives. They are bold, brave and effective. If we can all take a bit of their inspiration and bring a new woman's perspective to all aspects of life and fields of endeavor, we can hope to build ourselves a real culture. When we believe in the universal wisdom within us, how can we be frightened away from discovering it, or be indifferent to the best in ourselves?

PART FOUR

☆

THE WORLD
ACCORDING TO YOU

Creating Our Own Cultural Narrative

CHAPTER 18

VALUES

Values bind us together in the cultural narrative. Women's history and wisdom are virtually absent in this narrative, because they are debased according to male terms of what is important. We must alter this situation. Thus, the subject of values is an all-important mental, emotional and practical topic.

Values are mental constructions based on relative worth. They are standards we develop for judging what we think is important in life, knowledge and everything else. Values come into play with every personal belief and conclusion about an act or issue. They are the instruments of individual principles and preferences, and the grounding for our critical faculties. Ultimately, values lead to heightening our perceptions about life and death questions. It is crucial to know, therefore, where they come from, or how they got started.

The word, values, conveys meaning that is generally accepted by society. Unacceptably, is the fact that all values are skewed at the gender intersection of every level of relationships and the paternal system. We must adjust our concept of values to clarify and reflect the essence of our experience as women. What is in place is a system of social morality that has been rationalized absent of women's counsel.

Everyone has values issues and the first given pertaining to these issues is that women overvalue all things male. In other words, we conduct the entire process of our lives conforming to male priorities. This includes how we think about ourselves, because we accept that males basically value women as subordinates. Most of our inner and outer conflicts arise while at odds against ourselves because our identities are overloaded with male priorities. This creates the conditions of uncertainty and fear that cause us to wonder about our own basic worth.

We seldom think about values as a personal issue, because we are so busy helping and living up to all that is expected from us according to others' demands. The central zone of this preoccupation is, of course, the family and intimate relationships. The zone expands outward into the community, workplace and the world. Along this trajectory, women's empathy and support is expected by other groups or disciplines: race, religion, education, individual beliefs; others' personal relationships; refugees, foreign wars and any and all other impositions from around the globe that bombard our sympathies or moral indignation. Particularly if a woman is liberal, she is supposed to possess an infinitely approachable consciousness and identify with all downtrodden causes.

Healthy skepticism should greet the many demands made on our caring, as they are usually the consequence of patriarchal failure and deviousness and are often blatantly or deceitfully misogynistic. Take Poland, for instance. Jockeying for a position in the free world, Poland announced (2007) its government policy to export its "values" to the European Union. At the same time, this self-identified Catholic country, eliminated the Women's Ministry. This hints at how important it is to know what values means, both ideologically and politically, in light of the rising tide of fundamentalism around the world. Fundamentalism means patriarchal totalitarianism. The pressure to introduce Islamic law into Western democratic legal systems is another example of a totalitarian system of "values" that should raise the red flag for any woman who appreciates even the most rudimentary ideas about her own independence.

Like all male overreaching, ideas about what is "right" doesn't stop with life on terra firma. The imposition of their values continues after we're dead. We're expected to believe in the truth and consequences of stories that no one now, or ever has been, or will be, able to validate. Fantastical things: angels, devils, wings, horns! Grotesque things, like throngs of virgins awaiting suicide bombers—for heavenly deflowering, I presume. And the immeasurable cosmic phallus himself: guy-god, who invented and authored these prejudiced absurdities that are pawned off by patriarchal authorities as the ultimate in importance and truth.

Whatever the validity of the spiritual riddles and concerns that require our attention, all of them are at least one step removed from the fundamental ground of our being, which is the female-self and our experience of existence as women. This primacy anchors our moral reasoning, according to the precepts of our inborn rationality, combined with the feminine principle—the continuation and protection of life. Unfortunately, women's authentic principles often lie below the level of the collective consciousness and many of us spend a lifetime without them ever making it to the surface.

A serious life requires a search for alternatives for the things that trouble or inspire us. Because of the asymmetrical gender equation and male domination, women have been "estranged from their organic mesh with reality." Accordingly, there is no point trying to adjust our lives to conform with a world-or-any-other-view that does not relate to us. Our personal values analysis is an essential autonomous value judgment and the imposition of any external moral or ethical edicts that infringe upon or challenge the decision to question the entire patriarchal value system requires serious scrutiny.

The job of the values analysis is to sort out distortions that have a negative, uncomfortable or fictitious influence on how you think, feel and act. The things one must consider relate to questions you have about your own thoughts, not what people have told you to think. The goal is to make reasoned adjustments to your personal value system so that you can bring balance and harmony into your life.

.

What do you know and what do you just believe?
Linda Hogan, *Power*

Just as knowledge is not the same as belief, feelings are not synonymous with values. "But, but . . . I feel strongly about this!" You can't help the way you feel, but confusing feelings with values is a conceptual wrinkle that serves everybody else's needs but your own. The task is to straighten this out from an intellectual point-of-view.

Examining the origins of values usually taps into caring anxieties and gives rise to a degree of emotionality. The process evokes guilt about the quantity and quality of our caring; or fear about not passing muster with those who keep the moral books for our care account. And they'll be the first ones to let you know about it. Dependent for their lives—and gains—upon our historical gift of service, others generally attack women's autonomy as selfish individualism which separates itself from their needs (values). Such outside criticism is thus values motivated, so women should expect to feel the heat any time they don't do what they're told or don't value what they're supposed to.

> . . . our dominant society is a very imperfect one. It is a low-level, primitive organization built on an exceedingly restricted conception of the total human potential. It holds up narrow and ultimately destructive goals for the dominant group and attempts to deny vast areas of life.
>
> Jean Baker Miller, M.D.,
> *Toward a New Psychology of Women*

Whose Traditions?

To develop one's own critical faculties, the first lens to look through is tradition. American values and ideals, for instance, portray themselves as norms which we are all supposed to find think are the ultimate. Health, wealth and happiness; freedom, melting pot, one nation under God, mom and apple pie and democracy! As good as they all sound, many people find them alien to their own experience.

Women can look at the American principle of equality as hypocritical and a lie which conceals prejudice against women. The first values question, then, is this: how comfortable are you living with this lie? For some, the benefits of American life may outweigh any nagging ideological irritants. These people reduce the meaning in the ideals to the dream cliche and leave it at that. For others, the principles of equality and integrity are not a trade off.

But we are not others. We are individuals considering values in light of equity, feminism and the feminine principle; values which all go hand in hand. How, then, does your rightful stake in the culture, and the life of this country, balance out when considered in light of these principles?

At the various intersections of personal, social and cultural life, you will see that the contributions you make are disproportional to the benefits you receive as a result. The reasons for this are many and varied, but for women, the distortions can easily be observed on two levels: transference of interest and sacrifice.

Transference is recognizing the value of our personal stake in a particular ideal, but transferring its worth into the development or possession of another. The reward for this denial is reflected glory. Examples of this are the woman who gives her children everything and leaves nothing for herself; or who works year after year at menial jobs and domestic servitude to put her husband through medical school. In such cases, their success is her reward.

The sacrifice distortion is advocated by authority figures who pretend to a higher morality, while concealing their own lack of responsibility and cowardice. This sinister spiritual mutilation has had a profound effect on women throughout history and has nothing to do with what any human being will truthfully do for another. Whether it is a mother risking her life for her child, a fireman risking his for a victim, Terry Fox on his Marathon of Hope to find a cure for cancer, or people fighting for freedom, it is a profound force of nature that motivates the sacrifice, not fraudulent pieties about the ideals of human performance (or patriotism). With twisted values like this imposed over and above the traditional message that women are borderline important anyway, many women feel they don't have the right to expect or ask for their rights or their share of society's riches—much less demand them. But the demand for her sacrifice is always there. There's never enough of that.

The system and its power brokers like the values package the way it is. All sorts of mythologies, ruses, incentives, honors and exhortations are in play to safeguard the bogus values and positions of those who depends upon others' weakness in order to stay in control. For the power structure, changing values is a bad thing, not a good one. It is discouraged, not encouraged.

The reformation of values is a process. A reorganization occurs in the mind and this changes your life. As we grow, our past itself moves with us, taking on whatever character we give it. One by one, things change and as they do, you bring a character, a spirit and a mind to them. You bring your past disorder with you and it coexists with your new order. You are replacing someone else's values package with your own truth. The results are the product of an attitude, your own uniqueness, and the journey itself—not just the individual decisions. And what you end up with is invaluable.

Determining Your Own Values

To determine our own values we must think about the conflicts and contradictions in our lives, so we can get to know them. They are the bedrock of development. What are your uncertainties? What do you quarrel with yourself about in your own mind and personality? Where are the unresolved stresses; and is there a pattern here? What are the nagging questions? What are the conflicts of morality and purpose? Is this one big tangled mess that you'll never get out of? For some people it takes more than just thinking. Because we are conditioned to trust the construction of everyday reality, it is often a crisis or tragedy that shakes our faith and drives us to reconsider what we really believe.

When we start to clarify things, we are knocking at the door of the negated consciousness. What we once staked our life on, begins to show its soft underbelly. The illusions start to crumble, turning up false promises—falsely attractive, falsely important and often absurdly trashy. Unraveling the truth from moral pieties and impositions can seem like a life's work.

But your unconscious reorganizes you while you are in the process. Inevitably, we reach a comfort zone in our growth and begin to flourish in it. We discover that it does end and that there is an outcome; and that the outcome is one of the values of the search. When you get there, you may find something illuminating or you may end up with nothing but the belief that there was or is still something there. It doesn't matter. When you get to where you know you belong, your natural morality will be there, whether you attach a definition to it or not. It's the human condition. And yours is not someone else's to give or take away.

•

With the reexamination of values comes ambivalence. We are confused about what to keep and what to discard. This is where feminist knowledge comes in—the foundation whereupon we can clarify our judgment. The feminist standpoint is a rightful and equitable position from which we may test ourselves and others.

Valuing from the feminist standpoint is using your own values, arranging new combinations, and experiencing new sequences of conceptualizing events and phenomena to avoid thinking like men. It requires making the distinction between what is important and what is not and it should disempower any moral ideology that causes you conflict. Struggling to overcome the contradictions in this situation is not just the answer to a distressed mind or personality, but an evolutionary process. Man's genuine historical greatness has resulted from just such struggles and the time has come for women to meet the same challenge. The matter is one of recognizing the losses and tradeoffs in your value system—and rebuilding it.

In any exercise of self-recognition and reevaluation, one is adjusting for things unrealized against the backdrop of a formerly blank, negative or underdeveloped state. How far do you go in the new direction before you get to the point where you think you cannot afford to pull out? Any area of overvaluation becomes excessive and causes other values to deteriorate. In this case, human behavior is totally predictable. What was once a forbidden or hidden want or need, can explode into an obsession with a negative effect on everything else. So if you get the feeling you're going over the top, go back to the egg: where do you stand as a woman? In the values analysis, intellectual honesty clarifies the restraints that liberty must impose upon itself. This is where women have the advantage of their habits of caring and community. To women, values fuse individualism and community. How could one pretend to exist without the other?

Morality and Ethics

Many would argue that Judeo-Christian ethics are the basis of liberalism and democracy. I would argue that Judeo-Christian ethics are men's attempts at expressing natural law, which is the innate moral and common sense possessed by all human beings until it is brainwashed out of them. Whatever the origins of one's beliefs, most would agree on certain values: kindness is admirable, murder and incest are heinous, theft is antisocial, and the like. And they would strongly disagree on others; the amount of personal freedom from repression or injustice to which any individual is entitled, for instance.

Morality is neither simple, nor is it absolute. But it does seem to go hand in hand with sanity. Morality exists because life exists; not the other way around. Life has a lock on morality. Ergo, dogmatic patriarchal presumptions are illegitimate in that equation.

Morality Models

The hot morality model in vogue today is the **good and evil** one. The rhetoric of good and evil is childish. It is only suitable to provide parents with language to teach children how to behave and cope with the adventure of growing up. When applied to topics of political importance and the free will, it is silly. It indicates Americans' difficulties with getting beyond the adolescent stage of nationhood, which is also evidenced in things like insatiable greed and gluttony. Instructions to children are transformed into the exhortations of international diplomacy and we bluster along, fortifying our righteousness (us: good) and reviling the causes of our failures (them: evil). At this low level of moral acuity, almost anything the power structure does is justifiable and without knowledge about how our values and priorities are constructed, we tend to accept it.

Another fashionable way of looking at morals is the claim that **all values are relative**. This determines that the private psychological, emotional, economic and sexual drives of those who hold them, are as worthwhile as anyone else's. The moral imperative in moral relativity is, then, that we should accept enfeebling sentimentalities, perversions, banalities and the doctrinal absurdities of anyone who comes up with them, particularly when they are associated with a culture or rights group. And not only that. We are supposed to endorse these relative values, because political correctness, the symbiotic cultural pathology that compliments cultural relativity, drives us into going along with this type of thing. There is no end to the oddities and aberrations pawned off as morality or rights; you need only look and listen to find one right in front of you.

Another important model is our **legal system**. This crazy quilt patchworks into itself every human foible and reluctance, while advancing the myth of moral justice. "They" say it's the best thing we've got, living in a democracy, as we do. But the problem of power and corruption inherent in the law, as a result of one group's hierarchical authority over others, is where it all falls apart as an adequate moral and ethical model. Whether it works or not, it keeps going back to the individual authority and his or her traditional prejudices. The present-day conservative Supreme Court is an obvious example of the undependability of legal justice.

> It has been decades since the most privileged members of society—corporations, the wealthy, white people who want to attend school with other whites—have had such a successful Supreme Court term. Society's have-nots were not the only losers. The basic ideals of American justice lost as well.
> Editorial, "Justice Denied," *New York Times*, 5 July 2007

The **goddess movement** is a model that women have come up with of late to satisfy the need for myth and classification of spirituality—after rejecting the sexist doctrine of the male unigod religions. Goddess world is a panacea of peace and ecological harmony; nice to visit as theory, but can hardly explain away the human devastation and suffering in, say, a Hurricane Ivan. And what does the goddess counsel on how to liberate the victims of permanent war or feed the burgeoning global population. Nothing substantial, so far.

The grand opera of moral models is, of course, **organized religion** or mob morality. All of them share certain familiarities and flaws—like the one where they all claim that their particular god belief is the one true religion. Another is that they all reduce their religion, which is sold as a spiritual aid, to moral practice. And most religiosos overtly, or deep down, believe that the entire world should heel and follow, and that their doctrine should become the law of the land. This cunning impulse—to yoke the world with religious morality—is as inevitable as the moon rising. So thank goddess, that such a place as France exists, with a government committed to reliance on civil behavior as the fundamental principle in the rule of law; for now, that is.

Monotheistic dementia aside, in a developmental sense religious teaching is important as it expands one's psychology beyond autonomy and immediate relationships. Religious teaching widens the scope of one's observations and introspection, and the rituals are sociable and often motivate individuals to higher action. But like all models, they provide instruction at certain points of development only. They outlive their hold on our interest, as well as their usefulness. If in the process, one has honed her sense of compassion and learned the lessons of enjoying her own existence, then well and good. But one need not keep listening to the lessons of morality that began in childhood, and which we innately possessed in the first place.

Anyone whose intellect has been cultivated by religious doctrine faces a great swath of selective ignorance to be transversed before reaching the hills and vales of the exercise of autonomy. All down the line, important connections are missed that would provide clues to one's own personal legitimacy. Organized religion has also kept us inept by exploiting moralism for political purposes. The intransigent problems of poverty, ignorance, drug addition, sexual exploitation of children and the degradation of the environment are pushed down and drowned in this sea of moral deception. Patriarchal denial and neglect of such issues are not only indefensible but amoral. Nonetheless we still hold fast to the idea that the country was founded on Christian values and it is our collective duty as a nation to uphold them.

(There is a school of thought that the break with religion in the 60s has created a mass morality crisis. That since then, we have been trying to build a new moral code and haven't found a way to do it. This is unconvincing. It tries to fit contemporary life into the archaic religious paradigm, instead of attempting to articulate the evolution of moral philosophy. Common sense is an evolved faculty; so is morality.)

The Better Morality

When one disengages from religion's parasitic grasp on morality, one notices that the natural proclivity to behave in the interests of self-preservation and selflessness is still there and can be attributed to a natural system of morality. The moral impulse—the urge to do the right thing (whether we undertake it or not)—speaks to morality's innate existence and enduring order. Call it conscience, or a sympathetic intelligence to life and existence itself. It does not require an authority to dictate rules, duties, prohibitions and permissions. And it does not collapse in a crisis of faith or circumstances. Whatever the mind does or wherever passions lead us to resist this morality—creating evasions, alibis and endless contrivances to keep the ego separated from the truth—it is still there and always will be, waiting for us to do the right, and not the wrong, thing. Natural morality, then, is the better morality.

Self-generated decency and ethical behavior are the categorical imperatives of human survival—moral obligations unconditionally binding on all of us. When in doubt, you needn't rush to the nearest patriarch for guidance. Just check in with the feminine principle and consider the source of the irregularities in your judgments. Women approach morality ontologically. Without morality, what would be the point of our creation of human life? What would be the point of the trials and tribulations of evolution? How would we have hope, if we could not rely on natural morality?

Every rational human being shares with all others the desire to be a person of value—worthy of our own ethical scrutiny and worthy of the respect of others. When this person is at home living with others on the planet, this is moral being at the core, with core values—ones that are not easily scared off their mark, nor tainted by the hazards of fortune and vagaries of life. If the crisis of modern man is spiritual, I hope he's not looking to outdated religions for answers. If he looks into his core, he can find the things that connect him to others and to all things in the universe. These came when he was born of woman. And if he can't do this, then just tell him.

Differences between Women and Men

There is an ongoing debate about how women and men are different, or even if they are different. Of course women and men are different—in at least two profound ways. The first is mentally, the second behaviorally.

On the first count, men think differently than women because their values are formed by the narrative of a culture and history that issues from their own gender. From the time they are born, they listen to the catalogue of patriarchal pronouncements and assumptions. As they identify as male, so do they identify with the authority of this dogma. It leads them to assume that what women think, and have to say, is either substandard or subject to their vetting and approbation; that by default, they are entrusted to speak for women. They also assume that women's problems are not real, so can, therefore, be taken lightly or ignored altogether. In fact, women's issues are quite real: not to be trivialized and definitely not to be ignored.

The second important way women and men differ is behaviorally. As young males are socialized, they are taught to consider themselves superior to females, so males manufacture a great assortment of deceits and denials to prevent the exposure of limitations or failures that would depreciate their superior ranking. By the time they are grown up, men are busy chasing around the vicious circle of their own mythology, which behavior women not only don't understand, they usually don't want or need it, either. However, male cultural ideals coming with the force that they do, make it hard to escape getting sucked into the black hole of male belief and undertakings, at one time or another.

In both examples above, men set the standards of difference—they are right and they are better. The authority of women's experience is eternally second guessed or not worthy of consideration in the first place. These facts have great influence on the formation of women's values which relate to these differences.

When you reassess your value system, men are inevitably brought into consideration. Some of the best things in us have been honed as a result of identification with men, as have some of the worst. So be wary and be aware.

•

Try this little exercise. How do women and men think differently about the following things?

Female primacy	Tradition, religion	Strength
Female body	Women's intuition	Violence
Motherhood	Penis	Masculinity
Marriage	Femininity	Spirit, soul
Money	Misogyny	War
Mind, intelligence	Aggression, passivity	Rules
Death	Worldview, politics	Football (just
	Feminism	kidding)

Thinking through this list will help you get a grip on the positive and destructive influences of hand-me-down values. As well, it will suggest some of the losses and bad tradeoffs we make in pursuit of constancy and happiness. It may also add up to a coherent story about dissatisfaction and sources of pain—always a good thing to figure out, and get over. We often wrap ourselves up in the shell of our values as a way to deny and accept what we fear is amok in our general reality. But that is choosing a harder, rather than a better way to live.

> When I'm arguing with a woman, I'm trying to get her to see
> how *differently*, from her, I take things to heart.
> Roy Blount Jr., Be Sweet

*

> My feelings about men are the result of my experience. I have
> little sympathy for them. . . . I simply don't care. . . . It's too
> late for me to care. Once upon a time I could have cared.
> Marilyn French, The Women's Room

Value #1: The Human Voice

To "walk the talk" means to live up to our announced values: what we say is supposed to be reflected in what we do. This saying is a universal. We may not live up to what we say, but nobody is confused about what it means.

Talking the walk is something different. Only by raising our voices, were women able to pressure society to gain the rights we managed to win for all. But many have forgotten, or never learned, how to hold up their end in this dialogue. As a free woman, living in a free society, there is nothing more important than to speak up and speak out.

It is no mystery that the First Amendment—the right of free expression—is the most volatile of American privileges. This right is constantly being threatened due to the dynamics of power. All people in a position of authority get to the point where they believe that we, the governed or the "lessers," are supposed to hear only what they are saying—and that their assertions are irrefutable. To contradict—to speak against authority—is the only action that can change that tyranny.

Words have great transformative power. When you talk about something, you legitimize it. Language is the common point of reference in everyday life—the key to both personal survival and public citizenship. In speaking, you learn that language is malleable—the more you use it, the more you realize that you don't have to relinquish or compromise your values to arrive at common ground.

> Dialogue purifies thought.
> Mikhail Bakhtin, *The Dialogic Imagination*

The world would like women to keep our thoughts to ourselves and for the most part, we do. No one wants to hear what you have to say about the global warming, or having or raising children, or poverty, unless you fit the model of victim or guru or celebrity that the mass media deems acceptable for exploitation. In fact, what you have to say on important issues is usually discounted before you've even said it. Under this kind of pressure, it is easy for our intentions to break down in discussions; to end up as a lump in our throats that causes us to protect our cares and thoughts from future airing.

Women all share a common language which is at the heart of our trouble. We are all witnesses to our belief in equality, but that is hardly enough to ensure that the belief becomes a reality. Referring back to my premise (Chapter 4), what is missing in the culture is also missing in our speech and we are responsible for manifesting it:

VALUE #1
THE FREE SPEECH OF FREE WOMEN

It is by speaking that you control your situation in a civilized world. Nobody and nothing is more powerful.

Values of Independence

Values of independence are ones of which we are sole proprietor and manager (and includes love, though it is out of control more often than not.)

Your Sexual Body

All women fret about their body. This troubled relationship with our womanhood augments our problems of identity and development. We worry about our appearance, our weight, our wardrobe, our style; whether we should go under the knife; put out, have an affair. Are we using men or being used? Do we appear to be feminine and why do we equate losing the title "feminine" with social rejection? Am I pregnant?[24]

Controlling one's body is largely about power—meaning it is quite possible that men are controlling it for you. It's a gender thing: your body is always sexual—never not sexual. The comport of women's sexuality, like her mind, has been constructed under the system of male supremacy. How you value your body is the essence of survival. How you think about this affects your entire life.

Author Adrienne Rich talks about this phenomenon in *Of Woman Born*.

> I am really asking whether women cannot begin, at last, to *think through the body*, to connect what has been so cruelly disorganized—our great mental capacities, hardly used; our highly developed tactile sense; our genius for close observation; our complicated, pain-enduring, multi-pleasured physicality. . . . There is for the first time today a possibility of converting our physicality into both knowledge and power. . . . But the fear and hatred of our bodies has often crippled our brains. Some of the most brilliant women of our time are trying to think from somewhere outside their female bodies—hence they are still merely reproducing old forms of intellection.

Just because the restraints on women's sexuality have been loosened, does not mean one should take the idea of controlling their sexual body for granted. The history of civilization is seen as the triumph of the male over the natural sexual order. Man, whose obsession with the penis has been out of control since the beginning, transferred his failure of will to control himself onto woman, by blaming her for his raging incompetence and then subordinating her. The historical narrative abounds with stories. Odysseus subdues pigmaker Circe. Petruccio tames Katherine; ditto Benedick and Beatrice. Professor Higgins civilizes Eliza. Christianity triumphs over the "impurity" of women. Muslims enwrap them in bags and polygamy for purposes of sex, service and breeding. And some people cut off their clits. In Egypt, for instance, according to a government health survey conducted in 2005, 96 per cent of Egyptian women have suffered genital cutting and mutilation, also known as female circumcision. (*Source: "Voices Rise in Egypt to Shield Girls From an Old Tradition," New York Times, 20 September 2007)* In Indonesia, things are just as grim:

---

[24]To carry and bear a child or have an abortion is a private matter, regardless of legal or political claims to the contrary. Controlling your sexual body includes choosing to carry through with or terminate a pregnancy.

. . . according to a 2003 study by the Population Council, an
international research group, 96 percent of families surveyed
reported that their daughters had undergone some form of
circumcision by the time they reached 14. . . .Worldwide, female
genital cutting affects up to 140 million women and girls in varying
degrees of severity, according to estimates from the World Health
Organization. The most common form of female genital cutting,
representing about 80 percent of cases around the world, includes
the excision of the clitoris and the labia minora. A more extreme
version of the practice, known as Pharaonic circumcision or
infibulation, accounts for 15 percent of cases globally and involves
the removal of all external genitalia and a stitching up of the vaginal
opening.

(*Source:* Sara Corbett, "A Cutting Tradition," *New York Times*, 20
January 2008)

If you think any of this stuff disappeared with the sexual revolution,
think again. The meaning of sex in the sixties had much more to do with sex
getting easier for males, than it did with the expression and acceptance of
female sexuality. The double bind of dominance (more sex for males,
submission for females) did not disappear—it just retooled itself. Instead of
accepting that women's sexuality is sovereign to herself, men will have
nothing to do with such a claim. They have escalated their sense of
entitlement to women's bodies and having their sexual desires met with
women's willingness. Allan Bloom, author of *The Closing of the American
Mind,* expresses it this way:

> . . . it is one thing . . . to want to prevent women from being
> ravished and brutalized because modesty and purity should be
> respected and their weakness protected by responsible males
> and quite another to protect them from male desires altogether
> so that they can live as they please.

Respect and protect? This guy should have written "The Closing of the
American Fly."

Another interesting design on your desires is expressed by Sandor
Ferenczi in *Thalassa, A Theory of Genitality.* He describes the motive of
the male sex drive as "none other than an attempt . . . to return to the
mother's womb." Taken altogether, these kinds of things indicate that the

value you place on the sovereignty of your own sexual body is equivalent to survival itself.

•

How much is too much of a good thing? (Think of a gourmet meal coming back on you later because you ate too much.) Sex has passed out of the private and into the public realm and the entire society is obsessed with it—no holds barred. Not only that. Unless you're "liberal," then you must be some frigid freak, suffering from generations of repression, can't get off and nobody wants to screw you anyway.

Sexual exploitation—meaning dominant males forcing sexual behavior upon or from weaker members of society—makes for big kahunas and big business. It is a social and economic construction that everyone nods about, but only the participants see. There is no need to list the abuses and their impact on victims; we can hear about it every day. It is necessary, however, to point out that male force is submerged in sex itself and male power not only exercises, but legitimizes sexual degradation and violence against women, as a direct result or byproduct of sexual exploitation. This is a condition of everyday life wherever we live, so it behooves all women to be aware, be wary; and to definitely not be stupid about femininity or about feminism, either.

"To be a feminist and be anti porn is un-cool." Young Woman
The Current, CBC Radio, February 2005

I have heard young feminists make the case that women are free to express their sexuality as they wish and that it is males who are responsible for controlling their own violent impulses. And this is true on both counts, intellectually and politically. Living on planet Earth, however, we all have to constrain ourselves if we want to see the next sunrise. This relates as much to sexual expression as it does to every other curb we make on our own freedom and independence—if not more. Even when we do conduct ourselves according to sensible proprieties, it doesn't necessarily work. Women are often punished for being desirable, or just for being women. Bear in mind the "Tailhook incident" at the Las Vegas Hilton in 1991, where twenty-six military women were sexually assaulted at a gathering of Navy aviators. That had a double motive. One was sexual domination; the other was to "cut them down to size."

"You can't talk like that around a cowboy," Frank said. "Not
if you want to stay in one piece."
                                   Tom McGuane, *Nothing But Blue Skies*

Love and Romance

The French playwright and actor Molière said, "The great ambition of
women is to inspire love." How do we do this, exactly? "Conduct and
manners," according to Mary Wollstonecraft, in *A Vindication of the Rights
of Women* (1792), which "evidently prove that their minds are not in a
healthy state."

The practical, front line approach to inspiring love is to act on the belief
that serving others abundantly will do it. (Remember going in and cleaning
that guy's apartment while he was at work?) When this doesn't pay off in
love and devotion, but dependency mixed with a dash of contempt instead,
we are left with the pain of wondering why love has failed us.

The classic inspiration, however, is belief in the story of romantic love
itself. The love narrative tells us that a man will show up and satisfy all our
desires and emotional needs; replete with a utopian survival plan (manly
protection) and social formula (reflected power and glory) subtext. As it
turns out, neither he, nor we, can live up to the fantasy, and things fall apart.
After licking our wounds for a while or shorter, we jump into the fray again,
convinced that there was something wrong with this last one, but not with
the basic fiction itself.

We "fall" in love; with the idea of love and its huge emotional
promise—and the idea of a certain man and his huge potential for fulfilling
this promise. This abstract passion drives us forward, leaving important
things and people behind; knocking things out of kilter that we have taken
pains to create; and abandoning the quality we have brought to our lives by
making considered decisions as a result of insight and experience. The
Greeks refer to love as "the taking over of the rational and lucid mind by
delusion and self-destruction; or insanity."

"So what's wrong with that? Everybody does it," one may inquire.
Lots, if it's a pattern. It means we don't learn anything about ourselves or
our relationship with the world.[25] Thinking through and talking about how
we come to understand and value love goes a long way in preparing us for
future adventures of the heart. It will reveal many things that relate to

---

[25]Though love is a value of independence, it does not exist in a vacuum. Besides the
force of the object of our affection, social and cultural pressures and patterns also affect
the experience. Nonetheless, it's your passion—not someone else's.

projecting your needs and satisfaction into an implausible fiction. And a common tragedy it is. In fact, most people see love as the only happy ending of the cultural imagination.

> He was in a Romance, a vulgar and high Romance simultaneously; a Romance was one of the systems that controlled him, as the expectations of Romance control almost everyone in the Western world, for better or for worse, at some point or other.
>
> A.S. Byatt, *Possession*

Our profound feelings for others are ephemeral—a combination of satisfying, tormenting, obsessive and hyperbolic passions. How we manifest that love depends on our internal foundation, which must bear the weight of all our traits and appetites at the same time. Thus the overvaluation of any of them is bound to create some cracks at the base. This starts us wobbling around, trying to keep everything upright and together. From this angle, our whole life comes into perspective when we put a rational value on love.

The experience of a great and profound passion is one of the things that makes life worth living. But it is only a part—and must fit into all the other things you value in yourself as a human being. You don't have to give anything up for love—just the opposite. Love should bring bounty, sharing and plentitude to your life and that of others. A great love will take you very far in the journey of a happy life. A bad one will be a force in the opposite direction.

Some people think that love and feminism can't coexist or wonder "if there is love after liberation." A probable explanation for this, is that love inevitably produces a relationship of asymmetrical power, with the man at the controls. Love carries the seeds of emotional dependency, jealousy, obsession and fear; labor issues; and often leads to menacing conduct, violence and even death. Women not only became victims of their own love myth, but of men themselves. This is still a working construction. It has not been dismantled.

The only thing that will make it go away, is for women to accept the legitimacy of their own free will and build the underlying confidence that prevents her from compromising her values when faced with the prospect of love in her life. Instead of sacrificing our identity in the interests of a love partnership, we must come to expect that by being in love we get more out of life, not less.

The stereotype of romantic love is a patriarchal story and doesn't hold up for women who have to bear life and build it up from the beginning to the end. Byron, Shelly and Shakespeare are not our models, and have no credence in emulating women's lives from the point-of-view of emotion, expectation, or defining what is valuable. The romantic love story is particularly ridiculous in light of understanding men's dominant cultural power and patriarchal motives.

It is easier to get a trip on all this by creating the boundaries to protect yourself against the intrusions which compromise you in the name of love —and against your own self-induced mythology. When you realize a love that is a passion based on the admiration of individuality and the mutualities of communication and need—along with some weird chemical magic—then you know the feeling of the greatness of all life and love. Whether it will stick around or not, is up for grabs. Ludwig van Beethoven, in a letter to his lover, Antonia Brentano, wrote (in 1812): "Oh God, is not our love a heavenly structure and also as fine as the vault of heaven!" The last time he saw "Toni," she was leaving Vienna with her husband and four children. So as you can see, the rascality of love can befall the best of us!

The Job of a Lifetime

"What do you do?" is a major issue in the values agenda. In America, success has always meant making, or having, money. This means one must work and spend in order to have the identity and material goods that rate one's ability and standing in society.

The women's movement has placed very high emphasis on the right to a career for all women, as it means identity and independence from men and the patriarchal agenda. The demand was met by society with the logic of a different point-of-view: grow the labor, economic base. And we did. Most women work and still do not reap the payoffs of the American dream. The glamour in the cultural panacea of "career" hardly touches the real life struggles of most women. Add to that reality the negative implications created by conservative fundamentalism, global political strife, a degraded environment, bloodless labor laws, failed social and health care programs and the gap between rich and poor, and the struggles are getting worse, not better. Regardless of these facts, the emphasis in society is on how business and industry will suffer if women do not come up to the workplace standards of the labor-economic construct which is already in place.

We live in the capitalist system of the patriarchy. Capitalism is an elite megahoard, controlled by individuals who have accumulated its capital—which is the excess value that results from individual labor. Our careers and work life obviously lead us into this territory. Its merits and drawbacks are therefore serious topics.

Internalized in the philosophical engine driving capitalism is a moral concept called the "work ethic," originally known as the "Protestant ethic," derived from Calvinism. This concept is embodied in the corporate culture. It leads to conclusions such as "profits aren't what they should be"—read moral imperative. Then as a corrective action, the company lays off a thousand people just before Christmas, and asserts that this is the right thing to do. If one disagrees with this arrangement, there are alternative models and contraptions like Soviet socialism, or perhaps no economy at all, as a number of countries around the world have or do not have. While we wait for economics to evolve into something more ethical, capitalism is what we're stuck with.

Women have never required models or a moral supplement in order to work. And they certainly don't need to buy in on any moral level to the rat race of the masculine world, seeing that women are doing most of the work that underpins the culture already: it just so happens it's invisible. But so is, say, software, which in spite of its invisibility, has great recognition and dollar value as well. Women's invisible work, however, is not qualified as valuable, or even recognized as work contributing to the economy, according to patriarchal optics.

As women have established their foothold in man's world, running about in the capitalist maze is not, however, proof of a successful life. Nonetheless, there is enormous pressure on women to believe in this system, as well as hold up their stake in the competition. Examining your work values means looking at the time you spend, the tradeoffs you make for material goods and how the career or work package compromises your personal and intellectual development and relationships with others, the planet and your vision.

The idea of democratic capitalism is a psychological preponderance that weighs heavily on all of the labor and spending decisions we make. We are right to thank our lucky stars to be living in this country and not sitting on the ground somewhere in rags or a bag over our head, with sick and starving children clutching at our limbs and udders. But a panacea it isn't. The overvaluation of this package has led to problems that all Americans face and which are now climaxing and forecasting the future: declining population, lack of manufacturing base, imbalance of trade, exaggerated sense of entitlement, dumbing down of the population and on, and on. On a values level, we must acknowledge the social problems caused by the system and visualize how it robs people of the capacity to develop knowledge, resources, imagination and innovation.

It's not that plenty of conscientious, considerate people are unable to see the flaws in the system. They do, have done and continue to do so, and to put forth their findings. The point is, that we each have a responsibility to express our judgment about how things are conducted on our behalf. In light of millions of women and/or their partners working themselves to death and trying to rear families in a declining social structure, it is mindless to imagine that the American ideal is the best we can come up with. It is also a breach of our own principles. The job of a lifetime is living a full and free life—not being consumed by a vicious economic rat race.

> "There are enormous social consequences of our failure to look at the issue of work-life balance. But this fundamentally will shape the future of our society." David Ellwood, Dean, Kennedy School of Government
>
> María Cristina Caballero,
> "The Challenges of Women's Leadership,"
> *Harvard University Gazette,* 16 March 2006

The exploitation of women's work began eons ago, but its contemporary nature is particularly pernicious. We grow up with a model or ideal of female provision—mom and apple pie. Then we leave home and get onto the career track—from the convenience store, to middle management, to the board room, to the Executive Branch of the White House and everywhere in-between. We move into the phase of marriage- homemaker-motherhood, bringing our career along with us, for the reason that work is essential to our being and/or essential to the increased demands of the new and en-numbered economic unit. Everything about this path is seemingly rational. What's wrong with it, is that women are exploited by a system whose pathogenic nature destroys the experience of a full life by demanding extraneous labor for the purpose of relentless growth and profit for the few.

Evaluating the time-work construct requires you to truthfully answer what you love to do, what you find gratifying, what challenges and risks you would like to dare, what the payoffs are for what you put in, and what work has been put into the basic organization of your life which need not, and should not have to be done over again. Meaning, you don't have to "keep up with" the insane materialism of this culture. If you find what you are doing produces anxiety, torpor, anality, waste and greed, then you're probably making the wrong choices.

220 TALKING THE WALK

Like life, the truth about women and the workplace is messy. On this subject, an interesting juxtaposition turned up in the pages of the *Montreal Gazette* on July 17, 2004. One article was about female top dogs—the Executive Women's Alliance—gathering in Vancouver to jaw about the exhilaration of life in the board room, complain about subordinates' lack of commitment (give your life to your job and work all the time) and whine about getting old. In the same paper, one Jeffrey Garson told of bagging his law practice in Philly to become a shrink and career coach in order to get his work and life reconnected. So! Boardroom babes drop in and chill out, while lawyer dude drops out and tunes in. A tidy contradiction to remember, if one has any panaceaic ideas about job world fulfilling all of your heart's desires.

There is also the unsavory evidence that everything we've been demanding and doing has had no effect on the general perception of equality whatsoever. Recently Catalyst, the New York research firm on the subject of women's careers explained the meaning of it all in: "Needs and Goals Similar for Male, Female Managers." This must mean that working women have their priorities straight. Well no kidding! Glad to see it takes ever more research to come up with that one, for the umpteenth time. So, as with all major change, the jury on how we are perceived in the workplace and what it means to live a better life, is out. What we do know, however, is that women are not going back to a life of domestic gratification.

What is not being talked about, much less debated, is the questionable aspect of our system's labor strategy and the degree to which capitalist management promotes the exploitation of labor and keeps these tactics in place. The crashing collapse of socialism has silenced an important source of protest and if anything is left of leftism, it's only bedraggled rhetoric. To my knowledge, nothing since has captured the public consciousness that would inspire change. So it looks like the capitalist construction of the strong dominating the weak to further their own purposes will keep on keeping on. But nothing lasts forever.

> Twenty years ago, the gender debate centered on breaking the so-called glass ceiling that kept women out of executive suites, gaining equal access to the workplace and securing equal pay for equal work. Today, concerns more often revolve around reshaping the very architecture of Wall Street work in order to keep women involved. . . .
>
> Jenny Anderson, "The Fork in the Road," *New York Times*, 6 August 2006

Political Life

Freedom and citizenship, like free speech, are ultimate values and are maintained and protected in the political sphere of life. As Americans, we are united together in an ideological circle which has taken the ideas of the Enlightenment to its political apex: lucky for us. In this system, personal independence relies not only on democracy working for us, but also upon maintaining the rights and freedoms we already have. These cannot be taken for granted. How you value your political enfranchisement (women's struggle for the vote began with Abigail Adams in 1776 and ended in 1920 with the Nineteenth Amendment to the Constitution becoming law) will strongly define your sense of responsibility as a citizen.

Whether we know it, acknowledge it, accept it, like it or not, each of us responsible as an individual for what the collective does in our name. Here, there, anywhere and any time. We, the people, for instance, elect the leaders who send our military overseas to wreck countries and kill thousands and impose our views upon those remaining and exploit their natural resources. We are also the people who elect the purveyors of social, political and economic fraud on every level, division and segment of government. This is corrupt local, domestic and global politics and we own it.

Defining what is valuable about being a citizen is an absolute imperative for women living in our time. As our cultural values deteriorate, so do our democratic values.   There is great traffic in symbols and slogans of patriotism and nationalism these days. But waving flags and slapping yellow bows on trees will not repair an eroded democracy. Nor will rhetoric. Honorable ideals are reduced to slander and threats and used by one group against another. Rubbishy rhetoric is fodder for the mob, and the only defense against the mob is rational thinking and speaking out in protest.

This country is divided along the lines of pro and con political parties, leaving no room for debate on everything in between, which is where the real dialogue needs to take place. But creating that political reality would take more than universal will. It would also require putting faith in human decency and intelligence, instead of polar partisan power, to address and redress the human problems of which all political issues consist—including the one of power.

Our liberty relies on each of us, individually or in aggregate, standing up for our own stake in society and in our country. If we're not involved, then we deny the value we have placed on the changes in our lifetime that we identify with because we are women. Using your voice in the political sense is talking the walk.

"We want to live in a world in which we have such things as contentment, freedom, personal pride, opportunity for self-development, love, affection and spiritual purpose. We want to live in a warm world, a kind world, a human world. We want to be on good terms with ourselves and with one another. And whatever new program or governmental system fails to assist these very simple human desires is a ghastly failure, even if it produces more goods, greater wealth, more economic stability and more national power than has ever been produced or concentrated before." Dorothy Thompson

Peter Kurth, *AMERICAN CASSANDRA,*
The Life of Dorothy Thompson

Values of Relationship

Values of relationship are ones that are intimately connected with others. Their values are permanently interconnected with our own.

The Family

We are all part of a family.

Even if we announced our arrival as a foundling in a basket or were suckled by wolves, the family is a fundamental condition of living humanity, even in its negation. In another sense, we are all members of the common family—of womankind. No one questions the value of family. What we must question, is how we arrive at its valuation, why and how much importance we put on family and how separate we are as individuals from the family organization.

The power narrators say that the purpose of the family (as the primary unit of community) is the formation of civilized human beings who are loyal to the state which protects them. This makes for a stable political situation: control starts in the family and ends with the superimposition of elite rule over the individual.

The value of the family has enormous political currency. In America, within the religious fundamentalist definition, the family is husband and wife and as many children as show up without the interference of contraception or abortion, which conservative families don't admit to. This fundamentalist, husband-wife-brood model is the morally correct one in conservative circles. Dad is masculine, provider, chief achiever and authority. Mom carries out the paternal mandate while she makes the home, praises her fella and brings up righteous children who are being conditioned to take up the cudgel of patriarchal preeminence. In olden times, as in the reactionary now, dad sets the rules and mom holds it altogether. Business as usual, with the exception of one thing: mom's financial contribution.

The family is the place where the most profound aspects of life—birth and death—are intimately linked; and within these extremes, chaos inevitably occurs. While the family prepares individuals for life, powerful forces are at work shaping individuals to avoid individuality and stay in the cocoon. Or the alternative—avoid and escape the family tangle by asserting independence. If the "family values" promo included hypocrisy, callousness, narrow-mindedness and deceit; violence, incest, adultery, sexual repression, sexual obsession, rape, victimization, child abuse; hatred, coldness, impotence; fear, imprisonment and every other aberration; sexually transmitted diseases, AIDS, unwanted pregnancy and unbearable sadness as a part of the tale, then you'd have a complete picture of the deal you may be in for when you're part of a family.

Traditional families, which engender social patterns that have outlived their usefulness, are in trouble not only from pressure on the inside, but pressure from without.   The dependencies within the family and the correlative vulnerabilities, cause a flat kind of vision which makes for mutual resentment and automatic dismissal of the experience of people in the outside world. But alas, all family members have greater contact with the exterior than when these values were formed. The pressure from the outside to desist with obsolete gender roles and prescriptions of the traditional social structure within the family, force the consideration of reconciling traditional expectations with contemporary realities. Maladjustment, rebelliousness, stupidity, indifference, divorce, rage and abandonment are some of the responses to the error of forcing the idea of traditional "family values" down the throats of society.

The rational aspect of evaluating the family connection is one's basic attitude toward blood relations. How far does this value take us in our society and in our time? Does our loyalty to blood override all other values, in spite of the character, treatment and contradiction the family member has afforded us? Do we value this kinship to a moral extreme, even at the expense of our survival? Or do we attack the old images that have defined our clan ties?

Sophocles' story of *Antigone* is a classic example of the overvaluation of blood ties. Antigone's brother Polynices has been killed in battle, trying to seize the state. Antigone buries him in direct violation of King Creon's orders, thereby bringing death upon herself. In the play, the lesson is discussed in terms of the oversimplified ethics of both conflicting parties, and the lack of practical judgment and deliberation on the part of both Antigone and Creon. But what women have to look at, is what's wrong with Creon and her brother, not what is wrong with Antigone. What is the effect of belligerent male behavior on the basic unit of the community?

Another classic family story is *King Lear*. At the Shakespeare Lecture, McGill University, 23 March 2006, Professor Michael Bristol discussed this family saga in his talk, "King Lear is a member of my family." After describing the relationship of Cordelia and her father, and reminding us that in this family, almost everyone ends up dead, Professor Bristol concluded that "the family is not an ethical space." This is a good reference from which to begin to explore the behavior of family and our part in the family dynamics. How do we judge our blood kin and why? What are our emotional and intellectual boundaries? Do we start our values assessment from a position of self-respect, dignity and the feminine principle?

The inevitable and natural bonds of the family count as one of the greatest rewards one can have in this life. For women, it means marriage and childbearing, two additional institutions where gender makes a substantial difference between who's doing what and to whom, and who's getting what out of the relationship. This makes a package of three life structures where unconditional and perpetual commitment is undertaken on unequal terms: family, marriage, motherhood.

Hope, however, has come with the partial success of feminist logic over the traditional familial dogma. The limitation of women's freedom is no longer acceptable as part of the family deal—in theory. The feminist perspective on family has reformed the thinking of women and of men as well, to a degree. The problem is, that this is only true on a small scale. Whether enlightened family values influence the community and are moving into the big world beyond is an interesting query. It may or may not be happening, it's too early to tell. The restructured model of the contemporary family is pretty much confined to the level where women have been well-educated and schooled in the principles of equality and privileged in the sense that they have independent economic power and mobility, which most women in America do not have. The enlightened family model has a long way to go before it trickles down to households where authority remains vested in men.

Half my mother's brothers and sisters—there were nine of them—no longer spoke to her after this time. So all at once my mother was both orphaned and bereft of the idea of herself as a person protected by the inviolable carapace of family life. . . . She began to disintegrate. She began to drink.

Mary Gordon, *The Shadow Man*

Marriage

I married him because he was my Pegasus. On his back I would escape, arrive, begin. Love may be blind but I saw clearly enough. I just couldn't stop myself.

Anne Roiphe, *1185 Park Avenue*

Author Anne Roiphe comments in her book, *1185 Park Avenue*, that in 1957, when she married, "a female . . . had been quite conditioned to express her ambition through a male." But glomming onto her husband's idea of how to live proved not to be fulfilling. The marriage ended in divorce.

There are countless reasons that drive women to get married: to appease parents, it's the thing to do, having nothing else to do, everybody's doing it, I think it's time, to get out of the house, getting knocked up, to keep the man, for money or social status, because he has a good job, or for the experience are but a few. Since the fifties-style conditioning of women that Roiphe writes about in her book is no longer the boilerplate it once was, we have come up with countless other irrationalities so we can carry on as usual. Even when we claim to resent this time-honored escape from the responsibilities of self-actualization, the social pressure is always there. "Never been married?! Tsk, tsk, tsk." Women are still expected to tie their options to a man and engage in a dilapidated construction which more often than not, causes emotional and economic misery.

Examining one's valuation of marriage is wise at a time when so many of them end in divorce. A marriage that is disappointing, or worse, is dissolved by a divorce which is traumatic, or worse. After it's over, one usually looks back and can see where they went wrong and why they shouldn't have married this person in the first place. Maybe marriage and divorce is a rite of passage. It does make some people grow up. For others, it is the beginning of a pattern. Not only is the traditional marriage model inadequate, but so is the negative outcome.

Great mythology surrounds marriage and inspires much patriarchal faith. President George W. Bush is such a fan that he floated a proposal for a $1.5 billion miracle cure to promote "healthy" marriage—but mainly among the working class. One program in his administration's faith-based initiative package to promote marriage is operated by a Baptist church in Oklahoma

City. The idea of the program is to reduce the poverty allegedly caused by single-parent families. Pastor Young, who runs the program, is candid about its unequal logic, however.

> . . . men more than women need convincing on this point. Thus he sees it as an unhappy but unavoidable fact that women are this social policy's beasts of burden. Having already complied with social and economic pressures to work, poor women are now being asked to do something that their government had so far failed at: push their male counterparts into the cultural and economic mainstream.
>
> Katherine Boo, "The Marriage Cure,"
> *New Yorker*, 18 August 2003

On the uptown side, we have the multibillion dollar wedding business (incredibly, between $40 and $80 billion in 2007) urging us to tie the knot. Capitalism promotes the trappings of marriage. The more marriages the better! The more marriages per capita the better!! Women seem happy to buy into the spectacle, even though, in half of the cases, all they end up with is some stale cake and a photo album; and, of course, a guy who fails to hold up his end of her Cinderella fantasy about happily ever after. And who would blame him? It's a delusion.

One would think that the commercial trappings of marriage would bring on a severe dose of skepticism, followed by elopement, or city hall and a few toddies afterwards for the gang at the local tavern. Instead, the American hyper-marriage is passed off as a tradition to be observed by each and every bride, regardless of her age, nationality and the status of her hymen.

What tradition? In my marriage days, the white dress was a symbol of virginity (symbol, mind). As it turns out, the white dress is merely a fashion that was started by Queen Victoria when she married Prince Albert in 1840 (white satin and orange blossoms). Now the white wedding dress is de rigueur for boffing twenty-somethings and three-and-four-time divorcees, alike. The dress, the morning coats, the garter, the veil, the cake and the elaborate production—all are commercial inventions that have supplanted the basic ceremony which consisted of the words, I marry you. End of service.

The history of marriage explains both its private and public character. Privately, it was supposed to offer domestic stability, support in bringing up children, and guarantee lineage—at least it used to. Its public character fundamentally means that it is regulated by the state for all of the state's purposes. In the past, families essentially married other families, forging political and social alliances and economic advantages.

In the present, the companionate marriage, where the emotional bond is the end in itself, serves as the only reason worth mentioning for marriage: unless you're in love, you don't get married. This delusion (another one) ignores the actual reasons mentioned above and there are innumerable others. And of course, everyone assumes that respect and compatibility come as part of the marriage package.

The precondition to the marriage evaluation presumes that one accepts the fact that marriage between a woman and man changes their identity to wife and husband and that this will have a significant effect on the individual and the outcome of the married relationship. What kind of behavior can you expect from a man, in addition to what you already know before the big day? How will marriage affect your security; your social role? Will he be companionable and give you emotional support? Is he honest, trustworthy, fair and reliable? How's your sex life?

Are both of you willing or reluctant to discuss and enter into a pre-nuptial agreement? When it is drawn up, will you pay enough attention to its importance to see that it is structured so that any prejudice against women by your betrothed, his family, his attorney or the laws of the state you live in, are written out of this document?

Women lose things when they get into relationships and get married. It is very common to see a woman lose her identity, her individuality, her freedom, her energy; her apartment, car, career advantages, intellectual advantage; her friends; her money, time; her self-confidence, position in society, and on and on. When you examine your valuation of marriage, these are the places to look for the effect of marriage on your life. Make sure the numbers come up right.

> Even while marriage is declining in our culture, we cling to the romantic idea of soulmates: A 2003 survey found that 60 per cent of Americans—and 77 per cent of respondents in their early 20s—believe everyone has a true love.
> Erin Anderson, "Till next month do us part,"
> *Globe and Mail,* 9 June 2007

Motherhood

Motherhood is a reality at the very core of woman. No one has to make a case for it. Motherhood is not a value and not a right. As the fundamental pivot of human existence, it doesn't need to be qualified. It has, however, been co-opted and become a part of the morals package.

The idealization and sanctification of motherhood has resulted in innumerable myths (the mother of God), mischaracterizations (*the* defining experience in a woman's life), delusions (having a baby will solve my marriage problems) and platitudes (sacrifice anything for your children). In this interpretation, being a mother is not part of you, but defines what you are. Fortunately, life is larger than that.

Evaluating one's attitude about motherhood begins with defining the concept in the first place. Motherhood is the state of bearing and bringing up children. When they are no longer children, you are no longer in the -hood, which makes the condition one of finite duration. Once reached, it's time to reclaim the parts of your life you put aside and reconnect to your whole adult self. This presumes, of course, that one has made her own development an equal priority with the development of one's children. This is also the time when your kids are practicing being their separate selves, which you've been bringing them up to do.

Why do we value being mothers and how do we formulate these values? Can we possibly look at the value of children from the angle of motherhood? First you're a woman, a mother and then there's the child; instead of the reverse where the child defines your being. Can we focus on the subjective, "Why is it important that I be a mother?" instead of the objective, "I want to have a baby." How much sentiment, nostalgia, duty and outside pressure is brought to bear on our concept of motherhood?

Obviously, women's physical and emotional development is attached to the human life cycle. Life is valuable—the ultimate value—assuming the facts upon which life depends occupy the same status. When you add the rational dimension to the motherhood verity, the period of child rearing depends on the value of the mother's life first. The child is dependent with unconditional needs that mothering fulfills; not the other way around. Absent the rational dimension, motherhood is something inevitable that a woman is supposed to throw herself into, as though there were no option other than living for others. Options, therefore, should be the focus of the motherhood evaluation. If there are none, why do they not exist? Who eliminated them and what are the other solutions to mother becoming underling to the child? There is also the issue of timing in the motherhood equation and how children mesh with the flow of our lives. Many women "take time off to have children," which often means they relinquish the obligation to their own adult development. Some, of course, start bearing children before they've had a chance to develop an identity at all, which leaves their futures seriously compromised.

Being a Mother

Children, by their nature, believe that their needs are more important than their mother's life. These great egotists are the eternal agents for women's oppression. We go along with it. To protect their ego, we pretend that we don't have one of our own. Bringing up a child is creating reality. If we act subordinate, that reflection becomes part of them. So in the values analysis, what is it that you nurture? Their development or their ego?

If a woman fails to balance things out in the child's mind, when the child grows up, she models the same failure in her behavior and so it goes. This dynamic is the one that must be addressed by the woman in relationship with her children. When she sees it clearly herself and addresses it, all the little satellite egos are then capable of repairing themselves. Most kids "get it" and internalize the learning. But if they don't, the mother-child relationship will probably be permanently problematic.

Many children never lose their irrational expectations of their parents. These types believe highly in their own personal irresponsibility to deal with generational realities and tend to be mother scourges for the rest of their lives. As women commonly subscribe to the legend that mothers are always wrong, we are able to see solutions, but unable to act upon them. Instead of excising and cauterizing the roots of conflict and misunderstanding and demanding recognition as a free and independent woman, we treat our philosophical headache: "If I had it to do over, I would never have had them." This misplaced metaphorical band-aid can end up ruining our lives. Rather than imparting the wisdom that the mother has given the child the privilege of a life, women are still sucked into the "they didn't ask to be born" trap, hanging onto their role as goat in the ultimate blame game.

The mother-daughter relationship rates high on the motherhood misfortune scale, particularly in a time of cultural backlash, which is what we are in now. The repercussions and consequent repression affect mom; while daughter, being too young to understand its ramifications, tends to blame mom for everything, including her inability to think. This unique subset of the motherhood package—women's underdevelopment as it affects daughters' development—should be viewed with candor and intelligence, instead of misunderstanding and accusation. The healthy bond of mother and child is the process of helping the child to develop, while relinquishing control. But mom must also be affecting the process of her own growth and change, which will be reflected in her daughter's reality—for the better, not the worse.

> It's only when women are valued—independently of their relationship to other human beings—that daughters will no longer be afraid of being like their mothers.
> Jennifer Baumgardner and Amy Richards,
> *Manifesta: young women, feminism, and the future*

•

On the social level, it's always open season on women by the motherhood vigilantes. If women aren't breeding, something is amiss. And by some weird twist, this wrong is afflicted on the entire society! Working women; delayed childbearing; giving up children for a career; no kids equals selfish; no next generation and declining labor force! Such are the criticisms arrived at through patriarchal notions about what we are supposed to be doing with our lives and uteruses. Lurking in the subtext are insinuations about a woman's intellect, ambitions, independence and individuality, all of which create barriers to breeding. Instead of society adjusting, so that motherhood is part of a balanced life, it does the opposite, making motherhood even more difficult.

Becoming a mother is a woman's independent decision and has nothing to do with anything, or anyone, else. You are not your uterus and kids are not your immortality. You are not required to boost declining population figures, nor produce offspring for the labor force or military or pay into the social security coffers, contrary to what *The Empty Cradle*, Philip Congreve's book about fundamentalism and the birth rate suggests (and which hints at totalitarian solutions to remedy the problem of declining population). You are not obligated to be the vessel of a man's desire to keep his genes going and you are not required to produce grandchildren.

The Children's Story

The reader may be waiting to hear something about the children; and that, of course, is the problem. The children already have their stories, and on the motherhood level, they've been told at the expense of our own. Mothers have been denying their stories to satisfy the fables needed to keep the sentiment and nostalgia for childhood going. This scenario also makes possible the appearance of the bad mother, who is pitted against the sanctimonious expectations of perfecthood.

Charming though the genre may be, talking about children does not define your life—you do. The story of your life is one of expanding into your own potential—and children are part of that context, part of that whole life. You are not meant to deny them their history, but to tell your own in a different way. Motherhood has to be understood and valued in terms much larger than the diminutive constructs our identities have developed. So far, the motherhood story is sentimental hearsay, fueled by emotion and failure and irrational desires. These lead to distorted revelations which could only occur because the values that relate to this ontological condition are contrived by everyone but mom.

In her literary mystery, *Swann,* the late author, Carol Shields, talks about what gets passed on.

> I remember just how she said this. Generally I remember everything she says. The connective twine between us is taut with details. I have all her little judgements filed away, word perfect. There's scarcely a thought in my head, in fact, that isn't amplified or underlined by some comment of my mother's. This reinforces one of my life theories: that women carry with them the full freight of their mothers' words. It's the one part of us that can never be erased or revised.

Our individual motherhood narrative, having or being a mother, cannot be erased, but it certainly can be revised. This is the moment when it is more important than ever that women augment the motherhood mythology. We must tell the truth and apply the better ideas of a woman's life as we add to the cargo of all of our children's minds.

Truth Hurts; and Heals

Children grow up thinking that youth is superior to maturity, that motherhood is a life designed exclusively for their benefit, that their way is the right way and that mom has it wrong. Women's response, at this particular time in history, is to yield to this distorted message because they are unable to withstand the pressure from society and the youth-centered culture: "It's easier to give in than to fight with them."

The truth that hurts is that this is weak and destructive and that children are not capable of making mature decisions in their own interests. If it hurts a mother to realize she's weak inwardly and her passivity is destructive to her child, then one must face up to what is strong and positive. What values in your motherhood package make you strong and positive? These will turn out to be issues of womanhood, not motherhood. One must dare to turn the tables on a child's ego—forcing her to see life through a woman's eyes and life with a mother who conducts her life along an adult, and not childish lines. Of course it can be painful. But everybody has to learn that there are many centers to life's universe.

Having your own life can deliver truths that cause grievous hurts to a tender heart and mind. But the wounds of childhood heal, if they are tended by a woman who is committed to things beyond those important only to childish ways. However you handle it, when they are grown, they indeed will offer their objections to their upbringing and itemize your character flaws. Whether they speak them or scream them will indicate how well you've done.

> I've been all over the world, trying to find the key to the castle my mother and my heart are still locked up in.
>
> Roy Blount Jr., *Be Sweet*

*

> I hated my mom.
>
> Roy Blount Jr., *Be Sweet*

CHAPTER 19

STORY POWER

M ale power controls the cultural narrative, which is what we tell ourselves about ourselves. This power obliterates and invalidates women's take on reality. The following quotation points at the problem.

> Men may live more truly and fully in reading Plato and Shakespeare than at any other time, because they are participating in essential being and are forgetting their accidental lives.
>
> Harold Bloom, *The Closing of the American Mind*

Bloom confuses ontology (essential being) with abstraction (mind plus text) and values escapism (living fully in reading) over experience (unwilled life). He suggests, (inadvertently, I gather) how man thwarts his own evolution and in light of male power, ours with it. Bloom's thinking is disappointed, stale and incapable of imagining a better world. Nonetheless, he is a literary and cultural authority.

The following is a quickie version of what we, as cultural beings, should be telling ourselves about ourselves, using that old reliable, Darwin, as a catapult.

> In the past five hundred years, Americans (excluding Natives, who have their own stories) have continuously progressed from a social structure of strong enslaving weak, rich indenturing poor, the powerful controlling thought and

mobs controlling minds, to a state of law and order and universal freedom for all, but not in the case of women.

More recently, women have risen up to struggle against male domination—gaining ground, increasing momentum, and slowly surmounting the predictable patriarchal backlash to their progress. Women's struggles and reforms are a natural outcome of the human drive for freedom from oppression and, in turn, the survival of the human race.

Females distinguish themselves from males in this drive by their aptitude to alter, for the better, themselves and that which exists around them. Women apply new creative solutions to remedy situations and move them along. Males, on the other hand, tend to recycle old problem junk and give it a new name or go off on intellectual tangents from which they can seldom return.

Now, whereas those who maintain control of the Dominant Voice will support (or at least not laugh off the page) Bloom's theories, they will rail against my rendition of what we should tell ourselves about ourselves as something to be pooh-poohed and haw-hawed. Life described from the point-of-view which I have chosen elicits hostility and ridicule. So why is Bloom's claim any more credible than mine? Because: **The Dominant Voice prepares the ground for what we are to believe.**

What is worthwhile is decided from the phallocentric point-of-view. The power of the Dominant Voice decides what we are willing to listen to. It conditions us to automatically reject feminist ideas by branding them radical and anti-male, and therefore dangerous; and then proceeds to justify its assessment with the male versions of truth and real life. Rhetorical scare tactics emitted from the Dominant Voice result in women's fear of hearing. The ears and mind close off to broadening one's field of perception and understanding ourselves in relation to the conditions around us. This then, is the story, the tragedy, of our lives. Not Bloom's tripe about Plato and Shakespeare.

The Story of the Story

We live in the story of our lives. Our original minds and formative years are nurtured on the stories of our culture. These are combined with the residue of experience in our memory—an interconnecting fabric of accounts and snippets of the events, processes, thoughts and fictions we have grown up with, deliberately or not. Our bodies give us stories, too. And our emotions offer narratives that our minds could only dream of.

We connect with others and to the external world through stories. We join into the circle of life through culture. Culture can be described as an "environment of narrations that make self-evident sense in explaining human behavior." From this angle, the process of living ends up as an unending series of stories strung together—or a big anthology, selected over a long period of time—which we, as individuals, must make sense of.

And so we gravitate to story. Tellers of story. Books and news. Gossip. Movies and tv and bullshitters at the bar. The classic, the myth, the well-crafted "piece;" the Bible; titillating trash, theater, the presidential election. Visual arts, songs and music. Our memories, dreams, perceptions and imaginings. We lose ourselves and get embroiled in stories.

Through story, the kaleidoscope of human life is brought to mingle with our hearts and souls. Through it, we find the past and liberate the imagination. Intelligent response unlocks words to reveal the truth about human identity and behavior and the values that have shaped the story.

Story is two-sided: it implies an audience. Reader, onlooker, listener, keeping solidarity with the message; or, because of the teller's intention or hearer's aversion, exclusion. We all relate, or not, on a micro or macro level and anywhere in between. Because this is the medium through which we come to know ourselves, we must narrow down this grand narrative and evaluate it in terms of how it correlates with women's reality and intentions for the future.

Growing up female, we are conditioned to be seduced by story. Classical or trash, we are after that one thing: to be carried away. In the passionate tale, story and reader become reversible, locked together in the allure of patterns and imagery whose value we not only recognize, but are culturally poised to emulate. We become entrapped in the image of passionate seduction, and are unable to distinguish between the real and the contrived. And it may not end there. Many of us carry over the model into adult life, renaming it "hope." We hope that life will turn out like the tales of our cultural directives.

We lose ourselves in the story, believing that within the pages, our true selves can be found. Which is a tragedy, because we emerge from this story with romantic notions and frustrated desires, and indisposed to separate the fictions from the real world. The Cinderella story is the classic example. Told that we will be rescued from our limitations by a superior male who will cause us to live happily ever after, we are destroyed when the promise and its trappings fail, often tragically and irreversibly. This is as true today as it always has been. Only the jobs and decor have changed.

"Women are constructed not born," wrote Simone de Beauvoir, author of *The Second Sex*, meaning we're playing roles and wearing costumes. Stories lead us out of our essential character, claiming to know us better than we know ourselves. A million discoveries! Telling us what we have longed to find words for. Stories reveal the secrets of our kind—warning us against danger and against our own predations.

> In these readings, a sense that the text has appeared to be wholly new, never before seen, is followed, almost immediately, by the sense that it was *always there*, that we the readers, knew it was always there, and have *always known* it was as it was, though we have now for the first time recognised, become fully cognisant of, our knowledge.
>
> A.S. Byatt, *Possession*

Then they betray us, like Prince Charming does. We grow out of these stories. We will no longer be constructed. We have not found the promised man, the great career, the style, clothes, or allure of the drop-dead glamorous. Or maybe we have, but they've fleeted away, because we never learned how to keep them. We fall from the invented ease of the storybook scenario and wake up conscious; ready for the real push toward our individuality.

•

There is an omnipresent metaphorical frame through which we learn to know ourselves, the people and the world. This is the male worldview, and its values do not take into account the wisdom and experience of women, except where these serve its purpose. And there is a corresponding willingness in women—masochism even—that sustains and collaborates with this view. When we seek the truth at the essence of the story or image, we do so using judgments fabricated by male values (unless our texts have been vetted by feminist methodology—a rare occasion in the mainstream or at the grassroots level). The error may be inadvertent, but it is reality, all the same.

> Books make sense of life—the problem is that the lives they
> make sense of are other people's lives, never your own.
>
> Julian Barnes, *Flaubert's Parrot*

Julian Barnes is talking about being human, but by "other people" and "your own" he means men. He could be referring to women, though this is dubious, considering his rogueishness, literature and the world. If the gender declension were intended, it refers to two-dimensional, truncated, sentimental caricatures. But no matter. Despite our disillusionment, and in keeping with our social conditioning, we carry on with schizophrenic abandon, losing ourselves in male illusions: devalued, made small and less human than they, and not intended to share in the spirit of the thing. But we are meant to buy in, read it and, of course, praise it, which we more often than not, do.

We are co-opted into participating with their male characters and their sub-intelligent expressions of the female condition, therefore identifying against ourselves. We become allies in defiling our own common sense, as well as our sacred female imagery. We become a tangle of contradictions. The self created by our gendered storybook imagination is in contradiction with the nature of our experience. Who was to know?!

This phenomenon—buying into the dominant narrative—reveals a distinct lack of self-scrutiny. If you apply the same principles to a story, as you would to a person's words or behavior, would you still be willing to support it? When it argued or implied that you were inherently inferior to "other people" because of your gender? Can you face the fact that you've acted against your own identity and will live to tell of it? If you can do this, you are a great candidate for breaking the ground and creating the cultural environment for women's narrative to become an equal power.

Our Lives, Male Version

The story of womankind from the male point-of-view is the identity paradigm we grow up with: our lives, male version. This is a powerful force for the rationale of male order. Stories carry in them not only the hierarchical opposition of male and female, but the assumptions, presumptions and symbols that reinforce it. Story—how facts and ideas are related—has great social and cultural value to the patriarchy.

Sexist fundamentalism is ubiquitous. It begins with the tale of woman's manufacture out of Adam's rib. In language, the etymological relation of man-woman is inescapable; and "he" is the universal pronoun. The American myth of universal freedom is defined in male terms and it is the aim of conservative forces to perpetuate the myth at the expense of women's equal position in society and standing under the law.   Anti-feminist propaganda fuels the suppression of the story of women's progress.

And there is the neutrality myth.   Stories that claim to be gender irrelevant are structurally framed according to the hierarchical notions of the dominant ideology and resonate subconsciously with the power dynamics implicit in the story.   They are not neutral.   They convey the patriarchal agenda both directly and indirectly.   This lopsided account of life indicates that sexism and misogyny are an intrinsic part of the culture.   And we shape our characters in the matrix of this grand narration.

The depiction of gender inequality and male superiority in story gives men a great advantage.   The subject is seldom discussed, because the representation of women in texts is generally not up for discussion, unless she is the title character.   In these cases, she is observed from the point of male advantage, having been written from the point of male advantage, obscuring the situation further.   Critics may indeed attempt to deconstruct the story, but they do not, however, attempt to deconstruct the unacknowledged feminist issue.   Anna Karenina is analyzed as a woman trapped in a bad marriage with a kid, ravaged by love, who jumps in front of a train to kill herself.   But she is not assessed as a woman who acts out her ontological and philosophical principles to escape a rigged predestination. That would take a whole new book.

The values inherent in the cultural narration bind us together in dreams and sorrow, hope and fear—innumerable hearts and souls in universal agreement, without hardly ever drawing a convincing portrait of women. What is it, then, that resonates?

What are the alternatives against which we test ourselves?

What happens to our unknown—those hidden drives and untamed motives?   What is the value of "the canon," that narrative of grand ideas, to women?   If civilization is so valuable, where are the models, the lessons, that teach women how to grow into mature and independent human beings?   Jane Austin, George Elliott and Emily Dickinson simply don't cut it.   Three won't do.

The male version is the universal version.   In it, we are liars, tempters, sinners.   Consumptive martyrs.   A good or bad mom, a "caring but powerless mother," not loving-enough mother and a neglectful one.   The helpless twit, sleeper to the top, the bitch, gossip, pushover, nobody; blonde, moron, victim.   And another winner: pure womanhood which eventually reveals its dark underside. And the scenario is written in stone. Here in a nutshell is the classic stuff of storified woman in the male tradition. (And its female counterpart, the romance novel, is polar sexist slop.)

He says: Hello. I'll grind you down. I want to fuck you. You're trying to destroy me. You want to cut my balls off. You talk to much. I'd like you better dead. I'm leaving you. I'm a desirable seducer and I can have someone better than you. Even that 13-year old next door.

She says: I'll drop everything. I'm sorry. The government should have retrained you. What shall I be, slut or madonna? I love you. I can't live without you. What a great cock you have. I didn't mean it. I'd sacrifice anything for you. Don't go or I'll kill myself. Are you tired of me? I've seen the way that little bitch looks at you. Pray with me.

Author: Phew! Redeemed at last!

But time moves on, and so do the makers and consumers of narratives. The bedrock scenario continues to morph into new and improved versions of itself: bigger and better horror-porn, sadomasochism and other misogynies suitable for every imaginable medium and taste. And murdering women never gets stale.

•

Of course there are blips on the narrative horizon causing stirs in the gender universe. Males confirm, for instance, that although women should still be punished for refusing to stay cowed, if they have sex they needn't necessarily rehabilitate and die. (This may be on its way back, considering the present-day political tone.) Multitudes of talented women have taken up the challenge to voice their own minds with uncommonly interesting and significant results. There are brilliant models of female expression in every area of life. But the horizon is not reality. Considering the void, and the enduring political, social and cultural backlash against women's advancement, it will take evolution, not emulation, to exert the vision of women's truth and principles into this society and into life itself.

Myths and Ancient Texts

History, culture, everyday references, psychology and language are permeated by myth. Myths are set in the past and populated by archetypes. These characters act out human traits that are tricky to deal with, and have archetypal experiences, known as universals (experiences everyone can relate to.) Their job is to route us along certain paths of cognizance and instruct us on figuring out how we should behave, "or else." On the surface, most myths look like men blowing off steam, and worse—and women feeling the heat, and worse.

The uber story of myth is the devaluation of the goddess. Over time, the idea of woman has been systematically degraded, always reflecting man's jealousy of woman's creative power and his desire to usurp her position. Throughout prehistoric, ancient, Western, Eastern and Oriental mythology, the male has triumphed over the Great Mother. Her image has been sullied and her power denied; and language has been cleansed of female association. Male has become the great procreator and the mythic dimension of masculinity has shaped the generalized human experience and human mind itself. (See chart, "World Cultures," Chapter 6.) On the story level, women and their lives are minor incidents of the male experience.

Ancient myths once showed men and women locking horns in equal measure while playing out the rip-roaring drama of actually living. But once religion got a grip on the form, the story was not for learning. It became a powerful tool for social control. Good and evil told people how to behave and gender presumptions made sure women fell in line under male control. By now the Great Father was in charge and everything went downhill from there. On his watch, Lilith and Eve brought sin into the world and this primal characterization—woman as the carrier of sin and guilt—brought with it all other weaknesses, including innocence. Myth now had us domesticated, living apart from society with all of its threats and promise. We were now on earth to nurture, heal and mend the social fabric at home, living a life of suspended development and devoid of emotional and intellectual growth. Mature womanhood not wanted. Infantilism was the ultimate result and is obvious today in things like the rage for bigger breasts and clinging to the notion that forever young is a human right, rather than just a perky idea.

Mythology is the story of the male using brute force, deceit and theft to strip women of their primacy and forcing us to live in dishonor, on patriarchal terms, and within the constraints of male law and values. It is hardly any wonder that this take on life—the model and the reality—has caused a permanent derangement of our values and senses. And hardly any wonder that women have lost their survival skills, their language skills and their courage, and have relied on men for both solutions to, and protection from, their problems. And that women are frightened of commanding emotions, like those which drove the feminist movement of the sixties and seventies.

Mythology is a self-perpetuating form. Tales, folklore and the stories we use to try to understand the complexities of our reality, update themselves in language and symbols appropriate to the times. The distorted values result in powerful delusions, like the one against which we all pit ourselves at the present: the superwoman, meaning full-time career, marriage and motherhood. The patriarchal values package has conned women into thinking that this should be the status quo, and that anything less means failure. Can she or can't she? the myth goes. The sub-myth implies that it is best that she can't. Better she goes without the family package or without the power-money package.

When this story about work and family is told truthfully, by mature women and against the backdrop of the distorted worldview that determines our reality, then it *should* make the myth canon. It really would be helping us to figure out how to live more heartened and less harried lives. Meanwhile, we have to stomach the story of a tough broad, mentored in men's ways, clawing her way up to an infertile selfhood—competing for credibility with a harried mom defending her feminine role and who alas, never has time for romance. The story, as usual, is still fabricated by the tale tellers whose imaginations are ruled by the dominant narrator.

Two Sex Myths

Two contemporary myths about sexuality are worth considering in the context of creating a new narrative. One is the theory of sublimation; the other, the myth of women's sexual equality. The first is an airy fairy idea; the second is a more practical notion. Both profoundly affect perceptions about women's reality and how we think about our power to influence the culture.

Sublimation: the Myth of Culture

This is a male invention of why and how we live a life. The remarkable tale has been boilerplate philosophy and psychology since the beginning of both, and is still going strong today. Sublimation allegedly explains creativity and has taken on many versions. Freud, for instance, combines his "pleasure principle" with conquest and destruction and the life force, and attributes his amazing merger as the cause for the rise of society and culture. Here is a quickie about how the sublimation idea goes:

Men invented culture to elevate themselves above their own psychosexual urges. In other words, without this means of suppressing his base instincts (sublimation), life would be unfettered sex and we'd all be running around, willy nilly, fornicating ourselves into oblivion.

The sublimation pomposity could only be dreamt up by privileged dominators who, along with the brutes, enslave and coerce others to do the work of life, without which there is no survival, never mind culture. That is to say, the theory of "sublimation" is the intellectual perversion of the abject and useless.

The sublimation contortion predicates the story of the evolutionary blockage in male development. It is based on men's inability to accept female sexual independence, combined with the conceptual error of substituting this reality with dominance and violence, and in so doing, limiting his own growth. The inevitable by-product of this bizarre reasoning is the denial of his own female nature.[26]

This is self-deception of great magnitude and there is no end to the misery it has caused for everybody. The confusion is covered up by passions for abstract ideas and ideologies which inevitably collapse and revert to overt, rather than internalized, sadomasochism politics.

> This interpretation may follow easily from a society which has separated and assigned to one sex the only potentialities for action, decision and power.
>
> Jean Baker Miller, M.D.,
> *Toward a New Psychology of Women*

The normal female does not need to be orgasmic day and night. The erotic is all around us. Creative acts, social interaction, communing with each other; the manifestation of our labors, improvement, accomplishment;

---

[26] According to French feminist Hélène Cixous, a few men found a way around their self-inflicted repression. As Reynolds and Press describe it in *The Sex Revolts*, ". . . male avant gardists like Joyce and Mallarme were somehow engaged in *ecriture feminine*; they were able to rupture the strictures of patriarchal thought and syntax because they had special access to the "dark continent" of femininity."

process, progress and completion; art, literature, music, sights and sounds; the day and night; the glory of nature. Beauty, basic human goodness. Things that make you happy, content, feel good; the wonder of existence. All of this is erotic. Self-restraint is erotic, men are erotic, sex is erotic. Life is sexual and it is not pathology, it's life. Onanism, priapism and the addiction to orgasm are definitely not erotic. And it is our job to demystify, or demolish, concepts like sublimation, which are built on the suppression of the feminine principle and oppression of womankind.

Our Myth: Sexual Equality

> The failure of the American fictionist to deal with adult heterosexual love and the consequent obsession with death, incest and innocent homosexuality[27] are not merely matters of historical interest or literary relevance. They affect the lives we lead from day to day and influence the writers in whom the consciousness of our plight is given clarity and form.
>
> Leslie A. Fiedler, *Love and Death in the American Novel*

The narrative issue that Fiedler refers to above (writing in 1960 about Mark Twain's *Huckleberry Finn* and other towering American literary works), is a product of the gender split and the asymmetrical values which circumscribe male and female adult life. Men's identity is formed in relation to the world and women's in a relationship of intimacy with a man. Since the sexual revolution of the sixties, the human narrative has been augmented by the strong voices of many progressive women. However, the patriarchal corpus remains intact and has itself been augmented by the characteristic self-defense of the male against women's stand. There is not less macho posturing, homosexual flattery, and misogynistic "inspiration." there is more.

Sexual stereotypes persist. The male-dominated cultural canon endures. The dominant narrative is rehashed daily, by men and women alike, in every aspect of media and entertainment. Extreme pornography and soft core continue to dish up the slut. Film and television closes in on the clitoris. And the few durable nonfiction narrations that beg for mature dialogue about sexuality—the battle for women's reproductive control, child abduction into white slavery and prostitution, and ecstasy and erection drugs pushed on everybody—remain at the tsk-tsk stage. The sexualization of children and ludicrous statements like "blow-jobs-aren't-sex" as sustained by political

---

[27]This changed after the Stonewall riots in New York in 1969 which launched the gay liberation movement. Someone said it's no longer Joe and Huck, but Chuck and Buck.

rhetoricians, preteen girls and the media have not become topics of serious debate. So far, the culture seems to be "alright with it."

In spite of progress, the universal sexist narrative will remain intact. Women will be sexual objects. Women challenging the sexual order will be destroyed in court (rape, abortion, birth control) and worse. Fundamentalists will blab on about their providential arrangement of "godly males and beautiful women." Books like Margaret Atwood's *The Handmaid's Tale,* will be banned. The gaslighting will keep pace with the truth. Men and their lackey women will continue to make efforts to convince the world that women's version of reality is nothing but the twisted and paranoid spawn of her imagination. To expropriate a woman's body, or not, is never an issue from the male point-of-view, so don't expect empathy. They *will* defend their territory, which is what they consider your body to be. You can depend on it.

> The problem with the great literature of the past is that it doesn't tell you how to live with real endings.
>
> Marilyn French, *The Women's Room*

CHAPTER 20

YOUR STORY OF THE STORY

This section is where we get down to the basics of thinking through feminist principles as they may apply to saying what you think—or even think you think—but have not had the opportunity to express. Through the use of story, we can shape our language and view of ourselves in terms of larger and more potent truths. We decide where we stand, consider the narrative issues, and develop new ways of talking about all of it.

Texts—stories, myths, fiction, nonfiction—are the most manageable forms of communication to think about. They stabilize the complications of human affairs and make them accessible. Brief selections of text are used to stimulate thinking about things from new angles. In the process, we are applying feminist standards of importance and reasonableness as they relate to any and all external communication.

The sample texts which follow are chosen to represent a variety of random themes. There is no one type of statement, coming from one or another sex or particular genre. The authors are not necessarily icons of male chauvinism nor are they labeled as "good or bad." The texts are about subjects we can all relate to. They serve to connect you to a point of your own experience—an issue, character, situation, feeling, or any concept that the text might bring to mind. This connection is the point of departure for shaping ideas and expression to serve you, rather than constrain you. Along with the text is a statement of the theme and a brief summary of the content. Then you work with the text from your own point-of-view.

•

Your story of the story is about the difference that lies between the dominant cultural narrative of what it supposedly means to be a woman, and your life. The objective is to unearth and stimulate new descriptions of the female experience. The ultimate goal on the Road to Wisdom is to create meaning and a good place to start is accepting the fact that we've allowed men supremacy and collaborated in our own stereotypes and cliches, undercutting our goals and diminishing the possibilities in all relationships and aspects of life. This by no means suggests guiltiness, but rather that we increase self-knowledge and take deliberate action to set the record straight.

While working through this, one must avoid acting on two important impulses. The first is the tendency to perceive what the text describes according to its historical context. This would be jumping into the quagmire of traditional cultural authority. The point is to dislocate the hierarchical mental structures implicit in the text, not empathize with them.

The other impulse we must resist is falling into the polarity trap that all men are bastards. This powerful, reactionary deception prevents women from making accurate assessments about men at all. When we go in this direction, we are accompanied by the fear—and fallacy—that criticism of one aspect, implies condemnation of the whole.

This method is a feedback system, where women put their original imprint on the story of their lives in relation to our culture. We are creating stories that will be written into the narrative of the future; a future where the supremacy of the male narrative is a story of the past—or at least one that we are not afraid to attack or dismantle.

Sample Texts

Text #1

The center of courtly love is the convention of the inferiority of the lover to his mistress—or, more properly, to the Mistress, that physically undefined, faceless and history-less goddess, cruel, remote, and desirable. In a society where, by law and custom, women were disposed of at the will of their fathers and husbands, where it would have been considered a lack of manliness not to rape an unprotected lower-class female, and where the Church insisted upon the submission of wives to husbands and preached the essential unchastity of all women—in such a society, the lover pretended the most abject humility before an idealized beloved, submitted to her most outrageous whims without regard to dignity and in the teeth of reason.

Leslie A. Fiedler, *Love and Death in the American Novel*

THEME: Chivalry.
SUMMARY: Courtly love is the fallacious narrative about men in the thrall of women. The reverse is true. Men dominate women sexually and socially and religion preaches that all women are wanton.

Text/s #2

And the Lord spoke unto Moses, saying, Speak unto the children of Israel, saying, If a woman have conceived seed, and born a male child, then she shall be unclean seven days; according to the days of the separation for her infirmity shall she be unclean. . . . And she shall then continue in the blood of her purifying three and thirty days; she shall touch no hallowed thing, nor come into the sanctuary, until the days of her purifying be fulfilled. But if she bear a female child, then she shall be unclean two weeks, as in her separation; and she shall continue in the blood of her purifying three score and six days.

Moses, "Leviticus 12:1-5," *Holy Bible*

Behold, I was shaped in iniquity, and in sin did my mother conceive me.

David, "Psalms 51:5," *Holy Bible*

And when the days of her purification according to the law of Moses were accomplished, they brought him to Jerusalem, to present him to the Lord. (As is written in the law of the Lord, Every male that openeth the womb shall be called holy to the Lord.)

Luke, "The Gospel According to Luke 2:22-23," *Holy Bible*

THEME: Sex. Childbirth is a sin; women are dirty; all males are holy.
SUMMARY: Leviticus (1450-1410 B.C.): God tells Moses women sin by giving birth and must be purified. She is nearly ten times as impure if she bears a female child. Psalms (10th Century B.C.): David's mother is the

cause of his darkness and sin. Luke (A.D. 60): Mary purifies herself after Jesus' birth, then takes the child to the temple. God says all males born of woman are holy.

Text #3

> In 1959, just before going to Hayden, Judith wrote me a note asking me to safeguard her survivor files. I opened the file boxes soon after her departure. Along with the clippings, I discovered pages of handwritten annotations. I knew what those pages represented: they were the makings of poems. Yet this didn't matter to me. I believed that those pages, perhaps more than anything else, nourished Judith's illness. I told myself I had to act, to overcome my usual passivity. Judith could no longer cope. She desperately needed my help; our shared anguish had to end.
>
> A few days after she left, I threw away all her files.
>
> In 1965, I acted once again in defiance of Judith's wishes. She had wanted her journal to be read by one person—a man she deeply mistrusted but also needed—and then destroyed. Instead I saved it, hiding it as if it were my own secret life.
>
> But it wasn't; it was Judith's. And I've only just begun understanding what it meant for her to record that life.
>
> Martha Cooley, *The Archivist*

THEME: Husband destroys wife's papers which are the authentic record of her life.
SUMMARY: Judith asks her husband (the narrator of book) to safeguard her writings before she goes to the asylum. He decides they are part of her problem and throws them away. Later he keeps her journal which she has entrusted him to read and then destroy. Afterwards, he has insights into her and her work.

Text #4

> *Kate*: . . . Come, come, you froward and unable worms,
> My mind hath been as big as one of yours,
> My heart as great, my reason haply more,
> To bandy word for word and frown for frown;
> But now I see our lances are but straws,
> Our strength as weak, our weakness past compare,
> That seeming to be most which we indeed least are.

Then vail your stomachs, for it is no boot,
And place your hands below your husband's foot,
In token of which duty, if he please,
My hand is ready, may it do him ease.
Petruccio: Why, there's a wench! Come on, and kiss me, Kate.

William Shakespeare, *The Taming of the Shrew*

THEME: The rightness of the superiority of male over female.
SUMMARY: Virtually the final words of the play. After five acts of defying Petruccio's demands for her submission, Kate finally caves in—and calls upon the others to do the same. She begs off her previous stand with claims of pitiable weakness. She exhort all to lower themselves and be prepared to put themselves beneath their husbands' foot. Petruccio is happy and wants to kiss her.

Text #5

I have nothing to say about any of the talented women who write today. Out of what is no doubt a fault in me, I do not seem able to read them. Indeed I doubt if there will be a really exciting woman writer until the first whore becomes a call girl and tells her tale.

Norman Mailer, "Evaluations—
Quick and Expensive Comments on the Talent in the Room,"
Advertisements for Myself

THEME: Misogyny and dismissal of women writers.
SUMMARY: The only worthwhile writing by a woman would be the story of a whore's transition into a call girl.

Text #6

There was cleavage on display Wednesday afternoon on C-SPAN2. It belonged to Sen. Hillary Clinton. . . . The cleavage registered after only a quick glance. . . . Throughout Clinton's time as first lady, she wore clothes that were feminine and stately. . . . The cleavage, however, is an exceptional kind of flourish. After all, it's not a matter of what she's wearing but rather what's being revealed. . . . Showing cleavage is a request to be engaged in a particular way. . . .

To display cleavage in a setting that does not involve cocktails and hors d'oeuvres is a provocation. . . .

Robin Givhan,
"Hillary Clinton's Tentative Dip Into New Neckline Territory,"
Washington Post, 20 July 2007

THEME: Female politician has separate breasts.
SUMMARY: Woman in the South, in midsummer, wears less constricted clothing than usual in public. Her cleavage is noticeable and suggests provocative behavior.

Creating the Record

Even a small amount of text allows a high degree of access to its original intentions and ideas. A sentence can be used as a window into your own wisdom and a way to reveal reality.

When you contemplate the text with an independent mind, essential knowledge about the contents, and about you, yourself, is revealed. Independent means not in polar response to anything male. Polarities merely produce the opposite of what is already there. The challenge is to expand what we think and say about intention and implication.

Abstract from Feminist's Viewpoint

In a few words, the subject or issue apparent on the surface of each text is described from the standpoint of feminist knowledge, defamiliarizing the common context that pops into mind. Avoid thinking along the lines the culture leads us in; overcome the tyranny of our own conditioning to empathize with weakness, or genuflect to the power of what is presumably acceptable.

Text #1. *ABSTRACT—Love and Death in the American Novel*
This double-deceit—the humble lover and the powerful mistress—is the bedrock of the essential cultural lie. The narrative about "courtly love" acts as a cultural smokescreen that disguises the brutality of male sexual domination over women and women's abject powerlessness.

Text #2. *ABSTRACT—Holy Bible*
God and Moses set up all women as the scapegoats for sex and guilt in the beginning of Judeo-Christian ideology. Centuries later, Kind David is

still blaming mom for his lust and the desirability of Bathsheba. By the time we get to the New Testament, nothing has changed. In spite of Mary's "immaculate conception" by none other than God himself, and bearing the human-divine Jesus, Mary is considered dirty for giving birth.

Instead of addressing men's crude impulse to have sex with a woman immediately after she's given birth, they tar the mother with their filth brush.

Males escape any consequence for their part in both the going in (impregnation) and coming out (birth) in this arrangement because God says so. There is no way out of this male lust-guilt trap for girls and women who bear "mankind."

Text #3. *ABSTRACT—The Alchemist*
This story is about a man's destructive power over the expression of a woman's truth at the intimate level. She is deprived of authority; the meaning of her life is lost.

Text #4. *ABSTRACT—The Taming of the Shrew*
The denouement is a predictable reversal in the reality of sexist relationships. After putting up the good fight for her independence, Kate caves into self-denigration and groveling. Thus, Petruccio's position as dominant male is secure, as is hers, as the submissive female.

Text #5. *ABSTRACT—Advertisements for Myself*
Comments like this, which first appeared in 1959, are still in use; recently in "Art of the Feud," *New York Times*, 19 November 2006. A well-known woman hater, Mailer's persona as a literary figure is more valuable to the culture than are his misogyny and vile ideas about women, disreputable.

Text #6. *ABSTRACT—Washington Post* article
After decades in public life, newspaper prints that those bumps in Senator Clinton's front are actually breasts. Reporter attempts to expose a hidden sexual motive behind this revelation.

Transition Out of Text

The text is your symbol, symptom or cause. Now you begin to decide what, exactly, about this story or idea you will express. How does it relate to your thoughts, feelings, experience? With feminist knowledge in mind, what do you want to say about it? From this point, the narrative has no particular authority and by extension, the message of social and cultural oppression that the text implies is disabled.

This is where the keepers of the culture get riled. "You can't change the classics! You can't just take that out of context! Before he dies, the King (or whoever) says bla, bla. . . ." With the same assuredness that authors project their imaginations, perceptions or concepts, we in turn are conditioned with a complimentary assuredness to interpret them along the lines that they intend. This arrangement is what the keepers are trying to protect.

I use these texts to serve my values in my time and place and for my own purposes. I am contributing to the creation of a new narrative. I have no reason to justify the inadequate personal or historical nature of underlying its values or predicaments, as there would be no benefit in it. My agenda is to elevate thought by using texts that have passed cultural muster and relating them to women's reality—in retrospect.

The alleged "way," according to cultural mores, would be to exonerate the archive of its diminution and misogyny and attribute this to "the times," making it impossible to take women's experience seriously—this "seriously" also a value appropriated by the male. According to traditional criteria, one should understand, excuse because of circumstances and move on, which is the virtuous way for women to handle things—virtue being a part of the values package, spun off to romanticize and weaken women.

In real life, proclaiming the immutability of the cultural archives is nonsense, or a smokescreen to keep the patriarchal power intact and women in their eternal stupor about this issue. Patriarchal ethics are constructed on gender inequality. Just as males have used their imagination and power to keep the narrative devoid of plot, story or models to accurately portray or guide women, so can women rationally access our right to free thought and attack this strategy, and escape this trap.

Thus, we step out of this historical arrangement. This is chosen power. You, as a living, communicating human being are no longer at a disadvantage because of the dominant narrative. And because of this, you will find strength you never would have believed you had, in just a few words of text. Backed by feminist knowledge and the power of language, you need no longer be overshadowed by the repressive cultural narrative.

In And Out of Narrative Sexism

Fortunately, we have conceptual tools to use for our advancement. Using the feminist standpoint as an anchor, we open up the subject by highlighting certain generic angles. We start off with observations about intention and implication and take it from there. This provides a springboard for insights upon which to build original statements of how you really live in the world. What you're up against, why you don't back down; what you reject and why; what you expect from others; or demand of the world you have been too timid to challenge; take control, where once you were passive; speak, where you were silent.

We are looking for hidden meanings, faulty logic, conspicuous absences; finding both blatant and barely perceptible slights. We use our intellect in liberating our own consciousness from the many cultural derivations of women's presumed inferiority. We take the creative way to subvert what is allegedly reasonable but not; or overturn any inherent assumptions and claims that are flawed on the basis of overvaluation. And the central question is this: what means does the story take, or content imply, to reinforce asymmetry, inequality and inferiority?

Here are a few random ideas about where to look for traps in any narrative.

• Do the women's circumstances carry a personal history of underdevelopment without clarification of its external and internal causes?

• Does the author impose values on women's education or socialization without allowing her a response, destroying her in the process, i.e., forced stereotype?

• Does the writer make woman a victim (beware of "lover" or "assailant")?

• Is death a substitute for life (beware of sacrifice)? How is courage valued—in living for a cause, let's say; or dying for it? Whose cause? How, what does it benefit her (beware of martyr complex)?

• Is woman completely devoid of intellectual ability or volition or initiation, i.e., unable to address any issue whatsoever?

• Does the attractiveness of the charming male layabout minimize the successful female?

• Is the muse, dream girl, ghost, pawned off as creativity rather than a regurgitative tool used to mask creative failure in the face of the pressures to soldier on in the business of story making?

• Is original-sin woman in there—taking the wrap for everyone else?

We all identify to some extent with the moral and functional abilities of women in texts because we grow into life with these models in mind. This story review offers the practical experience of constructing our own escape hatch from this phenomenon. Sort out the facts of life from delusion and denigration. How does this particular story fit in? What does it bring up in your actual life?

Developing Story into Language

The stories we are creating are about having faith in a leap of consciousness. What is the story if you become your uncensored self, or if you speak against the fear of expressing your own power? Confidence is the key. As in any creative pursuit, there is no way to know in advance exactly where you are going. But bearing in mind feminist principles and knowledge, you can center yourself to avoid backsliding and unrealistic expectations. Whatever the subject material evokes within us, we are bound to find words for those thoughts. And if you can't explain "it," then the story is about what you can't explain.

> Mother kept her promise. She'd gotten up changed from her month in bed. For one thing, she was now inclined to say whatever was on her mind right in front of God and everybody. Even Father.
>
> Barbara Kingsolver, *The Poisonwood Bible*

Reframe the Story

Focus on any one of the six sample texts. What would be important for you to say in this situation or about this topic? What does it bring up in your actual life? Using the text as a tool, we establish our point-of-view from a feminist standpoint. We retreat from the demands of the conventional narrative; unrestricted, unrepressed mind wiping out personal inhibitions, based on false values. Do not constrain yourself to fit into what other important people in your life would expect you to say. The answer comes from opening your perceptions and widening your scope. What you want to say about it is your angle, or point-of-view.

From the angle you have chosen, what is right for you to say in order to transcend the constraints, or falsehoods in the text as they relate to your perceptions of reality? In the context of the issue in the text, specify your authentic position: where you stand. You have now created a new framework for what to think and say about the topic. Angle and reframing are the tools of discovery. They allow us to speak meaningfully and creatively, or with total abandon. There are no narrative boundaries. Your creative abilities have replaced the values of the dominant narrative in importance. And remember, we're on the Road to Wisdom, seeking the treasures of the negated consciousness. As adults, the creative imagination embodies truth, insight, instinct and experience. Rein in the fantasies. Save them for the fantastical.

While the simple polarity of man-woman is out, the text will nonetheless call for you to set yourself in relation to something. A person (man, woman, living, dead, imaginary), a group, institution, society, movement, place, symbol or an idea. (For example, at one point in her novel, *Power*, author Linda Hogan puts her protagonist in a little boat, at night, in a swamp, in the fog. Against an impenetrable world, Hogan lets her character fill in all of her thoughts.) Other or otherness (them, it) is a fundamental category of human thought. Make sure that "other" is never a man who is superior (he will think he is); but this obviously does not preclude a man having power over you.

We also have to factor in the idea that there are men in our life and they may be listening. Let it be known that they are in a new position of privilege: witnesses to the making of women's culture, and no longer a court of approval or disapproval.

•

What will happen when we talk about these things to others? We may be criticized and avoided. Difficult choices often mean difficult consequences that can cause uncertainty and suffering. Suffering, however, loses its teeth when one is committed to mature development and engaged in a fundamentally important process. In the place of sadness and silence, new energy will arise as a result of new dialogue and ideas. Envision a grassroots movement committed to saving our culture, and ourselves from the persistence of backwardness.

The 2 Minute Talking Liberation

Once you have determined what you want to say it's time for a venting. Hold forth for two minutes and say what it is you want to say. First off, tell it to your cat; or a portrait of Abraham Lincoln or the folks in Grant Wood's *American Gothic*. (In workshops, this can be done in groups of four or five.) Be a linguistic volcano. Say anything you want on the subject: direct, impulsive, untidy; without competition from men or hierarchies. Talk loud. Even with this short language exercise, you are telling your story—and beginning to convince yourself of its validity. Or use a recording device. Then try three minutes. Then longer. Then try it with a real live human "other" and let 'em have it! And voilà! You have started a conversation about something you've never spoken about until now. You are creating a brand-new addition to the human narrative.

> Will this story never end? My God, on and on and on. Only an atomic blast would end it.
> Marilyn French, *The Women's Room*

Pick a New Persona

Once you are familiar with the technique above, up the ante. While women are suppressed from creating the cultural narrative, so are we inhibited from discovering the myriad angles from which we might be able to express things. So put yourself in the real-life, real-world context as another character: of any class, religion, type, occupation—or just plain bad personality or character. (Think about everyone you saw on the subway or in the grocery store yesterday.) The morality of good character tells us that we must be consistent and stable and so we deny ourselves the creativity that comes with probing our underlying complexities; which, if we are fully human, are a turmoil of order and chaos competing for common ground. These buried stories are the raw material of language and the autobiography of knowing something about the human race; and we are not required to describe them under the constraints of time or number of pages, which the dominant narrators dictate. They are the stories of our life on earth. We need no one to edit or reorganize them; and we certainly don't need anyone to approve of them.

Use the text to inspire a persona—pick an angle of yourself that connects you to the material and to your position in the world in relation to this material: experience, reality, or someone you've thought of yourself as being.

It doesn't matter. It could be anything. A real side of you or anything you'd like to try on. *The skins of possible lives . . .*

In this part of the exercise, you judge yourself so you can discover or imagine what's inside you. You are positioning yourself to find out what you want to say and say it—and not according to standards of what's allowable and what's not. A woman has to be all kinds and types of people on demand from the outside. Here, by merely creating a linguistic exercise, we are changing that to a choice.

You could be a useless rich person, on the dole, hate your family. You could hate yourself. Be a shameless social climber. Obsessed with a major insight that permeates everything you think and do. Or a minor insight which sits on your shoulder, nagging. A wild egotist, devoid of life experience, have no class not even low class. Amoral or kooky. A packrat or a litterbug. Greedy, grasping, destructive. An ego-challenged wallflower.

You can be desperate not to be stupid anymore. Or passive. You can be mature with a character weakness. Anxiety ridden, neurotic, rebellious or complacent. Kinky, shabby, too tall or too short. A tyrant. Smarmy, or a nerd. Glamorous, rotund or fat or skinny. Awkward or a failure. A failure with men. Poor, swaggering, compliant or submissive. Unreliable, unethical, violent, furious, ignorant, adolescent or idiotic. An unsatisfied two-dimensional stereotype or a workaholic. A bimbo or a shrew. A self-satisfied poseur or a fake loser wannabe punk.

Maybe you're conventional, compassionate or hateful. Fair, arrogant, intellectual or uneducated. A liar. Under a spell, a hypochondriac, glutton, gourmande; harpie, fury, siren; slippery, seductive or a big blow bag. Or pregnant too often. A nun, hermit, CEO, a mad scientist. Brilliant; brilliant and nobody has ever told you that. Talented and aggressive. Talented with no ambition.

These angles are to encourage thinking of the many things we know about life; and about ourselves in relation to these things. These types may never have been nor never will be us; but that does not make knowledge about their experience disappear. What makes it elusive, though, is oppression and repression. These are life studies—people we've observed or encountered; know about or have heard about. Our experience of them becomes invisible, buried within ourselves; written out of our own narrative because we've been written out ourselves.

All things good and evil are inside us as knowledge, and it is the nature of the mind to reveal itself. Our wholeness as women depends on taking the blinkers off and accepting the shadows within us and all people; and life. Our natural morality depends on ridding ourselves of the hypocrisy visited

258 TALKING THE WALK

upon our nature over history. The way out is to develop ourselves into mature adults and speak out the truth about our own reality.

Afterword

Feminism is knowledge. We must take advantage of it and develop it. We all need to be fully confident about our position in the world and feminist knowledge helps us to attain that confidence. It benefits us in many ways—known, desired, unknown and at times, hardly imaginable.

We must establish feminist principles in the culture-at-large so that they are reflected back to us. This is particularly important in the information age. If we can break the grip of the dominant male voice on our psyches, we can create a new climate of perception. We can change the world.

I suggest keeping a notebook on the topic, "developing a permanent feminist standpoint." Record your true thoughts in your authentic voice. Stories, texts, thoughts, conversations, "what you plan to say to him or her;" retelling stories, responses to retelling stories; ways in which new perspectives are expressed in personal and social experiences; and the results of relating new values to your own experience. You'll be creating a new narrative—and creating history!

But above all, speak for yourself. Have an authentic conversation with the world. Language is ideational in itself, binding our thoughts together by expression. No statement is unimportant in the goal of developing the grassroots language of feminism. In the process of speaking, our stories will shape their own truth. In speaking, we liberate ourselves from the strictures of culture, and what is in us that has yet to be named. We are creating culture—the product of the collective female unconscious; not myth, but a culture of truth, daring and alternative possibility. Hope for our future lies in women's dialogue, devoid of patriarchal deceptions.

*

INDEX

political correctness and, 38
values and, 201, 210
feedback , 28, 37, 63, 104, 165, 171, 246
female, 5, 7, 77, 80, 83, 84, 123, 125, 126,
  182, 213, 225, 239, 242
academics, 30
authority, 158, 160
being, 123, 180
body, 87, 209, 212
circumcision, 212, 213
condition, 237
deity, 122
echo, 81
experience, 246
living, 7
narrative, 168
pathology, 91, 92
power, 52, 154, 190
reality, 13, 19, 25, 85
scholars, 31
social forms, 151
societies, 89
stereotypes, 181
students, 169
submissiveness, 132
subordination, 87, 137
upbringing, 160, 230
feminine principle, 7, 122-125, 140, 141,
  144, 148, 150, 154, 157, 158, 171, 172,
  175-177, 179, 181, 186, 202, 208, 224,
  243
femininity, 120, 125-127, 176, 181, 209,
  214, 242
feminism, 1, 8, 22, 25, 98, 104, 147, 191,
  194
  actually (defined), 1, 4, 13, 14, 18
  conservatives and, 25-27, 59, 136, 179,
    189, 206, 217, 222, 238
  cyclical nature of , 46, 56
  from model to angle, 56
  issues inside, 17
  language of, 6, 18, 19, 167, 168, 174,
    186, 259
  love and, 216
  men and, 98, 100, 101, 163-165, 195
  nuts and bolts of, 7
  radical, 16, 17
  See also grassroots feminism; second
    wave; standpoint feminism
feminist
  coalitions, 36
  collaboration, 35
  conservative, 27
  ideology, 142, 186
  issue, issues, 34, 238
  mandate, 182
  principles, 16, 50, 52, 87, 245, 254, 259
  standpoint, 7, 8, 60, 142-144, 146, 148,
    150, 152, 154, 156, 157, 167, 178,

193, 204, 253, 254, 259
See also activism, feminist; consciousness,
  feminist; dialogue, feminist, women's
  rights; identity, feminist; ideology,
  feminist; influence, feminist; issues,
  feminist; point-of-view, feminist;
  strategy, feminist; theory, feminist;
  thought, feminist; values, feminist;
  voice, voices, feminist, "War on
  Terror, Feminist Orientalism..., The"
feminist knowledge, 8, 13-16, 18, 25, 29-32,
  37, 50, 53, 55, 73, 84, 100, 101, 116,
  118, 140, 141, 146, 159, 160, 204,
  250-252, 259
feminist movement, 13, 23, 33, 34, 47, 50,
  105, 131, 133, 137, 138, 151, 241
Ferenczi, Sandor, 213
fiction, 70, 86, 160, 165, 215, 216, 245
Fiedler, Leslie A., 243, 247
first wave, 18
Foucault, Michel, 79
Fox, Terry, 203
framework, 6-8, 14, 55, 59, 80, 116, 140,
  141, 144, 156, 169, 255
fraud, 18, 69, 221
free
  expression, 141, 168
  society, 23, 25, 189, 210
  speech, 186, 211, 221
freedom, 30, 74, 76, 114, 149, 167, 191, 202,
  205, 221, 237
  sexual, 105
  women's, 13, 26, 34, 38, 112, 150, 192,
    214, 224, 227
French, Marilyn, 101, 210, 244, 256
Freud, Sigmund, 67, 69, 94, 96, 190, 242
Friedan, Betty, 19, 35, 42, 190, 191
Frye, Marilyn, 152
fundamentalism, 15, 16, 37, 70, 200, 217,
  230, 237

Gabel, Patricia, 176
gap, 2, 93-96, 120, 138, 184, 217
gender, 18, 22, 33, 36, 62, 68, 70, 72, 76, 88,
  100, 101, 126, 139, 141, 144, 178, 180,
  194, 223, 224
  asymmetry, 84, 146, 201, 253
  female, 15, 77, 125, 143, 212
  inequality, 87, 100, 142, 238, 252
  prejudice, 8, 35, 74, 155
  split, 84, 86, 87, 243
  story and, 237, 238, 240
  strategy, 83
  structure, 67, 83, 86, 101
  studies, 30, 131, 132
  values and, 199, 208, 243
  world cultures and, 64-68
generations, 8, 22, 36, 55, 61, 63, 86, 92,

and cultural relativism, 31, 38
deception, 207
failure, 70, 166
force, 84
ideology, 204
imperative, 13, 138, 206, 218
justice, 206
obligation, 123
philosophy, 186, 207
rules of nature, 124
morality, 3, 39, 40, 69, 186, 202
and ethics, 205
conflicts of, 203
crisis, 207
models, 205
natural, 204, 208, 257
social, 56, 199
See also better morality
motherhood, 36, 136, 137, 178, 209, 219,
224, 227-232, 241
motive, 101, 123, 137, 138, 142, 155, 156,
213, 214, 251
movement. *See* feminist movement; women's
movement; women's rights movement
movements, 16, 19, 28, 54, 59, 179, 189, 191
religious, 66
Ms. magazine , 104
multiculturalism , 31, 72
mural, 35
myth, 161, 163, 206, 235, 240, 259
American, 237
love, 216
neutrality, 238
sex, 241, 243
superwoman, 42, 241
unigod, 64, 67-70, 206
See also story; text
mythology, 65, 162, 209, 217, 225, 231, 240,
241
myths, 80, 93, 109, 122, 167, 228, 240, 241,
245

Nafisi, Azar, 31
narration, 169, 186, 238
failure of, 40, 46
narrative, 53, 68, 117, 122, 166, 167, 212,
238, 239, 246
authority of, 208, 209
common, 7, 48, 109, 185
controlling, 78
cultural, 4, 8, 25, 46, 59, 77, 103, 129,
197, 199, 233, 246, 252, 256
dominant, 147, 160, 193, 243, 252, 255
issues, 243, 245
love, 215. *See also* love story
motherhood, 231
patriarchal, 25, 106
sexist, 238, 244

unspoken, 5
values and, 203, 208, 221, 241
women's, 1, 4, 175, 195, 237
National Council of Women's Organizations,
99
native genocide, 33
negated consciousness, 94-96, 204, 255
New Victorians, The (Denfield), 81, 112,
129, 135, 138
New York Times , 27, 36, 78, 106, 109, 206,
212, 213, 220, 251
Newton, Isaac, 67
Nickle and Dimed (Ehrenreich), 137
Nietzsche, Friedrich, 67, 69, 137
Nine Parts of Desire (Brooks), 31
Nineteenth Amendment, 221
Nobel Peace Prize, 195
nonfiction, 243
Norton, Eleanor Holmes, 35
nosharia.com, 71

Of Woman Born (Rich), 212
"Older-and-Wiser Hypothesis" (*New York
Times*), 109
opposition, 8, 14, 23, 35, 45, 79, 85, 138,
149, 154, 168, 172, 191, 193, 237
of male and female, 237
to equality, 44, 149, 177
to feminism, 17, 26, 45, 175
oracle, 78-80, 112, 160, 185
our lives, male version, 237
our men, 100-102
overreaching, 86, 180, 200
overvaluation, 77, 180, 204, 216, 218, 223,
253

*Passionate Minds, The Great Enlightenment
Love Affair* (Bodanis), 63
passivity, 17, 89, 123, 209, 231, 248
patriarchy, 7, 25, 47, 56, 64, 79, 80, 83, 84,
95, 114, 144, 177, 194
capitalist system and, 62, 217
definition, 60, 61
destruction of, 28-30, 140
forming an identity in the, 89, 90
hidden forces of, 61, 83
loss of self in, 91
overvaluation of, 180
status in, 121, 166
story and, 237
when criticized, 100
Pelosi, Nancy, 48
persona, 125, 194, 251, 256
philosophy, 26, 56, 86, 123, 152, 186, 191,
194, 207, 241
Planned Parenthood, 150
point-of-view, 4, 6, 25, 29, 37, 82, 141, 173,
217, 254